Defensive Positions

HARVARD EAST ASIAN MONOGRAPHS 381

Defensive Positions

The Politics of Maritime Security in Tokugawa Japan

NOELL WILSON

Published by the Harvard University Asia Center
Distributed by Harvard University Press
Cambridge (Massachusetts) and London 2015

Printed in the United States of America

The Harvard University Asia Center publishes a monograph series and, in coordination with the Fairbank Center for Chinese Studies, the Korea Institute, the Reischauer Institute of Japanese Studies, and other faculties and institutes, administers research projects designed to further scholarly understanding of China, Japan, Vietnam, Korea, and other Asian countries. The Center also sponsors projects addressing multidisciplinary and regional issues in Asia.

Parts of chapters 1 and 3 are based on an article that appeared as "Tokugawa Defense Redux: Organizational Failure in the Phaeton Incident of 1808," *Journal of Japanese Studies* 36, no.1 (2010): 1–32. I gratefully acknowledge permission to reproduce that material in this publication.

Library of Congress Cataloging-in-Publication Data
Wilson, Noell, 1971–
Defensive positions : the politics of maritime security in Tokugawa Japan / Noell Wilson. — 1st edition.
pages cm. — (Harvard East Asian monographs ; 381)
Includes bibliographical references and index.
ISBN 978-0-674-50434-9 (hardcover : alk. paper) 1. Japan—Foreign relations—1600–1868. 2. Japan—Politics and government—1600–1868. 3. Coast defenses—Japan—History—17th century. 4. Coast defenses—Japan—History—18th century. 5. Merchant marine—Security measures—Japan—History. 6. Shipping—Security measures—Japan—History. 7. Japan—Defenses—History—17th century. 8. Japan—Defenses—History—18th century. I. Title. II. Title: Politics of maritime security in Tokugawa Japan.
DS871.7.W55 2015
355.4'509520903—dc23

2014032846

Index by Mary Mortensen

♾ Printed on acid-free paper

Last figure below indicates year of this printing
22 21 20 19 18 17 16 15

To my father,
William Lawrence Howell III
1944–2002

Contents

Maps and Figures

Maps

Figures

Acknowledgments

This book would have not been possible without the generous institutional and financial support I received over many years. In particular I would like to acknowledge funding from the Fulbright Japan–U.S. Educational Commission, which permitted me to carry out the bulk of my research in both Tokyo and Fukuoka from August of 1999 through December of 2000; as well as a 1999 Harvard University Reischauer Institute of Japanese Studies Summer Research Grant; a 2003–2004 Harvard Graduate Society Dissertation Write-up Fellowship; a 2007 short-term research grant from the Northeast Asia Council of the Association for Asian Studies; two summer fellowships from the University of Mississippi in 2008 and 2009; and a travel grant from the Duke University Libraries. I am also very grateful for a map subvention that I received from the Department of History and the Croft Institute for International Studies at the University of Mississippi.

I began this study while a graduate student at Harvard and am especially indebted to the long lunchtime discussions and challenging questions of my dissertation advisor, Hal Bolitho, as well as to Dani Botsman, Al Craig, Wayne Farris, and Andrew Gordon, who all provided critical feedback and moral support at multiple stages of the project. In addition to their guidance, my work also benefitted in important ways from the camaraderie and intellectual companionship provided by fellow graduate students Jeff Bayliss, Jamie Berger, Marjan Boogert, Christine Kim, Ted Mack, Hiromi Maeda, Noriko Murai, Hiraku Shimoda, Eiko Maruko Siniawer, Amy Stanley, and Laura Wong.

I owe a special debt of gratitude to three historians with whom I worked extensively in Kyūshū during the early stages of research, and in subsequent visits: Yoshida Masahiko, Professor of History, Kyūshū University; Miyazaki Katsunori (then director of the Kyūshū University

Research Institute of Cultural History and now Professor of History at Seinan Gakuin University); and Matsuo Shin'ichi, now associate professor of History at Siebold University of Nagasaki, who were tireless sounding boards, patient archival tutors, and wonderful guides to Kyushu cuisine. Kajiwara Yoshinori, professor of History at Fukuoka University was very generous in allowing me to audit his seminars and in including me in his graduate symposia. Hibi Kayako, now curator at the Meiji University Museums, spent countless hours patiently guiding me through handwritten texts. I am also grateful to Rikitake Toyotaka of the Fukuoka City Library for shepherding me through their archives. Fukaya Katsumi, Professor of History at Waseda University, kindly allowed me to attend his research seminars over the course of a year as I learned to decode local manuscript texts. Taniguchi Shinko, now Associate Professor at Waseda University, was an indefatigable tutor as she guided me through the intricacies of *kanbun* grammar. While in Tokyo during the initial stages of research, an informal writing group composed of Barbara Ambros, Steve Covell, Betsy Lublin, Hiromi Maeda, and Duncan Williams was also critical in helping me develop the early stages of my argument.

At the University of Mississippi, Joseph Ward, chair of the History Department, and Kees Gispen, director of the Croft Institute for International Studies, were enthusiastic advocates of this project, both in encouraging research grant applications and in arranging a semester's leave in the final stages to allow me to finish revisions. Judy Greenwood, head of Interlibrary Loan, and the rest of her staff were fabulous supporters in tracking down difficult-to-locate texts and then convincing the lending libraries to allow me to borrow them.

Numerous mentors and colleagues, beyond those listed above, gave generously of their time to provide feedback at significant turning points in the development of the project, including Erin Chapman, Oliver Dinius, Peter Frost, Susan Grayzel, Joshua Howard, Theresa Levitt, and Joseph Ward. I owe a special thanks to Kären Wigen, who painstakingly commented on a penultimate draft of several chapters, and to Catherine Phipps, who generously line-edited a final version even as she was meeting a manuscript deadline of her own. I am also very grateful for the opportunity to develop the core arguments through dialogue following presentations sponsored by the Midwest Japan Seminar, the Vanderbilt University History Department, the Association for Asian Studies, and the University of Mississippi History Department Colloquium. My sincere thanks as well to Marie Anchordoguy and Kevin M. Doak, Coeditors of the *Journal of Japanese Studies*, Martha Walsh, Managing Editor, and their anonymous readers, for extensive comments that served as a spring board for the manuscript.

I extend my sincere thanks to William Hammell, previously director of the Publications Program at the Harvard University Asia Center, who initially expressed interest in this project, and to his successor, Robert Graham, who along with tireless editor Deborah Del Gais, shepherded the book to completion. I deeply appreciate the thorough comments of three anonymous readers whose feedback improved the argument, structure, and flow of the book in important ways. I would also like to express my appreciation to Scott Walker of the Harvard Map Collection, Harvard College Library, for the beautiful maps.

Finally, my greatest gratitude goes to my family, who have sustained my spirit and energies throughout the project that never seemed to end. My mother Shirley was there at every stage, often at a moment's notice, taking care of children, walking the dog, and making sure everyone was well fed. My siblings Catherine and Will played an important role in repeatedly drawing me to family vacations, especially when I was tempted to remain at home in my "writing cave." Elliott, Winnie, and Hugh, my terrific trio of children, served as important daily reminders that approaches to spreading Nutella could be just as fiercely debated as theories of state formation. But in the end, my most important supporter of all was my husband, Gary—editor, cheerleader, and dad extraordinaire—who continually reminded me, over more than a decade, that all things worth having require a wait.

Note to the Reader

All dates in the body of the text are presented according to the Gregorian calendrical system. Dates in footnotes, however, are cited in the "year/month/day" format and follow the Japanese lunar calendar in use during the Tokugawa period.

Introduction

Woodblock prints of Nagasaki from the 1680s, such as the *Nagasaki dai ezu* (Great picture of Nagasaki), typically emphasized Nagasaki's role as an international commercial entrepôt and center of foreign cultural exchange. These images accentuated the exotic other by situating the Dutch trading compound at Dejima in the foreground, offering insets of stereotypical foreigners in their native dress and magnifying the scale of Dutch East India Company merchant vessels. Such attributes proved attractive to a consumer of prints who might never visit the port but still aspired to vicariously participate in its cosmopolitan environment. Privileging the features that sold these panoramas, however, meant that important indigenous characteristics of the port were minimized. Even though trade was predicated on security, artists pushed the harbor garrisons to the margins of these seascapes and seemed to add the hillside forts as an afterthought. The gargantuan Dutch trading vessels were drawn up to three times larger than the military compounds, when in reality the proportions were reversed.[1] These deliberately rendered compositions suggested that the artists themselves, and the print-buying public in Edo and beyond, were more interested in evidence of the regime's internationalism than in symbols of Tokugawa martial power.[2]

Yet within a few years of the publication of the first *Nagasaki dai ezu*, a new version of the print appeared, this time underscoring the military

1. *Nagasaki dai eizu* (1680s), housed in Tenri Central Library, Tenri University, Tenri, Japan, reproduced in *Kohan Nagasaki chizu chō*, p. 3.

2. Nagasaki in the late seventeenth century was already emerging as a tourist destination because of the allure of the strange and exciting Chinese and Dutch residents. See Yamori, *Toshizu no rekishi, Nihon-hen*, pp. 176–79, 428–35.

character of Nagasaki. Although the image and its proportions remained virtually unaltered, newly added captions highlighted three key military features of the port. First, they identified the compounds of Kyūshū lords, whom the shogunate required to maintain residences in Nagasaki as a base of operations in case of military attack. Second, the captions noted the responsibility of daimyo domains for the harbor's defenses, revealing local military actors as the cornerstone of Tokugawa security. The caption placed in the water space between the two primary garrisons of Tomachi and Nishidomari read, "Approximately 4 *chō* distance [roughly 442 yards] between batteries, manned by the lords of Saga and Fukuoka in alternating years." Finally, whereas a grid of Nagasaki's city streets occupied the lower right-hand corner, more than half of the image now featured the long, narrow harbor extending into the open sea. The inclusion of the distant reaches of the ten-mile-long bay introduced the informed viewer to the outer harbor islands, which had been increasingly fortified in the mid-seventeenth century.[3]

Short of redrawing these panoramas to put military functions first, however, these maps could not adequately convey the critical political significance of either the garrisons or the appointment of Fukuoka and Saga domains (territories of local lords) to manage them for the Tokugawa. After all, Nagasaki, the largest Tokugawa port until the mid-nineteenth century, served as the only permanently fortified harbor for the first two centuries of the early modern period in Japan. When the shogunate confined the Chinese and Dutch trade to Nagasaki in the 1640s, it also demanded that local domainal troops guard the port. This system of domain-executed coastal defense was later adapted to guard the Kantō region, home to the Tokugawa capital of Edo in central Japan, and to Ezo (later known as Hokkaidō), the northernmost of the four main Japanese islands. Indeed, the maritime security system first developed in Nagasaki became a touchstone for fortifying treaty ports throughout the realm in the 1850s.

This book examines the development of early modern Japan's coastal defense by focusing on the role of domains in this system and the political implications of their involvement for Tokugawa state formation.

3. Second version (*Karasen raichō zu, Nagasaki zu* [1689–90]) reproduced in *Kohan Nagasaki chizu chō*, p. 5; Takeda, *Sakoku to kokkyō no naritate*, p. 158, argues for Nagasaki's importance in the early seventeenth century not merely as a cultural and economic sphere but also as the center of a defensive zone facing the East China Sea.

My thesis is that domainal autonomy in the execution of maritime defense increased across the Tokugawa period (1603–1868) so that daimyo ultimately challenged Tokugawa authorities as the primary military interface with the outside world. Excavating this story makes three main contributions to our understanding of Tokugawa history. Coastal defense reveals both the rise of unanticipated domainal autonomy in military affairs and, through it, the attenuation of the shogunate's control of the monopoly on violence, which contributed to the Tokugawa fall from power. Third, this political evolution reflects how domain-managed coastal security comprised the critical third element—in addition to trade and diplomacy—of Tokugawa external relations. This trajectory first identifies control of the realm's proximate water spaces as an extension of the Tokugawa monopoly on violence to domains once the domestic wars of Tokugawa unification, ending with the suppression of the Shimabara Rebellion in 1638, were complete. Empowering coastal domains with increased military agency to guard these littoral zones critically diluted the shogunate's central control of the use of force. By the 1850s, troops in the central Kantō region and in Ezo would become soldiers for hire, instead of samurai merely fulfilling their lord's military obligation to the shogun, turning the original early seventeenth-century daimyo-shogunate contract on its head. The foundational arrangement of early Tokugawa political consolidation—the daimyo's promise of military service to the shogunate in time of crisis in exchange for daimyo autonomy in his home domain—was now fractured. Thus, the very political tool the first Tokugawa shoguns had thought would preserve their hegemony ultimately precipitated the shogunate's dissolution. The story of Tokugawa maritime defense is the history of this undoing. The inability of the shogunate to combat these unintended consequences reveals important structural challenges in Japan's transition from an early modern system of parcelized local maritime defense to one of centralized national security embraced by world powers in the nineteenth century.

This book is a study, then, of how the organization of coastal military forces and the decision making behind defense policy shaped the broader political culture of the Tokugawa period. Defensive arrangements in Nagasaki, where we begin our story, and later at Hakodate and Yokohama, have critical implications for our understanding of both coastal defense strategy and Tokugawa state formation writ large. In Nagasaki, and at later sites, the three central actors in military affairs were:

(1) the shogunate, the Edo-based architect of coastal defense policy; (2) the magistrate, who nominally supervised the domains' defense activities; and (3) the domains, which interpreted and implemented the shogunate's directives for defense with varying degrees of autonomy. Negotiations among these three key agents of Tokugawa maritime security reflected the bureaucratic turf battles within an early modern polity where lines of responsibility were fluid and situation dependent. These discussions, beginning in the 1640s, revealed that contrary to the predominant interpretation in extant scholarship, the desperate efforts of mid-nineteenth-century Japanese to shore up coastal security were not a new or reflexive response to Western pressure. Instead they were the culmination of two hundred years of deliberate strategies for securing the Tokugawa realm, beginning in Nagasaki.

The Nagasaki system of defense was not a formal blueprint, but rather an organically evolved arrangement for guarding Nagasaki harbor in which the two Kyūshū domains of Fukuoka and Saga alternated responsibility each year beginning in 1641 for posting troops to secure the port. Over the first century of their existence, these duties developed three interrelated functions—protection from Western attack, enforcement of trade restrictions (anti-smuggling campaigns), and guardianship of Dutch merchants in port—each of which augmented domainal military agency beyond the limits anticipated in the shogunate-domainal military contracts of the early seventeenth century. Not only the mechanics of fortifying seaside garrisons, but also the politics of troop mobilization and funding, were experimental arrangements in which domains gained increasing agency vis-à-vis the shogunate because of the diminishing authority of its regional proxies, the magistrates. By the late eighteenth century, and with the emergence of the Russian threat in the north, we see what was a singular, institutional anomaly become a prototype as Nagasaki's military arrangement was replicated in Ezo and later in the Kantō region.

By employing coastal defense as a new analytical lens to examine how local actors, in negotiating external security, transformed larger Tokugawa political culture, this study addresses two critical lacuna in our understanding of Tokugawa state formation. First, by approaching maritime defense as a story of negotiated military authority, rather than merely (lack of) artillery and naval development, it recuperates maritime security as fertile ground for exploring the political landscape of early modern Japan. Tokugawa coastal defense has long been overlooked as a productive topic for historical study because its lessons of technological inadequacy are assumed to be so obvious. Yet, viewed from the perspective of its own internal logic, the maritime defense culture of Tokugawa Japan was dynamic and malleable, and the key developments were organizational rather than technological. In Europe during this period, the Industrial Revolution and accompanying firearms development had made technological innovation the defining element of military progress, making "machines . . . the measure of man."[4] Within such a framework, the fundamental Tokugawa military problem was guns, not soldiers, equipment more than strategy and leadership. Scholars, both Japanese and foreign, have accordingly dismissed the historical significance of Tokugawa defenses because of their technological obsolescence in the mid-nineteenth century. Analyzing Tokugawa inadequacies in this way illustrates a continuing explanatory prejudice in history, described by Jeremy Black as "technological bias . . . in accounting for military development."[5] This book reclaims maritime defense as a critical arena for understanding Tokugawa political development.

Second, this study reveals how the system of maritime security emerged not in response to Western imperialism, as conventionally argued, but rather in the early seventeenth century as the third Tokugawa shogun, Iemitsu (r. 1623–51), became interested in extending military control into proximate water spaces.[6] The two earliest shoguns, Ieyasu (r. 1603–5) and Hidetada (r. 1605–23), were preoccupied with indigenous, land-based threats to their hegemony in the form of rival lords rather than with potential attacks from the sea. By the late 1630s, however, Iemitsu had completed the construction of a stable, agrarian-based domestic order, in which new legal and financial institutions both disciplined recalcitrant lords and established a predictable stream of rice revenue to fund the shogunate's bureaucracy. With internal affairs well managed, the 1640s became a decade of expanding Tokugawa control of the surrounding seas. The shogunate ordered coastal and island guard

4. Adas, *Machines as the Measure of Man*, pp. 366–67. Adas explains how in the nineteenth century, "advances in metallurgy and machine tooling made possible great increases in the size, range, accuracy, and rate of fire of both artillery and hand weapons."

5. Black, *Rethinking Military History*, p. 9.

6. Representative examples of maritime defense as a response to imperialism include Bolitho, "The Tempō Crisis," p. 124, and McClain, *Japan: A Modern History*, pp. 129–34.

posts erected across western Japan to watch for suspicious foreign sails, including twenty-one sites in Satsuma and multiple locations in the Ryūkyū Islands. But only with the fortification of Nagasaki harbor in 1641 did the shogunate define its sphere of proximate oceanic sovereignty by ordering domainal troops to permanently garrison coastal guard stations.

Within two years, the shogunate stretched the reach of its sovereign rights into the unclaimed waters of the larger East China Sea, beyond "sight of land," which had previously delimited the boundary of Tokugawa jurisdiction at sea.[7] In 1643, when Dutch officials asked the shogunate how it would respond if they attacked Chinese merchant vessels, the Japanese replied that this action would not be a problem so long as it occurred outside Japanese territory (*ryōiki*) and its immediate vicinity (*shūhen*), meaning the maritime border defined by Mejima Island, located some hundred miles southwest of Nagasaki, and its proximate waters in the East China Sea. Significantly, the term used to represent "territory" in this response—a compound of *ryō* (meaning "territory" or "dominion") and *iki* (meaning "sphere")—was usually employed to denote land-based authority. The transfer of this concept to oceanic spaces revealed the shogunate's interest in controlling maritime regions as it had land-based territories. That same year, when a Dutch ship carrying Christian-related items approached Mejima, it hid these articles, demonstrating that it recognized Japanese authority to prohibit Christianity in the surrounding waters.[8] Without a navy to enforce it, this projection of sovereign rights into the East China Sea basin well beyond the four main islands of the Japanese archipelago was short-lived. Yet it represented the

7. Yamamoto Hirofumi, *Sakoku to kaikin no jidai*, p. 110, observes that the notion of proximate water spaces as an integral part of Tokugawa territory emerged with the creation of a system of coastal defense in the early seventeenth century in which the shogunate ordered that foreign ships that violated sovereign oceanic boundaries (the limits of sight from coastal lookouts) proceed to Nagasaki. Adam Clulow has posited the notion of Hirado as a "maritime domain" because it focused so intently on cultivating oceanic trade between 1609 and 1641, the year the Dutch commercial post shifted to Nagasaki. Clulow, "From Global Entrepôt to Early Modern Domain," pp. 4–7. By contrast, this study suggests that the shogunate's creation of the Nagasaki defense system precisely in the year of the Dutch transfer reveals the creation of a broader "national" maritime orientation surpassing that proclivity held by particular domains.

8. Takeda, *Sakoku to kokkyō no naritate*, p. 160.

shogunate's interest in exercising political authority over maritime regions, something no previous Japanese government had been capable of achieving.

Closer to home, in 1644, the shogunate commanded all domains to compile provincial maps (*Shōhō kuniezu*) for defense purposes. Officials requested particular attention to the details of the coastline and its waters, including the direction of shore winds, currents, and tide fluctuations.[9] These maps, as well as the lookout posts that prompted residents to alert local authorities when they spotted unknown ships, embodied the broader political and social process of integrating littoral zones, particularly those bordering the southern island of Kyūshū, into the Tokugawa order.

The early Tokugawa regime had been a terracentric polity, privileging land-based agriculture and commerce over aquaculture and sea-based trade, a proclivity similar to the strategic worldview of Qing mandarins in neighboring China, who largely ignored maritime regions because challenges to power had historically originated from the continent. Yet unlike these Manchu rulers, who began to systematically defend coastal areas only with the advent of Western pressure in the 1840s, the Tokugawa focused on securing littoral regions fully two centuries earlier.[10] The shogunate's strict regulations limiting trade to Korea, China, and Holland did not arise because of a turn inward and disinterest in the maritime world. Rather they came out of a commitment to more effectively secure the external relations it wished to maintain. The system of Nagasaki defense was as much a vehicle for regulating interaction with commercial partners and guaranteeing their safety while in port as for repelling potential military threats to Japan itself. Indeed, it became the primary institution for enforcing the exclusion edicts of the 1630s. This early seventeenth century shift in the Tokugawa shogunate's vision of the utility of the military potential of its subordinate domains—from agents to suppress internal revolt to instead military gatekeepers to the external environment—becomes apparent only when we consider maritime defense as a crucial facet of the role of the monopoly on violence in larger Tokugawa state formation.

9. For the military origins of these maps see Yonemoto, "Maps and Metaphors," p. 117.

10. For Qing policy see Leonard, *Wei Yuan and China's Rediscovery of the Maritime World*.

The Role of the Local in the Monopoly on Violence

The Tokugawa interest in, and growing ability to enforce, maritime sovereignty catalyzed an important shift from the fragmented, ad hoc manner in which proximate ocean spaces had been governed by local magnates in fifteenth- and sixteenth-century Japan.[11] Although state-sponsored maritime defense represented an important hallmark of the centralized military control of Tokugawa authority, it could be effective only if implemented by parties in the coastal areas with local knowledge. Even as the Tokugawa began to issue edicts from the 1630s, outlining for the first time how maritime defense would be incorporated into their centralized monopoly on violence, the domains referenced in these documents became the chief intermediaries through whom the Tokugawa negotiated their defensive relationship to littoral spaces.

The coastal defense system produced heightened domainal autonomy for two reasons. First, maritime security in Tokugawa Japan was entirely defensive. Tokugawa coastal installations guarded against anticipated maritime attack rather than mobilizing expeditionary forces for land campaigns. As an island nation, Japan did not face the constant possibility of assault that confronted polities surrounded by potentially antagonistic political units on land. This key distinction created a breathing space for the shogunate to devolve greater military authority to local elites. Second, since the Tokugawa control over the use of force comprised what Eiko Ikegami has termed a "*collective* monopoly on violence," which was exercised by a social class of warriors, instead of civilian bureaucrats as in Europe, daimyo could claim relative autonomy over the mobilization of their troops even if their dispatch theoretically represented the will of the shogun.[12] Historian Mary Elizabeth Berry identifies daimyo discretion over local military matters as a fundamental characteristic of the "mediated conduct of Tokugawa rule" through which the shogunate indirectly discharged its prerogatives, such as protection of the polity. She characterizes these mediations as "systemic features of the early modern state, rather than foils to its integrity."[13] Yet the evolution

11. Shapinsky, "With the Sea as Their Domain."
12. Ikegami, *The Taming of the Samurai*, p. 152.
13. Berry, *Japan in Print*, p. 231.

of coastal defense as a *permanent* charge, rather than a periodic military levy (*gun'yaku*), granted Fukuoka and Saga domains at Nagasaki (and later other domains in Ezo and the Kantō region) a singular, standing military agency that implicitly challenged the shogunate's Confucian claim to safeguard the realm. Although the structural ironies of this arrangement did not surface on a politically momentous scale until the 1850s, they pervaded the execution of coastal defense duties in subtle ways that gained increasing significance across time.

Coastal defense was not merely the product of hinterland functionaries implementing the orders of their superiors in Edo, but rather a more complex negotiation among the three agents of nested, and frequently competing, military authority: shogunate, magistrate, and daimyo. Nagasaki, where our story begins, possessed a distinct administrative structure. It was the only one of the four Tokugawa "gates" that was a direct shogunal territory (*tenryō*) and not a domainal land administered by a local lord, as were the other three portals of Tsushima, Satsuma, and Matsumae.[14] This singular classification as the only portal before the nineteenth century that was a Tokugawa territory meant that a resident Tokugawa proxy, the Nagasaki magistrate (*bugyō*), de jure administered its commercial, judicial, and defensive responsibilities. The presence of this administrative intermediary, who was absent in the other three portals, placed the domains executing the port's defense in almost daily contact with a direct proxy of the shogunate. Yet because of this very structure, domains were partially insulated from direct correspondence with Edo-based shogunal officials, giving them greater latitude to contest or resist the decisions of the magistrate. Scholars generally emphasize that the Nagasaki magistrate increasingly gained economic and diplomatic authority across the Tokugawa period.[15] But examining the third category of the post's administrative purview—harbor defense—reveals that the magistrate's influence in military affairs in fact diminished over time as domains supplying troops acted with growing independence.

Evaluating the distribution of military authority in coastal defense rests on understanding how the shogunate's putative monopoly on violence,

14. Matsumae, too, was a shogunal territory (*tenryō*) for two different periods in the late eighteenth and mid-nineteenth centuries, as discussed in chapter 5.

15. For example, see Suzuki, *Nagasaki bugyō no kenkyū*, and Earns, "The Nagasaki Bugyo," pp. 68, 70.

identified by Max Weber as the foundation of political stability in the early modern world, was partitioned and delegated. Domainal actors have long remained absent from analysis of military force in the Tokugawa period because so few internal disturbances after the 1638 Shimabara Rebellion required the mobilization of daimyo-led troops.[16] Yet the projection of this monopoly of the use of coercive force in Nagasaki, through Fukuoka and Saga domains' garrisons, helped broadcast Tokugawa martial power to both foreign and domestic audiences. The locus of control of this power, however, was ambiguous. As early as the 1690s, the Dutch physician Engelbert Kaempfer remarked that the harbor's domainal troops were "beyond the jurisdiction of the governors [magistrates]," even as they were mobilized "in the name of the shogun."[17] Although Nagasaki defense duty had been created to extend the reach of state-sponsored violence to foreigners, the actual level of central oversight varied. Whereas James White argues that the extent of shogunal "monopoly" increased across time at the "expense of other subnational actors—primarily the feudal lords or daimyo," the incremental expansion of domainal military autonomy in Nagasaki, and later at treaty ports, suggests the opposite.[18] By 1844, daimyo had definitively supplanted the Nagasaki magistrate as the preeminent military authority in Nagasaki, appropriating leadership of the port's security. A parallel development emerged in the next decade in both Yokohama and Hakodate. Although this shift became most pronounced with growing concern about Western incursion after Russian envoy Adam Laxman's arrival in the 1790s, it had begun as early as the mid-seventeenth century, as domains exploited ambiguities in the distribution of military authority to aggrandize their own power.[19]

16. Anne Walthall and James White both emphasize the rarity of mobilizing domainal samurai troops to quell peasant protests. Walthall, *Social Protest and Popular Culture*, pp. 36, 138; White, *Ikki*, p. 48.

17. Kaempfer, *Kaempfer's Japan*, p. 153.

18. James White observed in his important study of state growth and popular protest that the "defining aspect" of the Tokugawa state was "the creation of a governmental monopoly of the legitimate use of physical force," in sum, the classic hallmark of early modern state power identified by Max Weber as a "monopoly on violence." White, "State Growth and Popular Protest," p. 1.

19. Works such as Robert Hellyer's examination of Kyūshū trade, David Howell's analysis of Hokkaidō fisheries, and Brett Walker's study of Ainu-centric

Coastal Defense and Tokugawa History

The paradigm of Tokugawa seclusion, or *sakoku* ("closed country")—the idea of an early modern Japan isolated and unengaged with the outside world—is long since disproved. Indeed, current histories frame Tokugawa foreign relations with some variation of selective engagement, emphasizing that tight state control of external affairs was not a reflection of xenophobia, but rather a deliberate, rational strategy to construct a Japan-centered regional diplomatic and economic order. Yet absent from this rich field of scholarship are studies of the construction of maritime defense installations and consideration of how these domain-managed coastal security initiatives comprised a critical third element—in addition to trade and diplomacy—of Tokugawa external relations.[20]

As early as the 1970s, historians such as Asao Naohiro began to explore Tokugawa maritime restrictions as a vehicle for modulating engagement with, rather than rejecting outright, the outside world. Yet as these scholars pieced together the details of state-to-state relations, they largely ignored local agency.[21] Building on this pioneering work, Ronald Toby's study of shogunal diplomatic relations identified the core of

commerce have long challenged Edo-centric interpretation of Tokugawa diplomacy and economics, yet the shift of attention to the local has only recently reached maritime defense studies, predominately in work by Japanese scholars. See Hellyer, *Defining Engagement*; Howell, *Capitalism from Within*; Walker, *The Conquest of Ainu Lands*. Representative Japanese-language scholarship includes Matsuo, *Edo bakufu no taigai seisaku*; Kuroda, "Shōhō yonen no nanban sen raikō jiken"; Miyake, "Kōkaki ni okeru Edo kinaki keiei." A related influence creating an image of top-down defense has been the disproportionate attention given writings on coastal defense by Kantō-based intellectuals—such as Hayashi Shihei, Honda Toshiaki, or Aizawa Seishisai—who were largely unaware of on-the-ground fortification projects and troop rotations in Nagasaki. Studies such as Bob Tadashi Wakabayashi's analysis of Aizawa Seishisai consider this scholar's treatise as evidence of the frequent discussion of maritime defense in the abstract, but one without concrete action at the water's edge. Wakabayashi, *Anti-Foreignism and Western Learning*.

20. Indeed, Mark Ravina's important study of the nature of Tokugawa "lordship" asserts that "having ceded authority over diplomacy and foreign affairs to the shogun, the daimyo were dependent on his competence to defend the Tokugawa order." The present study reclaims daimyo, and their troops, as critical actors in defending the realm. Ravina, *Land and Lordship*, p. 15.

21. Asao, "Sakokusei no seiritsu."

seventeenth-century international affairs in East Asia as political and commercial negotiations among state actors.[22] Even as this project highlighted the role of the Tsushima Sō daimyo (lord of the island domain situated in the strait between Kyūshū and the Korean peninsula) in mediating relations with Korea, its primary contribution to our understanding of Tokugawa foreign affairs was analyzing how the shogunate deliberately projected authority through formal diplomatic channels to legitimate a new regime. Toby explained part of the shogunal interest in constructing an image of state power through foreign relations as a response to an unstable East Asia, particularly the Chinese dynastic change, whose civil wars might destabilize Japan. Indeed, his analysis of Iemitsu's intelligence-gathering network in Nagasaki, Tsushima, and Korea—managed by a "foreign policy control center" in Edo—defined regional geopolitics as the most critical security concern of the mid- to late seventeenth century.[23] In Toby's analysis, diplomacy, not military preparedness, was the linchpin of Japan's security: "The ability autonomously to manipulate foreign states and foreign monarchs in the formative years of the dynasty served both to assure the physical security of the Japanese homeland and to prevent the subversion of the state from abroad, on the one hand, and to legitimate the new Tokugawa order on the other."[24] From this diplomatic perspective, Nagasaki was a critical information conduit, but not significant as a fortified defensive zone.

This seminal vein of scholarship dismantled the "closed country" paradigm with studies that proved the vibrancy of Edo-centered seventeenth-century Tokugawa diplomacy. This revisionism then progressed to examine the specific local sites through which international exchange occurred. The reconceptualization of critical littoral zones as gateways rather than barriers produced the four-portals construct of Tokugawa foreign relations, first proposed by Arano Yasunori. Arano posited that international affairs occurred not primarily between Edo bureaucrats and representatives of foreign states, but rather through local agents at the four central ports of Matsumae in Ezo, Tsushima, the Ryūkyū Islands (southwest of Kyūshū), and Nagasaki.[25] Daimyo intermediaries at each of these sites interpreted and implemented Tokugawa

22. Toby, *State and Diplomacy in Early Modern Japan*.
23. Ibid., p. 162.
24. Ibid., p. 242.
25. Arano, *Kinsei Nihon to higashi Ajia*.

directives for commerce and diplomacy, including the Matsumae, the Shimazu in the Ryūkyūs, and the Sō in Tsushima, as numerous studies have explored.[26]

Building on this emerging field, Robert Hellyer analyzed the Tokugawa era as a period of increasing commercial and diplomatic engagement with the outside world, prompted by larger forces of globalization.[27] By focusing on the role of Satsuma and Tsushima domains in mediating Tokugawa trade, Hellyer framed the early modern Japanese economy as integrated into world markets, an important corrective to the notion of a Tokugawa realm connected primarily to its regional trading partners. Yet in this study of Tokugawa "engagement," maritime defense enters the narrative only in the 1860s, as a response to Western encroachment. Treating coastal defense as a significant policy concern starting only in the mid-nineteenth century obscures its role in the previous two hundred years of Japanese history, during which it was a critical element of mediating external relations.[28]

This book reframes our understanding of early modern Japanese coastal defense, challenging its previous portrayal as a xenophobic reaction to Western pressure in the nineteenth century and instead casting it as part of a longer-term process, both shogunal and domainal, to extend military control to water spaces. The story is divided into two parts. The first part explores the creation of Nagasaki defense as a complex system of external relations with three overlapping military goals between 1640 and 1840. The second half examines how the integration of Tokugawa Japan into an era of naval power in the nineteenth century both shifted "national" security beyond Nagasaki and adapted the harbor's defense system as a template for the treaty ports.

Part 1, "The Evolution of the Nagasaki System," focuses on the development of the Nagasaki defense system through the early nineteenth century. Although the creation of a defensive prototype was not a conscious goal of Tokugawa officials in 1640, or even labeled as such as it

26. Representative examples include Walker, *The Conquest of Ainu Lands*, and Ravina, *The Last Samurai*.

27. Hellyer, *Defining Engagement*.

28. Kamishiraishi Minoru's work *Bakumatsuki taigai kankei no kenkyū* is an important corrective to this tendency.

evolved, in this study the notion of a "Nagasaki model" is a discursive shorthand to represent the military arrangements in Nagasaki built on a fluid political relationship between shogunate, magistrate, and domains. In Nagasaki, we trace how a triad of local (Fukuoka and Saga domains), regional (Nagasaki magistrate), and central (Tokugawa officials in Edo) actors negotiated the evolving military and policy parameters of the harbor's security. The in situ execution of defense developed three distinct but interlocking functions (each examined in a separate chapter): (1) defense against foreign military incursion, (2) enforcement of commercial restrictions, and (3) protection of Dutch traders. The overlapping nature of these duties revealed an early modern political culture of openness to institutional adaptability, while also exposing the debilitating limits of ambiguous expectations.

Chapter 1, "Localizing National Defense to Nagasaki," lays out a novel spatial paradigm for understanding realm-wide defense by identifying the Nagasaki system as a prototype that would later be replicated across the polity. The refinement of this experimental blueprint between 1641 and 1685 reveals early Tokugawa conceptions of maritime sovereignty, as well as how the system originally functioned in its primary role as guard against anticipated Western attack. The second chapter, "Smuggling and the Chinese Interim of Coastal Defense," examines the reconfiguration of the Nagasaki system to exterminate Chinese smuggling at the turn of the eighteenth century, when domestic economic upheaval required stricter regulation of the outflow of precious metals. The new fiscal threat relocated Fukuoka harbor guards and firearms from Nagasaki to the Genkai Sea in Northern Kyūshū, aggrandizing domainal military authority vis-à-vis the Nagasaki magistrate. Yet, while the tri-domainal coalition of forces sandwiching the Shimonoseki Strait—Fukuoka, Kokura, and Chōshū—received the first standing permission in the Tokugawa period to use mortal force against foreigners, imprecisely defined maritime borders there led domains to prioritize successful attacks in their own sovereign waters over effective policing of the trans-maritime region. This fundamental weakness highlighted the importance of designating core defensive nodes (such as Hakodate and Yokohama) as shogunal territories so that coalition domainal forces might avoid conflicts over disputed maritime sovereignty in the future.

Chapter 3, "Defending Dejima," explores how the Tokugawa structured Nagasaki defensive rotations around the cycles of the Dutch trading season, integrating protection of these unarmed, commercial guests as the primary, sustained incarnation of domainal military responsibility in Nagasaki. "Guardianship" of the Dutch fostered singular semi-private relationships between Fukuoka and Saga domains and the Dutch merchants, which provided these lords prestige and information available to no other domains on an equal scale. This history of privileged access to the Dutch trading compound at Dejima convinced the Nagasaki magistrate to allow the Saga lord, Nabeshima Naomasa (r. 1830–61), to board the Dutch warship *Palembang* in 1844 for a tour of up-to-date Western armaments that would catalyze Naomasa's leadership of the mid-nineteenth-century arms race.

Part 2, "Applying the Nagasaki System to the Realm," shifts to examine new defensive nodes as the Tokugawa crafted a maritime security plan that stretched the length of the archipelago, reflecting the emergence of the nation in new spatial terms. The fourth chapter, "Pan-Daimyo Collaboration and the Fortification of Edo Bay," examines how the extensive marital and political networks of Saga lord Nabeshima Naomasa, cultivated through his domain's core role in defending Nagasaki, positioned him as the primary architect of the revolution in maritime defense in mid-nineteenth-century Japan. This chapter traces his embrace of a new "inner harbor (*naime*)" defensive strategy and his construction of Japan's first reverberatory furnace to produce cast-iron cannon, both of which were later adopted in the Kantō region. These two interlocking projects illustrate how defensive reform in the years from 1845 to 1853 was a cooperative effort among key daimyo and scholars of military science rather than an antagonistic, inter-domainal rivalry as conventionally argued.

Chapter 5, "Reconfiguring Coastal Defense at the Treaty Ports," looks at how the creation of the treaty port system in the 1850s appropriated reformulated versions of the "Nagasaki model" throughout Japan, most clearly in Yokohama and Hakodate. Comparing improvements to defensive infrastructure and oversight at the three most important ports at midcentury demonstrates that the military organization of the maritime perimeter was dynamic, and not the "anachronistic space" it is often depicted as being. Unlike when the Fukuoka and Saga lords first embraced their 1641 Nagasaki duty as a vehicle for reconfirming their loyalty to the Tokugawa, without the explicit promise of monetary or political benefit, domains securing the Kantō region and Ezo between 1840 and 1862 obtained cash payments and new territories as direct compensation for their maritime military service, turning the foundational daimyo-shogunate contract on its head. In spite of the shogunate's attempts to centralize military affairs with the creation of new bureaucratic posts, these officials ultimately focused on diplomacy as the key to Tokugawa security, further devolving coastal defense responsibilities to the domains.

Thus, the military defeat of the Tokugawa in 1868 was not primarily the product of the shogunate's failure to build political consensus in a society wracked by both foreign diplomatic pressures and internal social fractures. It was the specific outcome of a military culture in which domains, over multiple centuries, had been increasingly encouraged to cultivate their own defensive capabilities. Although the shogunate permitted these semiprivate initiatives with the understanding that they would be used to secure the Tokugawa realm, the domains that experienced greatest success with them ultimately decided that Tokugawa hegemony was not worth protecting.

PART I

The Evolution of the Nagasaki System

CHAPTER ONE

Localizing National Defense to Nagasaki

In 1641, the Tokugawa shogun Iemitsu appointed the lords of Fukuoka and Saga domains to the newly created office of "defender of Nagasaki harbor" (Nagasaki *keiei yaku*) to protect Japan's largest port city from foreign incursion. He then imbued this assignment with an illustrious lineage, one that stretched back more than 1,000 years and linked these lords to the imperial court. Within weeks, Iemitsu's senior councillor Doi Toshikatsu asked eminent Confucian scholar Hayashi Razan to research the precedent of Kyūshū-based defense as a tool for legitimizing this new duty.[1] Hayashi was certainly aware of the thirteenth-century repulsion of the Mongols from Fukuoka, but he went back further in time to offer the example of Empress Jingū, a mytho-historical figure who had allegedly invaded the Korean peninsula from northern Kyūshū in the third century. To guard against a retaliatory strike, she had named her grand minister, Takenouchi no sukune, to the post of "bulwark against foreign attack" (*ikoku no osae*). In comparing Iemitsu to Empress Jingū, Hayashi deliberately situated his Tokugawa master within an incontestable tradition of Japanese maritime power. Taking the analogy a step further, he then likened the Kuroda and Nabeshima daimyo (the lords of Fukuoka and Saga domains, respectively) to Kōra Daimyojin, the spiritual embodiment of Takenouchi, suggesting that the domains merely represented the most recent incarnation of Japanese bastions against foreign incursion. Thus from the inception of the Nagasaki assignment, these auspicious parallels allowed the shogunate to rest the defense of

1. *Saga ken kinsei shiryō*, vol. 1, no. 2, pp. 691–92.

the entire Tokugawa realm on the security of Nagasaki, and so emerged the Kyūshū origins of early modern Japan's national defense.

During this first stage of Tokugawa coastal defense, which developed in Nagasaki between 1640 and 1685, the two domains of Fukuoka and Saga began to guard the port in alternating years as their appointment by Shogun Iemitsu required. Within this period of organizational experimentation, these two domains and the magistrate, the Tokugawa proxy in Nagasaki, negotiated their political and military powers as a multi-tiered chain of command was streamlined to grant domains increasing authority of military oversight in Japan's only international harbor. This initial stage of Nagasaki's fortification reflected Tokugawa willingness to incrementally delegate growing military agency to local daimyo.

The absence of attack by Western vessels soon cemented the idea that shoreline defenses, rather than a naval fleet, would form the cornerstone of maritime security. By 1685, the Tokugawa interpreted the coastal garrisons in Nagasaki as a defensive "success" and established these static artillery fortifications as the foundation of maritime protection. As most Tokugawa coastal armaments were still technologically equivalent to those on board Western vessels, a significant gap had not yet emerged (as it would in the nineteenth century) between the Tokugawa claims to military power as the foundation of its legitimacy and its ability to assert this claim to both foreign and domestic audiences.[2] Yet whereas most artillery pieces in seventeenth-century Nagasaki were in fact firearms on loan from the Tokugawa, the soldiers manipulating them were domainal samurai. This disjuncture rendered Nagasaki defenses Janus-faced, projecting collective Tokugawa martial might outward to external audiences while operating domestically to help define the role of domains in the larger process of state formation.

Conventionally, Nagasaki defense has been interpreted as yet another category of domainal military corvée obligations (*gun'yaku*), an addition to alternate attendance, construction projects, or quelling of domestic unrest already required. Yet its broader significance lay in that it first delegated the Tokugawa "monopoly on violence" to domains to now

2. The disjuncture between the shogunate's forceful claim to maritime authority yet inability to exert it (a fundamental element of Brown's "flamboyant state") would not emerge until the eighteenth century. See Brown, *Central Authority and Local Autonomy*.

include the use of force against foreigners. The creation of a standing, permanent military duty, at a site far from Edo, allowed the domains of Fukuoka and Saga to appropriate increasing military and political authority as the magistrates became progressively preoccupied with the economic affairs and general management of a port city whose population increased from 25,000 in 1614 to more than 40,000 by 1659. By century's end, Nagasaki's population reached 64,000 inhabitants, the highest total of the Tokugawa period and a number that ranked it just behind the castle towns of Nagoya and Kanazawa, making it the sixth-largest city in Japan.[3] Even with the assistance of numerous city elders and the administrator of Tokugawa lands (*daikan*) outside of Nagasaki city proper, the task of overseeing the affairs of a city this size—including management of the only resident foreigners in Japan (both Dutch and the Chinese)—was formidable, in fact according to some scholars, as demanding as overseeing any of the five shogunal cities in the realm.[4] Most of the foreign sailors stayed only temporarily while their vessels were loaded with outbound cargo, but one estimate calculates that the Chinese population alone may have reached as many as 10,000 during the years of greatest trade.[5] Nagasaki was host to greater volumes of foreign trade—and greater numbers of Japanese residents—than any of the other three international portals of Matsumae, Tsushima, or the Ryūkyūs. Given the variety of the city's activities, one can see how the magistrates, overwhelmed with the complexity of their administrative duties, might readily delegate military affairs to domainal soldiers so that the magistrates could focus instead on commercial and judicial matters. This critical delegation of defensive responsibility to domains, an incomplete and inexact partitioning, would produce escalating political tensions for the remainder of the Tokugawa period. This chapter is the story of how that partitioning developed during the first decades of fortifying what would become the longest permanently defended port in Tokugawa Japan.

Although the historical significance of early modern Nagasaki is often limited to its role as a conduit for foreign culture and as an entrepôt of international trade, it possessed a palpable military feel for a harbor that was not in fact a castle town and therefore lacked a resident samurai

3. *Nagasaki kenshi, taigai kōshō hen*, pp. 372–73.
4. The other four at the time were Edo, Kyoto, Osaka, and Sakai.
5. Gramlich-Oka, "Thorn in the Eye of the Shogunate," p. 51.

population. Even during the normal, peacetime dispatch of domainal guards to Nagasaki, these troops might number as many as 2,000 in the city. Indeed, the lodging of Fukuoka and Saga defense forces throughout the city's wards has led one historian to characterize late seventeenth-century Nagasaki as "under martial law."[6] Yet this simultaneous mobilization of troops from different domains frequently juxtaposed Fukuoka and Saga samurai, men keenly aware of how their lords emphasized the identity of their domain's rowboats, barges, and troops with public display of their family crests on flapping pendants and banners. When a ship entered the harbor, the first heraldic displays its crew would see sported the flags of an apricot flower in a tan field or a white circle surrounded by a red field, symbols of the Saga and Kuroda daimyo houses, respectively. Both were displayed simultaneously on board the harbor guard boats or fluttering from the garrison encampments as the domains competed from day to day in executing their duties, just as the Tokugawa had hoped to encourage superior performance through rivalry by assigning two domains to defend Nagasaki. The undiscerning foreign visitor, unable to identify the provenance of this military regalia, might easily interpret these harbor displays as a show of Tokugawa force. Yet, the flags of the Tokugawa hollyhock were instead tucked away at the magistrate's inland residence, out of sight of ships entering the wharf area. Still, samurai and commoners in Nagasaki, as well as the Dutch and Chinese who regularly traded there, understood this pageantry as a contest of ritual not only between the domains of Saga and Fukuoka, but also between both domains and the Nagasaki magistrate. The story of this negotiation in Nagasaki is a critical foundation for exploring the broader history of coastal defense in the Tokugawa realm at large.

Pre-Tokugawa Defense of Nagasaki

Jesuit missionaries had first identified Nagasaki's attractiveness as a harbor three decades before the Tokugawa rise to power. In 1571, when the site of the future city was still a minor hamlet of some 1,500 inhabitants, Jesuit Padre Belchior de Figueiredo sounded the southwest Kyūshū shoreline in search of a trading port to replace the one at Fukuda, in neighboring Ōmura domain, which was judged vulnerable to typhoons

6. Hesselink, "Two Faces of Nagasaki," pp. 181–82.

approaching from the south.[7] The Society of Jesus subsequently resettled exiled Japanese Christians from their home territories to Nagasaki, striking an alliance with the Christian daimyo Ōmura Sumitada (Dom Bartolomeu), whose vassal oversaw Nagasaki lands, and made the port a permanent safe haven for Christian converts. During this period, the growing hamlet centered around the Tsuru Castle of Nagasaki Jinzaemon Sumikage, a retainer of Ōmura Sumitada from 1558 to 1570.[8] Around 1573, when neighboring lords envious of Sumitada's profits from the foreigners threatened the Nagasaki colony, an Ōmura vassal reportedly entreated the Portuguese and their Japanese followers to flee to the woods. But the Christians refused, having protected their compound with a palisade and ditch. According to Luis Frois, writing soon after, "Thus the place which today is Nagasaki became a fortress."[9]

Although these early efforts produced an ad hoc garrison for refuge during local conflict, less than a decade later, Alexandro Valignano also recognized the strategic value of Nagasaki for solidifying his order's presence in East Asia. Ambitious chief of the Jesuit mission in China, Japan, and India, Valignano envisioned the protected harbor as a permanent military colony where native Japanese Christians would reinforce the Portuguese presence in Japan. In a document written during the summer of 1580, he outlined his interest in developing Nagasaki as an armed harbor:

> For the welfare and preservation of Christianity the fortification of the two harbors taken over by the Church, Nagasaki and Mogi, is of great importance. Both should accordingly be protected with forts and equipped with munitions, weapons, and artillery for defence. . . . In the first year [the superior] should spend on the defence installations as much as necessary. Thereafter, 150 ducats out of the anchorage fees of the Portuguese should be applied to this purpose. Both fortresses are to be armed in a manner to withstand any attack. In order to secure Nagasaki even more, as many married Portuguese are to be settled there as will find accommodations in the town. In case of siege these will be taken into the fort and will reinforce it. The Superiors are to take care that the inhabitants increase, and that they are equipped with all necessary weaponry.[10]

7. Nishimura, *Kinsei Nagasaki bōeki*, p. 33; Takeno, *Han bōekishi no kenkyū*, p. 40; Pacheco, "Founding of the Port of Nagasaki," p. 307n26.

8. Toyama, *Nagasaki bugyō*, p. 9; *Nagasaki kenshi, taigai kōsho hen*, pp. 50–51.

9. Translation of Frois quoted in Elison, *Deus Destroyed*, pp. 92–94.

10. Ibid., p. 98.

Soon after, Valignano observed that in addition to its naturally protected location, Nagasaki had become an even safer port city because of the fortresses and moats built along its perimeter.[11] The fortification of the larger bay, however, did not yet extend to the promontory of the Nomo peninsula some ten miles to the southeast because these lands belonged to other territorial magnates.

In 1588, after subduing Kyūshū in his quest to rule the Japanese archipelago, Toyotomi Hideyoshi made both Nagasaki and Mogi (a port on the south side of the Nomo peninsula) his direct territories and named Nabeshima Naoshige (one of the most powerful warlords in Kyūshū) to the post of administrator of Nagasaki (*daikan*). Since Portuguese ships from Macau had made Nagasaki their port of call since 1571, Hideyoshi used Nagasaki foreign trade to procure lead and gunpowder from Europe for his Korean campaigns of the 1590s.[12] By the time rival warlord Tokugawa Ieyasu rose to power in 1600 following Hideyoshi's death, Nagasaki was not only the destination for Portuguese vessels but also the most important international harbor in all of Japan.

Localizing National Defense to Nagasaki

Despite a clear sixteenth-century preference for Nagasaki harbor by both foreign and domestic traders, Tokugawa Ieyasu centered his power base in the Kantō plain, making the island of Kyūshū less appealing to him as a center of Japan's foreign relations. Only three months after the death of his political rival Hideyoshi, in late 1598, Ieyasu invited Spanish ships to trade at Uraga (see map 1), the promontory closest to his nascent castle town at Edo. He soon courted trade with Spain via both the Philippines and Mexico in an attempt to establish a port in Edo Bay that would rival that of Nagasaki and nearby Hirado (home to Portuguese and Dutch traders, respectively, in Kyūshū).[13] In a last-ditch effort to recenter foreign commerce in the northeast, in 1613 Ieyasu encouraged Dutch traders to establish a second commercial house at Uraga. As Hendrick Brouwer, the Dutch factor (head of the commercial station) at Hirado,

11. Valignano quoted in Takeno, *Han bōekishi no kenkyū*, pp. 43–44.

12. Elison, *Deus Destroyed*, p. 92; Nakamura, *Kinsei Nagasaki bōekishi no kenkyū*, p. 75.

13. Takeno, *Han bōekishi no kenkyū*, pp. 74–75.

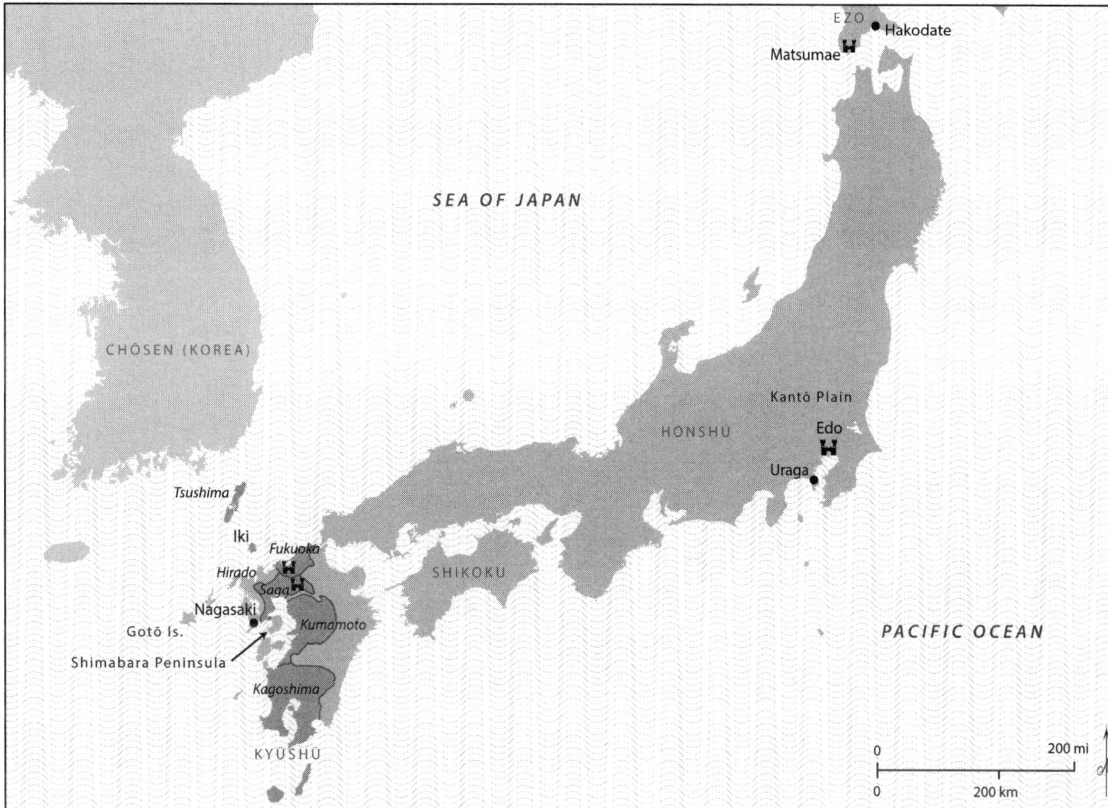

MAP 1 Important ports and defended coastal sites in early seventeenth-century Japan.

argued, however, Dutch merchants were well treated in Hirado and had already invested considerable funds in constructing warehouses there, so they decided to focus their attention on developing this single trading site.[14] For the Dutch, as well as Portuguese and Chinese trading in Kyūshū, Nagasaki and Hirado were more attractive trading destinations than Uraga not only because of these merchants' historical presence, but also because the trade winds and ocean currents that carried vessels northward from Macau, Indonesia, or the Asian mainland flowed almost directly into the southwest corner of Kyūshū.[15] In 1616, following a string of unsuccessful negotiations between Japan and successive governors-general of the Philippines, Ieyasu's vision of establishing an international port in his home territory came to an end.

While reflecting European preferences for trading at a port in southern Japan, the decision to fortify Nagasaki in the 1640s continued Ieyasu's strategy of ensuring national security by protecting carefully selected coastal nodes. In the 1590s, when he first laid claim to the Kantō region, Ieyasu had inaugurated a maritime garrison system along the Uraga coast to protect against attack by rival warlords. Following Tokugawa victory at Sekigahara in 1600, during the first two decades of the seventeenth century, shogunal officials labored to create domestic peace and construct a defense for the emerging capital city centered on Edo Castle. In 1616, Shogun Hidetada, Ieyasu's son, integrated Kantō-area coastal security into his bureaucratic structure with the creation of the post of Shimoda magistrate to defend Edo Bay from potential attack by adversaries and infiltration by missionaries.[16] The primacy of maritime security within the broader administrative responsibilities of the Shimoda magistrate became so well-known that by 1636, the Dutch factor Nicolaes Couckebacker referred to the holder of that position, Imamura Masanaga, as "director of Edo harbor affairs."[17] As this Dutch moniker revealed, contrary to terracentric histories that highlight a land-based state-building campaign during the early decades of Tokugawa rule, shogunal interest in securing proximate water spaces was evident from the start. Yet this was not a permanent, domain-managed system. The subsequent defense of

14. Suzuki, *Tokugawa Ieyasu no Supein gaikō*, p. 97.

15. Ibid., p. 12.

16. Ibid., pp. 12, 220.

17. Quoted in Suzuki, *Tokugawa Ieyasu no Supein gaikō*, p. 221; *Hirado Oranda shōkan no nikki*, vol. 3, p. 316.

Nagasaki demonstrated that the shogunate's vision of maritime security encompassed more than a single site and would integrate new, permanent executors—the domains.

Coastal Defense in the Early Modern World

The Tokugawa development of coastal defense in the 1640s as part of a system of land-based maritime security was not an idiosyncratic response to regional security concerns by a state that had rejected naval power. Rather it came at a time when new static, coastal fortifications were being constructed around the world. Sea power was still often understood from a land-based perspective. Even as broader Europe experienced a "naval revolution" by the mid-1600s, these very states became increasingly dependent on coastal forts as the scope of their overseas colonial acquisitions surpassed what their warships could effectively protect.[18]

The early fortification of Nagasaki mirrored contemporary developments in Europe, relayed to the Tokugawa by the Dutch. There, maritime states of the mid-seventeenth century, such as Britain, had come to realize that shore defenses were a necessary second line of defense to reinforce their naval power. Japanese coastal garrisons, however, developed from a tradition of castle building at strategic inland points to prevent land-based assaults. Hideyoshi's two attempted invasions of the Korean peninsula in the 1590s prompted a departure from this custom when Japanese forces constructed roughly twenty-five castles on the southeast coast of Korea to serve as the cornerstone for defending the harbors it occupied. Western lords in Japan also built substantial castles on the shorelines of the islands of Iki and Tsushima in the Tsushima Strait, and in northwestern Kyūshū at Hizen-Nagoya, to serve as staging grounds for these invasions. These fortifications commanded a panoramic view to allow long-distance scouting; they did not provide protection for soldiers engaging hostile ships in gunfire at the shoreline.[19] When the shogunate ordered Nagasaki harbor fortified in 1641, the boom of inland castle building following the Tokugawa settlement had ended. Nagasaki, the sixth-largest city in Japan, remained the only urban center of comparable size without a castle-fortress even as it became the defensive

18. Black, *Naval Power*, p. 42.
19. Turnbull, *Strongholds of the Samurai*, pp. 188–89.

center of Tokugawa maritime security. The decision to break with tradition and fortify the long, thin harbor entrance with a series of hillside garrisons lining the shore reflected the Tokugawa commitment to finally engage threats at the water's edge.

During this period, new technological developments in artillery, such as increased range of accuracy and mobility of cannons, made shoreline defenses feasible for the first time in a variety of world regions. In the 1540s, Henry VIII (r. 1509–47) became the first English monarch to consider building coastal forts. He anticipated attack by Catholic powers in continental Europe committed to restoring the pope's authority in England after Henry had established himself as the head of the Church of England.[20] The English navy grew to a standing fleet during Henry VIII's reign, but as a fledgling military organization, it still proved insufficient to protect the home islands, making land-based fortifications a critical second line of defense.[21] Although the navy expanded to become the largest in the world by 1650, its structure still reflected the fact that its leaders perceived maritime affairs in a "distinctly land-based context."[22] Even after Oliver Cromwell and the New Model Army seized control of the government in 1649, the navy was considered an extension of terrestrial defense. This privileging of the army over the navy was nowhere more evident than in the practice of commissioning new ships with the names of successful civil war battles on land, such as the *Naseby*, named after the first major conflict of the English Civil War.[23]

As a result of these developments, the early 1600s saw a period of port fortification throughout the major harbors of East Asia to protect colonial entrepôts, and the shogunate learned from seamen in Nagasaki of this increasing militarization of maritime trading centers. By 1640, when the Tokugawa began to fortify Nagasaki, the commercial perimeter of East Asian waters was already well garrisoned, with the notable exception of Japan. At the port city of Cavite in the Philippines, adjacent to the Spanish colonial capital of Manila, the deeper harbor could better accommodate galleon trade, prompting the governor-general, Juan de Silva, to construct the triangular fort Fuerza San Felipe between 1609 and 1616.[24] In the immediate aftermath, from 1617 to 1626, the Jesuits in

20. Morley, *Development of Coastal Defense*, p. 7.
21. Rodger, *Safeguard of the Sea*, p. 221.
22. Mack, *The Sea*, p. 74; Black, *Naval Power*, p. 39.
23. Rodger, *Command of the Ocean*, p. 1.
24. Javellana, *Fortress of Empire*, p. 30.

Macau fortified their recently acquired territories against attack with the Monte Fort and other rock bastions on the peninsula.[25] Between 1624 and 1634, Dutch merchants on Taiwan constructed Fort Zeelandia at the city of Anping as the Dutch East India Company's base of operations on the island. During that same decade, their Spanish rivals built a fortress in the Bay of Jilong in northern Taiwan, and soon after one at Danshui.[26] The Dutch also fortified Batavia, the home port of the Dutch East India Company in Indonesia, as a walled city in the 1630s, in response to concerns about native resistance to their presence as well as misgivings about potential attacks from British commercial competitors, whom they had ousted a decade before. That Nagasaki was the only harbor among all of these sites in which the indigenous government, instead of a colonizing power, fortified a port to its own advantage was a powerful symbol of Tokugawa ability to assert its military power both at home and in the broader East Asian maritime world.

Defensive Legacies of the Shimabara Rebellion

Even as the nascent shogunate negotiated the administration of a garrisoned Nagasaki, it prioritized quelling Kyūshū-wide disturbances, rather than guarding against attack on the port proper, thus leaving Nagasaki without resident troops. It charged the early magistrates there not just with overseeing defense and trade in Nagasaki, but also with managing Tokugawa control over the broader island of Kyūshū, where the shogunate still perceived discontented daimyo and the spread of Christianity as imminent challenges to Tokugawa hegemony. These early magistrates were daimyo in their own right and controlled a sizable retainer band in their home provinces. Yet, they did not reside in the port city, but rather in their respective castle towns, in part due to their regional duties, but also to prevent them from profiting from clandestine Nagasaki trade.[27] The first magistrate, Terasawa Hirotaka (1592–1602), lived in nearby Karatsu domain, an easy journey from Nagasaki should an emergency require his presence or the immediate dispatch of troops. His appointment began a line of daimyo magistrates that continued until 1633.

25. Garrett, *The Defenses of Macau*, pp. 9–18.
26. Andrade, *How Taiwan Became Chinese*, p. 80.
27. *Nagasaki kenshi, taigai kōshō hen*, pp. 67–68.

Not until the 1637 uprising on the Shimabara Peninsula (just east of Nagasaki) heightened concern about the seditious, and aggressive, influence of Christianity in Kyūshū did the shogunate design a permanent system for defending the harbor. In this rebellion, 20,000 to 30,000 peasants, frustrated with oppressive taxes and angered by a recent famine, revolted against the local authorities. Since some of the rebel soldiers had previously fought under Christian generals during the battles of Tokugawa consolidation, and many combatants carried banners inscribed with the names of Catholic saints, the shogunate readily interpreted the disturbance as justification for ousting the Christian Portuguese from Japan. The only way to ensure their expulsion, and the future security of Japan, was to fortify Nagasaki harbor against a predicted vengeful return of Portuguese gunboats.

The rebellion shaped the structure of Nagasaki's defense in several ways, but the most dramatic revision was the augmented military agency extended to domains. The superlative performance of coalition forces confirmed the shogunate's idea of securing the port with a composite army from multiple domains in Kyūshū. The specific contributions of Nabeshima (Saga domain) and Kuroda (Fukuoka domain) forces to quelling the rebellion reinforced the military acclaim their forebears had won in Hideyoshi's Korean expeditions of the 1590s (which had first demonstrated the fitness of their houses to secure Nagasaki). Although leading the final assault on Shimabara Castle was critical to their appointment in Nagasaki because it reconfirmed the loyalty of Nabeshima and Kuroda to the Tokugawa, their ability to engineer a military success was equally important. Saga domain contributed more than 34,000 troops at Shimabara, more than any other domain, and roughly a third of all forces. Yet, the shogunate ultimately punished Nabeshima Katsushige, the Saga lord, for allowing his troops to attack Shimabara Castle ahead of official orders. Eager to prove fealty to the Tokugawa after his father's forces had belatedly joined Ieyasu at Sekigahara, Katsushige was likely equally motivated by the thirst for victory—and for the chance to outperform rival daimyo.[28] Fukuoka domain mobilized some 20,000 troops, roughly a fifth of the total forces, with contributions from the branch domains of Tōrenji and Akitsuki. Although Kuroda Tadayuki's father had demonstrated his loyalty at Sekigahara, Tadayuki also owed the

28. Nakamura, "Shimabara no ran to Saga han," pp. 65–66.

Tokugawa a strong showing.[29] He had been censured in 1625 for building a vessel, the *Phoenix* (*Hōō maru*), that was larger than Tokugawa regulations permitted. Further, he narrowly avoided attainder during the daimyo "house disturbance" (*ie sōdō*) of 1632 when he escaped a charge of treason by shogunal courts. At a time when the allegiance of outside (*tozama*) lords to the Tokugawa remained suspect, the superlative performance of these two outside daimyo in battle distinguished them as generals the shogunate could trust to oversee a national security emergency.

Shimabara was the last significant domestic military conflict of the Tokugawa period until the battles of the Meiji Restoration in the 1860s. Rather than ushering in a culture of demilitarization, however, it relaxed laws governing samurai movement across domain lines, enabling composite forces to mobilize more easily for joint defense efforts. *Buke shohatto* regulations ("Codes of conduct for warrior houses"), the core Tokugawa laws guiding behavior of the warrior class, forbade domains from sending forces across the borders of their own territory because of concerns about potentially seditious collusion. In the codes' revisions just prior to the outbreak of the Shimabara Rebellion, Article 4 restricting troop movement had read, "In Edo as well as other provinces, regardless of what situations may occur, the men of a province shall guard their own territory and await [shogunal] orders."[30] Keeping to the letter of the law, Kumamoto and Saga domains initially refused to dispatch reinforcements to aid the Shimabara lord because they lacked official shogunal permission to send troops. The shogun Iemitsu must have been greatly pleased when his inspector in Funai reported that these were the reasons for Kumamoto's refusal.[31] Until this time, the shogunate had encouraged domains to control disturbances without pulling forces from across *kuni* (provinces, whose borders dated back to the ancient period) lines.[32] This limitation was designed as a tool to prevent a trans-domain

29. *Fukuoka kenshi, Fukuoka han tsūshihen*, 1:234.

30. Ishii, *Kinsei hōsei shiryō sōsho*, vol. 2, p. 3, quoted in Irimoto, "Iemitsu seiken," p. 34.

31. Nakamura, "Shimabara no ran to Saga han," pp. 59, 65. Iemitsu's reaction quoted in Irimoto, "Iemitsu seiken," p. 34.

32. *Kuni* were territorial divisions of administration during the ancient period. In the Tokugawa era, they were merely geographical units, but they often transcended domain boundaries. For an important discussion of the use of *kuni* as categories of military "containment" in the Tokugawa period, see Wigen, *A Malleable Map*, esp. pp. 232–33.

challenge to Tokugawa power, as can be seen in the sequence by which unrest was to be forcibly quelled: (1) by forces of the same domain where the disturbance occurred, (2) by adding samurai from other domains within the same *kuni*,[33] and (3) as a last resort, by the call of warrior reinforcements from domains in other *kuni*.[34] But costly delays during the Shimabara Rebellion, resulting from the need to receive official permission for troops to cross domain lines, prompted the shogunate to revise Article 4 of the *buke shohatto*:

> In the previous year's edict (1635), it was ordered that whatever incident may occur, you shall guard your own territory, referring to private altercations within your home territory (*kunidokoro*). However, incidents in which the wishes of *kōgi* [public authority, or shogun] are opposed, or of robbery, are a different matter. Henceforth, remember this well. If anyone disobeys the law of the land, [act] in accordance with the requests of the neighboring domain. If your numbers are small, plan to join forces with surrounding troops.[35]

If anyone, including foreign actors, broke shogunal law, daimyo now had permission to send troops across domain boundaries and to suppress the intransigents without waiting for specific instructions from Edo. Shogunal orders for Nagasaki duty would invoke this new protocol in 1642 by granting permission to neighboring domains of separate provinces (Saga and Fukuoka were component domains of Hizen and Chikuzen *kuni*, respectively) to work together in a territory outside both of their borders.[36]

In addition to sparking these legal changes, the Shimabara Rebellion also shaped the pattern of Fukuoka and Saga domains' alternate attendance trips after they assumed Nagasaki duty. During the uprising,

33. In the Shimabara Rebellion, for example, forces of Kumamoto, a constituent domain of the same Higo *kuni* as the site of the simultaneous uprising in nearby Amakusa, had been mobilized. Although Shimabara proper (the eponymous origin of the disturbance) was a constituent territory of Hizen Province (*kuni*), and Kumamoto part of Higo Province, Kumamoto forces were initially mobilized to quell the simultaneous uprising in Amakusa, part of Higo Province.

34. Nakamura, "Shimabara no ran to Saga han," pp. 59–60.

35. Fujii, *Edo kaibaku*, pp. 259–60; Kuroita, *Tokugawa jikki*, 3:102.

36. Fukuoka, Kokura, and Chōshū forces used this latitude in sending troops across domain borders to repel Chinese smugglers in the early eighteenth century, as discussed in chapter 2.

several neighboring daimyo were absent from their castle towns—either in residence in Edo or en route—making the immediate dispatch of proximate troops difficult. The structure of Nagasaki duty thus accommodated alternate attendance, allowing for Fukuoka and Saga to make their trips to Edo in off-duty years to ensure that at least one of the two lords was always present in Kyūshū to oversee a potential defensive emergency in Nagasaki.

The anti-Christian sentiment that escalated following the rebellion led the shogun to prohibit Portuguese trade in mid-1639, making a military presence there critical to guard against resistance by recalcitrant captains. Along with this prohibition, the shogunate issued new regulations for the western lords of coastal provinces, especially those in Kyūshū. The decree read: "From here forward that country [Portugal] will secretly send priests, and we must prevent their ships from landing on our shores." To that end, each domain was ordered to place "trustworthy fellows along its coasts, and if any ship arrives, it shall be carefully inspected."[37] A second order accompanied this edict, commanding domainal troops to escort to Nagasaki all foreign ships that drifted to shore after being blown off course (Nagasaki *kaisō rei*).[38] This second directive further centralized foreign interaction in Nagasaki, making standing defenses there crucial to respond to defiant vessels. In Saga domain, these orders led to the creation of several lookout posts, including one at Fukahori, at the seaward end of the promontory south of the city, which would be transformed into an important harbor battery two years later when permanent Nagasaki defenses were officially implemented.

As Nagasaki emerged at the center of Kyūshū defenses, Edo experimented with various combinations of *fudai* daimyo (hereditary allies considered loyal to the Tokugawa) and magistrate authority in overseeing domainal troops. Initially shogunal officials and hereditary lords were given supreme command in emergencies. But following the prohibition of Portuguese ships, Shogun Iemitsu took a first step toward assigning local, often outside (*tozama*) daimyo responsibility for Nagasaki security. Summoning five outside lords in Kyūshū with domains bordering the sea to Edo Castle, he ordered them to report to both Edo and Nagasaki if any foreign ships arrived along their shores, and to confer with the *fudai* daimyo of Shimabara and the western inspector,

37. Nakamura, "Shimabara no ran to Saga han," p. 95.
38. Ibid., p. 96.

Kōriki Tadafusa, should an altercation occur.[39] Iemitsu also appointed the guardian of Himeji Castle and grandson of Ieyasu, Matsudaira Tadaaki, as commanding general of all domain forces sent to confront foreign vessels.[40] These measures placed a *fudai* daimyo enfeoffed in a distant part of Honshū (Himeji was several days' journey from Nagasaki) in charge of assembling emergency forces in Nagasaki. Thus, the resulting pre-1641 system was a *fudai*-centric hierarchy of decision making in which the wielders of authority had scant knowledge of the geography of Nagasaki harbor and comparatively few forces at their personal command in easy range of the port.[41]

De jure oversight lay with remote *fudai* officials, but execution was local. Although the shogunate expelled the Portuguese in 1639 following the Shimabara Rebellion, the next year a Portuguese mission returned to reestablish commerce. When they anchored, Ōmura domain torched their ship and Saga forces executed sixty-one sailors for violating shogunal law. The day after the ill-fated vessel's thirteen remaining crew members departed for Macau, Edo issued an order to all domains calling for lookout posts and reinforcing instructions to send every foreign ship, including Chinese vessels, to Nagasaki.[42] One of the domains that implemented this order with greatest alacrity was Fukuoka, whose lord established lookout posts at five locations along the domain coast: Himejima, Nishiura, Aijima, Oshima, and Iwaya.[43] Moreover, the domain assigned guard boats to three islands in the Genkai Sea—Rojima, Shirajima, and Okinoshima—to make daily surveillance rounds, with the retainers of the Fukuoka chief retainer used as reinforcements. For the short term, Nagasaki was secured by an ad hoc amalgam of domainal

39. Fujii, *Tokugawa Iemitsu*, p. 173. Takayanagi and Ishii, *Ofuregaki Kampō shūsei*, p. 629. These five men were Hosokawa Tadatoshi, Arima Toyōji, Tachibana Ryūsai, Kuroda Tadayuki, and Nabeshima Naoshige. Hosokawa was daimyo of Kumamoto domain, Arima of Kurume, and Tachibana (also known as Shigemune) of Yanagawa. All five were *tozama* lords.

40. Fujii, *Tokugawa Iemitsu*, p. 174.

41. This *fudai*-centricity, which continued even into the first decades of the Nagasaki defense system, reflected Tokugawa hesitancy to completely trust *tozama* (outside) daimyo (such as Fukuoka and Saga) well into the mid-seventeenth century.

42. Nakamura, "Shimabara no ran to Saga han," pp. 96–97; Kawazoe and Fukuoka komonjo o yomu kai, *Shintei Kuroda kafu*, vol. 2, "Tadayuki ki," pp. 179–80.

43. Kawazoe and Fukuoka komonjo o yomu kai, *Shintei Kuroda kafu, Kuroda kafu sakuin, nenpyō*, p. 890.

forces. Three hundred troops from Shimabara were to guard the city of Nagasaki, while an additional 110 Ōmura samurai and foot soldiers—supported by three ships and fifty-nine sailors—protected the harbor.[44]

Edo officials—anticipating retaliation from the Portuguese—started to consider basing a formalized, permanent security force for Kyūshū in Nagasaki. Eight months later, in early 1641, the shogunate made Fukuoka domain responsible for the defense of Nagasaki, and nearby Gotō and Ōmura domains were similarly appointed to guard their own coastlines, in exchange for reduced alternate attendance. The following year, the shogunate named Saga domain as Fukuoka's military partner in Nagasaki. With these new assignments, the creation of a composite defense force had begun: one in which not only the provision of troops and weapons in Nagasaki but also broader decisions about their mobilization and defensive strategy would gradually fall to this single pair of domains.

Establishing a Composite Force Defense

The most effective method of securing Nagasaki might well have been to transform it into a seaside castle town like neighboring Fukuoka, with a fortress and adjacent housing for thousands of samurai. Understanding why this scenario did not develop is key to explaining the selection of Fukuoka and Saga as the port's defenders. Further, it clarifies why the distribution of military authority between the magistrate and daimyo in Nagasaki defense became so contentious. Having two adjacent domains shoulder responsibility for defending a *tenryō* (a direct Tokugawa territory; Nagasaki had become one in 1604) was the least expensive way for the shogunate to secure its port, even if a permanent samurai population would have more quickly responded to an emergency. But even more critical than delegating expenses was retaining a shogunal monopoly on trade and information about the outside world, control that might have been compromised were port activities administered by a local lord rather than a bureaucratic appointee, such as the magistrate. Thus, the Tokugawa could not have realistically considered transforming the area of Nagasaki into a domain privately administered by a local warrior family with its attendant retainer band.

44. *Hirado Oranda shōkan no nikki*, pp. 88–89, quoted in Nakamura, "Sakoku no keisei to Fukuoka han," p. 30.

At the same time, the Nagasaki magistrate from the late 1630s onward did not possess sufficient personal retainers under his command to mount a preliminary defense while awaiting reinforcements from the neighboring domains, because he was no longer a daimyo. The military limitations of the magistrate were largely the result of Takenaka Shigeyoshi, whose misconduct during his tenure as magistrate (1629–33) had prompted the shogun to declare daimyo ineligible for the post. Takenaka was lord of Funai domain in Bungo, with an assessed income of 20,000 *koku*. Extant documents do not allow precise calculations of the size of the Funai retainer band in the early Tokugawa decades, but a domain of this income would have likely put some 2,000 retainers at a daimyo's service in an emergency.[45] Following Takenaka's financial malfeasance and suicide in 1633, however, the shogunate ceased to assign daimyo to the position of magistrate, instead appointing two *hatamoto* officials—direct Tokugawa retainers of impressive rank but middling income—to serve jointly. Since these individuals had only some twenty to thirty subordinates under their direct command, access to military troops from a nearby domain became critical.

Given that Nagasaki remained a shogunal territory, without its own resident samurai population, and given the military limitations of the magistrate's modest retainer band, the final configuration of Nagasaki military security hinged on the assignment of neighboring domainal forces to create a composite defense for the port. The two domains delegated for this duty—Fukuoka and Saga—seem to have been selected for two main reasons: the past military success of their hereditary daimyo lineages predating Shimabara and their specific geographical locations. Fukuoka's appointment in early 1641 came barely a year after the burning of the Portuguese ship, reflecting the new urgency of defending the city. The specific charge given to thirty-nine-year-old Kuroda Tadayuki was to prevent uninvited foreign ships—specifically Portuguese *galeota* but other foreign ships (*ikokusen*) as well—from landing on Japanese shores.[46] That Nagamasa, Tadayuki's father, had distinguished himself by sailing at the vanguard of Hideyoshi's 1592 attack on Korea and tak-

45. When ordered to supply reinforcements for the harbor seven years later, Ōmura domain, with an assessed income of not quite 30,000 *koku* (one and a half times that of Funai) had dispatched 2,600 men.

46. Kawazoe and Fukuoka komonjo o yomu kai, *Shintei Kuroda kafu*, vol. 2, "Tadayuki ki," pp. 182–83.

ing Changwon Castle in the first month of fighting undoubtedly enhanced the martial reputation of the Kuroda lineage.[47] Similarly, Nabeshima Naoshige rose to power in Saga in part by leading some 12,000 Saga troops into battle in Korea. This performance also anchored his family pedigree, making Saga worthy of becoming a military guardian of Nagasaki.[48]

The physical locations of the domains also complemented each other, offering a comparative advantage for the shogunate's broader security goals that allowed them to edge out other potential candidates. For example, Ōmura and Shimabara domains had supplied the interim defense of the port and were adjacent to Nagasaki (and thus might have dispatched forces more quickly). But because those domains' assessed incomes were only 27,900 *koku* and 40,000 *koku*, respectively, their retainer bands were not large enough to shoulder primary defense of the harbor.[49] By contrast, Kumamoto domain (an outside territory located just across the Ariake Sea from Nagasaki) was far wealthier than Fukuoka or Saga, with an assessed income of 515,000 *koku*. Moreover, its castle town was closer to Nagasaki than that of Fukuoka. Nonetheless, Iemitsu is said to have thought Fukuoka's military capabilities superior. Satsuma domain, with its large military and considerable wealth, presented another possible choice. While the shogunate briefly considered pairing Satsuma domain with Fukuoka, it ultimately rejected this idea to allow Satsuma to focus on managing the Ryūkyū trade, which profited both the shogunate's coffers and its strategic interests in the East China Sea.[50]

When combined as a pair, Fukuoka and Saga (the seventh- and tenth-wealthiest domains in Japan, respectively) promised a more effective joint choice than other combinations.[51] Saga domain territory fell on both sides of the shogunal lands of Nagasaki, meaning that portions of its retainer

47. Maruyama, "Bakuhanseika no Genkai nada kōtsū," p. 6; Kawazoe and and Fukuoka komonjo o yomu kai, *Shintei Kuroda kafu, Kuroda kafu sakuin, nenpyō*, pp. 870–73.

48. Maruyama, "Kyūshū: kinsei no maku ake to tenkai," p. 66; Jōjima and Sugitani, *Saga ken no rekishi*, p. 71.

49. Shimabara's assessed income was less than a tenth of that of Fukuoka.

50. Nakamura, "Sakoku no keisei to Fukuoka han," p. 33.

51. See Craig, *Chōshū in the Meiji Restoration*, p. 11. Among other Kyūshū domains, Satsuma was the second largest in Tokugawa Japan, and Kumamoto the sixth, but for reasons discussed previously were not seriously considered. Kyūshū contained four of the ten largest domains.

band were already stationed on the peninsula south of the city. Thus their commitment to port security came not just out of obligation to the shogunate but also from interest in protecting their own lands.[52] Located on the Sea of Japan coast, Fukuoka was the closest domain to mainland Asia (other than Tsushima). It had historically served as a buffer zone for continental threats—especially during the thirteenth-century Mongol invasions—and might again provide a front-line defense were China ever to menace Japan.[53]

Saga and Fukuoka initially operated in a hierarchical and complex system of layered oversight in which other actors retained the right of supreme command. As the directive assigning Nabeshima Katsushige to Nagasaki service read: "If a galeota [Portuguese ship] is to land, [as Matsudaira Shimosa no kami],[54] Inoue Chikugo no kami,[55] Kōriki Settsu no kami,[56] Baba Saburōzaemon[57] and Tsuge Heimon[58] have been [instructed], you are to confer with them."[59] In case of an emergency, Katsushige was to consult with three sets of individuals: the Nagasaki magistrates in Edo and Nagasaki; key *fudai* officials, such as the lords of Shimabara and Himeji; and the Tokugawa inspectors who reported directly to the central shogunal council.[60]

In spite of this cumbersome decision-by-consensus structure that privileged authorities outside Kyūshū, both Nabeshima Katsushige and Kuroda Tadayuki worked to establish their personal imprint on the responsibility, exhibiting an eagerness to excel that suggested they wanted to ensure that this newly created post became a hereditary office. Soon after receiving his charge, Katsushige consulted with three senior councillors to draft a detailed five-point plan for Nagasaki duty. Katsushige

52. In *Treasures Among Men*, p. 105, Harold Bolitho also alludes to the importance of proximity.

53. Kawazoe and Fukuoka komonjo o yomu kai, *Shintei Kuroda kafu*, vol. 2, "Tadayuki ki," p. 184.

54. Himeji lord, Tadaaki.

55. Tokugawa grand inspector.

56. Shimabara lord, Tadafusa.

57. Nagasaki magistrate then in Nagasaki.

58. Nagasaki magistrate then in Edo.

59. Nakamura and Takano, "Nagasaki keibi to zaisei," p. 50; Maruyama, "Tokugawa seikenka ni okeru sankin kōtai," p. 977.

60. A system of two magistrates serving simultaneously but alternating duty in Nagasaki was in place at the time.

was apparently interested in codifying semi-independent action. He recognized the critical role of Saga in defending Nagasaki harbor given that Fukahori, an allied territory governed by Saga advisers, would be the first point of contact with Portuguese vessels.[61] The main elements of his plan included (1) ascertaining the intentions of Portuguese ships from Fukahori, the Saga promontory bordering the east entrance to Nagasaki harbor, and then forwarding notice to Nagasaki; (2) allowing the Portuguese crew to go ashore (with guards attached) and then sending news promptly to Nagasaki; and (3) stationing 200 to 300 men at Fukahori.[62] Although this document recognized that Saga should obtain permission before dispatching guard boats, Katsushige managed to insert his domain as both an executor of defense and a creator of its underlying policy.

Katsushige also cautiously tested the latitude of his new authority in construction and shipbuilding projects. Although the 1609 edict ordering the destruction of all ships over 500 *koku* caused domainal navies to wane, Katsushige nonetheless worked to strengthen the Saga domain fleet after being charged to protect Nagasaki. A letter of 1646 revealed his interest in building a small hut at the Fukahori promontory to house gunners and other soldiers. It also stated that the domain would request permission from the Nagasaki magistrates to build seaworthy ships of 300 to 350 *koku*, as well as ships considered very large, of 400 *koku*, for use in case of emergency, which was understood to be the unexpected appearance of a foreign vessel.[63] Despite a clear need for these vessels, Katsushige's correspondence revealed his concern about the shogun's perception of his interest in amassing a naval fleet: "Given that this is an 'on-duty' year and provisions are lacking, I should [even] send boats to the Fukahori battery, but since this might seem suspicious, I recognize that I should not."[64] Even as both domains invested considerable resources in fulfilling their charge, they had to be cautious lest the shogunate interpret their attempts to execute harbor duty as having seditious overtones.

Kuroda Tadayuki, too, tested the extent of his newly acquired influence when in the spring of 1647, while in Edo on alternate attendance,

61. Maruyama, "Tokugawa seikenka ni okeru sankin kōtai," p. 981.
62. Ibid.
63. *Nabeshima ke monjo*, p. 378, quoted in Takeno, *Han bōekishi no kenkyū*, p. 155.
64. *Nabeshima ke monjo*, p. 718, quoted in Takeno, *Han bōekishi no kenkyū*, p. 156.

he sent a message to his neighboring daimyo, Ōmura Suminobu, asking for special permission to borrow a small tract of land at Tokitsu. For the previous six years, Tadayuki had traveled to Nagasaki several times a year as joint head of the harbor defenses. For some time now he had wanted to construct a simple shelter in the port of Tokitsu, where he could rest after crossing the Ariake Sea and compose himself before entering Nagasaki to meet the magistrate. Once Suminobu agreed, Tadayuki consulted with the senior councillor Sakai Tadakatsu to avoid friction over this unprecedented construction outside his own domain. Receiving shogunal permission, Tadayuki soon dispatched a carpenter and supervisor from among his retainers to build the rest house. It was finished not a moment too soon, for immediately afterward, in the sixth month, two Portuguese ships arrived in Nagasaki, supplying the first serious test to the harbor's defense system and cause for Fukuoka to send both its troops and their lord to Nagasaki.[65]

The construction of a small building in a tiny port town en route from Fukuoka to Nagasaki is unexceptional at first glance, but a closer look reveals three important details about domestic defense at the time this Tokitsu rest house was completed. First, since Fukuoka and Saga had been appointed to Nagasaki duty in 1641, a wave of defense-related construction had ensued. Initially, temporary huts had been constructed at the two main batteries guarding the harbor, Nishidomari and Tomachi, with buildings dismantled and rebuilt at the change of domain guard in the fourth month of each year. But gradually permanent structures replaced these makeshift quarters. The Tokitsu rest house reflected the increasing permanency of a fledgling defense system. Second, the need for rest houses such as the Tokitsu annex reveals the growing regularity of the Nagasaki defense cycle. Rest stops were necessary because the Fukuoka and Saga lords now traveled to Nagasaki three times annually during on-duty, or *tōban*, years: in the fourth month (at the annual change of domain guard between Fukuoka and Saga); in the seventh month (when Dutch merchant vessels arrived); and in the ninth month (when the Dutch departed). Third, the location of the rest house in Ōmura territory demonstrated the auxiliary role domains other than Fukuoka and Saga would play in the initial years of Nagasaki defense.

65. Kawazoe and Fukuoka komonjo o yomu kai, *Shintei Kuroda kafu*, vol. 2, "Tadayuki ki," pp. 192–93.

Domainal Agency Following the Return of the Portuguese

The first incident in which foreign vessels tested the efficacy of domain-led defense of the Tokugawa shoreline was the simultaneous arrival of two Portuguese ships in Nagasaki requesting trade in 1647. The appearance of the ships, which carried an ambassador from Lisbon, immediately raised concerns since their flags did not match the Dutch design, and they were fortified galleons rather than the smaller *galleota*. In response to their arrival, the Nagasaki magistrate asked neighboring domains to send troops and requested that Fukuoka, on duty since the fourth month, increase its forces.[66] After receiving orders from the shogunate to depart from Nagasaki, the Portuguese set sail without incident. Indicative of the still marginal policy role of Fukuoka and Saga domains, only top advisers of Shogun Iemitsu in Edo participated in emergency discussions of how to respond.[67]

In this year, Fukuoka and Saga's military leadership in the harbor appears to have still been probationary. Before the final, peaceful departure of the Portuguese, ten domains sent a total of 55,528 troops to defend the harbor. Saga and Fukuoka sent the largest forces, of 11,730 and 11,350, respectively. Although these domains contributed more than 40 percent of the total number of troops, the shogunate continued to perceive that *fudai* daimyo were the most loyal representatives of its interests. Thus, the commanding general of the coalition forces in 1647 was a *fudai* lord, Matsudaira Sadayuki of Iyo Matsuyama, whom the shogunate named to the post of Nagasaki commander (Nagasaki *tandai shoku*). Matsudaira Tadaaki of Himeiji had been the post's first appointee five years earlier, directed to collaborate with the Nagasaki magistrate should a ship arrive in the port. The same held for Sadayuki. Even though Sadayuki contributed only 11 percent of the troops (6,300 men) and hailed from distant Shikoku, his position as a *fudai* leader elevated his power over decision making.

Although *fudai* actors officially oversaw emergency mobilization, participating domains on the ground maneuvered to assert their agency in the military response. Matsudaira Sadayuki, the Nagasaki commander,

66. Ibid., 2:3–4.
67. Kuroita, *Tokugawa jikki*, 3:491.

finally arrived on the thirteenth of the seventh month along with Saga, Kumamoto, Yanagawa, and Karatsu forces.[68] Once Sadayuki, the Shikoku lord, arrived, he met with Kuroda Tadayuki and assured him that he would send forces were the shogun to order an attack on the ships. But Tadayuki argued that Sadayuki's most important role was to give orders, and since Fukuoka was the on-duty domain that year, his forces would attack—alone, if necessary. Sadayuki replied that since he had just been appointed three years earlier, he could not simply be present without making further contributions.[69] Tadayuki apparently felt a strong sense of ownership over Nagasaki duty and would maneuver as much as possible to keep it under his control.

An analysis of this episode from the perspective of Fukuoka also indicates that the magistrate was not as firmly in control of military matters as previous accounts suggest.[70] A previous edict issued by the shogun's councillors in 1645 prohibited domain troops from engaging the enemy without express permission from the shogunate.[71] Yet the conduct of domains during this incident in 1647 demonstrates that the chain of command was not always strictly observed—and that violations might go without punishment. After receiving news of the ships' arrival, the following day Ōmura sent 3,000 troops to Nagasaki without waiting for an official request from the magistrate.[72] Kuroda Tadayuki sent troops four days later, on the twenty-ninth, after receiving explicit orders from the Nagasaki magistrate on the twenty-seventh.[73] He had departed for Nagasaki on the twenty-sixth, however, without the express permission of the magistrate.[74]

68. Kawazoe and Fukuoka komonjo o yomu kai, *Shintei Kuroda kafu, Kuroda kafu sakuin, nenpyō*, p. 892.

69. Kawazoe and Fukuoka komonjo o yomu kai, *Shintei Kuroda kafu*, vol. 2, "Tadayuki ki," p. 202.

70. The image that emerges from the shogunate-centric documents of the *Tsūkō ichiran*, the primary sources conventionally used to analyze this incident, suggests significant military control of the magistrate.

71. This edict from 1645/2 is recorded in Ōmura documents and cited in Kimura, "17 seiki chūyō bakuhansei kokka," pp. 109–112, and Matsuo, "Porutogaru shisetsusen," p. 61.

72. Matsuo, "Porutogaru shisetsusen," pp. 62–63.

73. Kawazoe and Fukuoka komonjo o yomu kai, *Shintei Kuroda kafu*, vol. 2, "Tadayuki ki," pp. 195–97.

74. Ibid., p. 194, says he leaves on the twenty-sixth, but the *Kuroda kafu nenpyō* (p. 892) says he and Fukuoka troops departed on the twenty-seventh. Since the

Similarly, once in Nagasaki, Tadayuki continued to resist magistrate directives. On the twenty-ninth, one of the chief retainers of Hirado domain, Nagamura Uchizōsuke, repeatedly petitioned the magistrate to allow troops from his domain to join the harbor defense in order to demonstrate the loyalty of the Matsuura house. His request was rejected because the magistrate concluded that Hirado shores, too, needed to be well guarded.[75] Rebuffed by the shogunal proxy, Nagamura then obtained an audience with Tadayuki, head of harbor defense that year. Nagamura invoked the long history of good relations between the Kuroda and Matsuura houses and ultimately received permission directly from Tadayuki to station Hirado boats near the Nishidomari battery as part of the line of ships preventing the Portuguese from departing.[76] Clearly, the orders of the magistrate were not inviolate. Viewed from the perspective of these daily negotiations, the 1647 incident suggests that Tadayuki, the Fukuoka lord, gained considerable authority by strategizing to establish himself (or at least the on-duty domain) as the primary arbiter of defense matters.

This incident also reveals the unanticipated utility of appointing Fukuoka domain to Nagasaki duty, since the Kuroda lord could leverage the wealth of Hakata merchants to support his security obligations. During this period the Nagasaki administrator (*daikan*) was Suetsugu Heizō, a descendant of a well-known merchant named Suetsugu Kōzen (1546–1630) based in Hakata, the flourishing commercial center of Fukuoka domain. During the month the ships were present, Suetsugu procured—at great cost—twenty-five small ships to send to Nagasaki for a possible attack on the Portuguese ships in the harbor. Each ship was manned with two sailors from Nagasaki, who received two *shō* (just under a gallon) of rice per day as payment. Tadayuki's retainers—Tanaka Gorōemon, Tsuda Ichinojō, and the lord of the Minagi branch of the Kuroda family, Kuroda Sanzaemon—shouldered the cost of the twenty-five ships, some 1 *kan* 250 *me* silver.[77] Hakata merchants Itō Kozaemon and Oga Suemon provided

---

nenpyō was compiled from the Annals of the Kuroda House, it seems likely the first source is correct.

75. Ibid., pp. 202–3. After arriving in Nagasaki, the daimyo of Gotō, Ōmura, and Hirado were each told to return home in order to supervise protection of their own shores.

76. Ibid., p. 203. Also mentioned in Yamamoto, *Nagasaki kikiyaku nikki*, pp. 53–54, although he does not specify his source.

77. Tanaka seems to be Gorōbei from Kawazoe and Fukuoka komonjo o yomu kai, *Shintei Kuroda kafu*, vol. 2, "Tadayuki ki," p. 198, who is mentioned there in conjunction with Tsuda Ichinojō and Kuroda Sanazaemon.

the rice stipends for sailors and spent an additional 10 *kan* silver to requisition twelve merchant ships from Hirado, Kokura, Ōmura, Amakusa, and Nagasaki that would be loaded with brush and used as fire boats to burn the Portuguese ships if necessary.[78] In return for providing the straw to burn the ships, Oga received a fifty-person allotment of rice as a reward, a tremendous sum for a merchant.[79] These examples provide an important early indication of how the domain parceled out the expenses of defense to high-ranking retainers as well as merchants, revealing that Nagasaki duty was not perceived as the sole preserve of the samurai: financing the execution of the monopoly on violence was in fact the responsibility of the whole domain.

Reforms following the departure of these Portuguese ships further underscored the role of Fukuoka and Saga in Nagasaki defenses and codified the most basic rules governing its execution. First, the shogunate ordered the lords of Saga and Fukuoka to remain in their domains during off-duty years until the Dutch merchant ships departed in the ninth month (at the end of their summer trading season). This duty was called supplemental guard (*kaban*) and ensured that both lords would be close at hand should an emergency arise involving the unarmed Dutch vessels (which were required to hand over all weapons to Japanese authorities while in port). Requiring both lords to remain in Kyūshū during the trading season foreshadowed the increasing importance of their oversight. From 1648, these daimyo departed their domains on alternate attendance in the tenth month, returning in the second month of the following year. This change reduced their stay in Edo to about three months (instead of the conventional six to twelve), earning them the mocking moniker "hundred-day daimyo" (*hyaku nichi daimyō*).

In addition to codifying daimyo movement, the shogunate ordered both Fukuoka and Saga to begin building the infrastructure to make their duty more visually imposing to incoming vessels and to accommodate increasing numbers of troops. They constructed thirty-nine modest buildings at the two main batteries of Tomachi and Nishidomari, which were located across from each other on the north and south sides, respectively, of the inner harbor.[80] At the same time, the shogunate

78. Nakamura, "Sakokusei no kakuritsu to Fukuoka han," p. 6.
79. Takeno, *Han boekishi no kenkyū*, p. 237.
80. Nakamura, "Sakokusei no kakuritsu to Fukuoka han," p. 7.

ordered Ōmura domain to build seven gun batteries in the inner and outer harbors even though only two of the sites fell within Ōmura domain.[81] The on-duty domain was assigned responsibility for the three inner-harbor posts (Otao, Kōzaki, and Megami) closest to the city center and considered most important; responsibility for the four outer-harbor posts fell to the off-duty domain. Sources differ about the number of weapons added to the harbor batteries during these initial reforms, but it seems that about ten cannon and nine smaller firearms were divided among the on-duty posts, and twelve guns were distributed among the four off-duty posts. These weapons included both shogunal pieces on loan from Osaka Castle and arms owned by the individual daimyo houses, prompting domainal reforms to make order out of this mélange. Tadayuki not only required his retainers to establish specific banner designs for each division of Fukuoka troops posted in the harbor; he also ordered the standardization of shot and barrel size of firearms, hinting at the difficulties soldiers likely encountered in finding ammunition to fit their diverse weapons.[82]

The final change stemming from the 1647 incident was the compulsory establishment of Nagasaki residences (*yashiki*) for fourteen domains from southwest Japan (map 2). Each was permanently manned with high-ranking officials who would gather information and facilitate communication in time of emergency.[83] Fukuoka and Saga were two of six domains (including Kumamoto, Tsushima, Kokura, and Hirado) required to post officials in this residence year round. The eight domains of Kagoshima, Hagi, Kurume, Yanagawa, Shimabara, Karatsu, Ōmura, and Gotō were required to station officials only between the fifth and ninth months, when the Dutch were in port and thus the possibility of attack perceived to be greatest.[84]

Even with the increasing regimentation of their obligations in Nagasaki, however, Fukuoka and Saga did not always adhere to the letter of

81. Otao (Nagasaki territory), Kōzaki (Nagasaki), Takaboko (Saga), Kage no O (Saga), Naginata Iwa (Saga), Shirasaki (Ōmura), and Megami (Ōmura).

82. Kawazoe and Fukuoka komonjo o yomu kai, *Shintei Kuroda kafu*, vol. 2, "Tadayuki ki," pp. 245, 247.

83. Yamamoto, *Nagasaki kikiyaku nikki*, pp. 66–68. The "intelligence officers" did not acquire the title of *kikiyaku*, however, until sometime between 1751 and 1771.

84. The prevailing trade winds, which favored sailing ships at that time of year, made the arrival of unexpected guests most likely during this season. Nakamura, "Sakokusei no kakuritsu to Fukuoka han," p. 11.

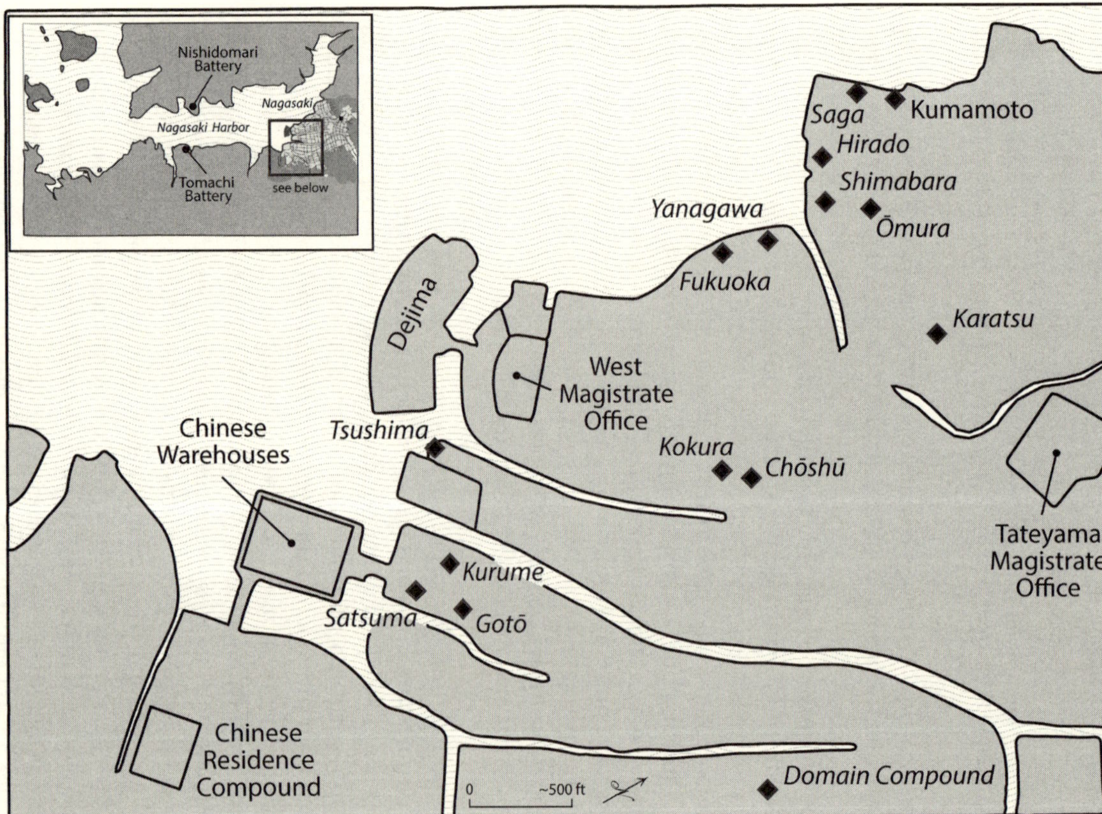

MAP 2 Nagasaki harbor batteries and domainal residences, late seventeenth century (Hellyer, *Defining Engagement*, 33; the harbor map is adapted from Fukuoka shi hakubutsukan, *Genkai nada no Edo jidai*, 116).

the law. Surprisingly, they were not censured by the magistrate, Nagasaki commander (*tandai shoku*), or shogunate for violations, suggesting Tokugawa tolerance for experimentation during the duty's formative stages. Despite early efforts to impress the shogunate with their loyalty, once the domains secured their posts and successfully negotiated an emergency, they exercised greater latitude in executing their duty. After the 1647 reform period, the on-duty domain became technically responsible for posting 1,000 troops in Nagasaki. As early as 1666, however, both domains dispatched considerably fewer than this number: Saga sent only 680 troops to Nagasaki, and the following year, Fukuoka sent only 830. At the end of the Enpō era (1673–80), Fukuoka sent 790 troops and Saga about 700. By the beginning of the following century, in the Shōtoku period (1711–15), Fukuoka sent some 900 men and Saga about 800. That no Tokugawa official protested these shortcomings suggests diminishing concern about a foreign attack. Further, it revealed the inability of the Nagasaki commander, absent from Nagasaki and a *hatamoto* magistrate without troops of his own, to compel Fukuoka and Saga domains to dispatch the full complement of soldiers.

The death of Shogun Iemitsu in 1651 spurred a strategy to ensure continued vigilance in Nagasaki during transitions in either shogunal or Fukuoka and Saga daimyo leadership. After this point, the shogunate named the lords of domains closer to Nagasaki as commander. While Matsudaira Tadaaki and Matsudaira Sadayuki had hailed from southwest Honshū (Himeji) and Shikoku (Iyo Matsuyama), respectively, the final two Nagasaki commanders were Kyūshū men: Ogasawara Tadazane of Kokura domain and Okubo Tadamoto of Karatsu domain. The appointment of these individuals in 1662 and 1663, respectively, resulted from the rise to power of a young shogun, Ietsuna (r. 1651–63), who, at barely twenty, "physically weak," and controlled by advisers, hardly prioritized the Nagasaki service that his father had created.[85] Filling the post of Nagasaki commander with local daimyo who would be committed to Nagasaki security out of self-interest was prudent.

The death of Kyūshū lords also figured into this new arrangement of appointing local Nagasaki commanders. Kuroda Tadayuki, who had supervised Fukuoka's presence in Nagasaki since the defense system's inception in 1641, died in 1654. Nabeshima Katsushige, who had led

85. Hall, "The *Bakuhan* System," p. 165; Totman, *Politics in the Tokugawa Bakufu*, p. 211.

Saga's role in port since 1642, died three years later, in 1657. This meant that all three creators of the Nagasaki system—the shogun Iemitsu and two daimyo—died within just six years. The new Fukuoka and Saga lords, Kuroda Mitsuyuki and Nabeshima Mitsushige, were both in their midtwenties, had spent their lives far away in Edo, and had certainly never managed the unexpected arrival of a foreign vessel. Clearly, external oversight continued to be necessary until these new leaders had demonstrated their fitness to protect Nagasaki.

Nagasaki Military Authority after 1670

The Portuguese did not return after 1647 and concerns about foreign attack receded in midcentury, shifting the core responsibility of Fukuoka and Saga domains to daily surveillance of Nagasaki trade. As peacekeeping emerged as their primary role, the shogunate insisted less and less on *fudai* oversight of port security. The most important individual leaders were now the local lords, who visited the harbor on average three times per year and provided troops from day to day. The retainers of these lords best understood the geography of the harbor, its tidal shifts, and its wind patterns, all key for defensive strategy. Thus, when Ogasawara Tadazane died shortly after assuming the office of Nagasaki commander in 1663, Okubo Tadamoto of Karatsu took over, but on his death in 1670, the position was eliminated.[86] While the abolition of this post may indicate some decline in shogunal concern about the defense of Kyūshū, it more likely signaled a recognition that actual control of defense now lay with Fukuoka and Saga domains and the magistrate.[87]

Following the abolition of the Nagasaki commander post, however, no edict filled the gap to specify the relationship between the Nagasaki magistrate and the domains in defending the harbor. Eliminating this office exposed the military dependency of the magistrate on the domains—and the structural ambiguities created by the absence of a unified command during emergencies. The fracturing of military authority in Nagasaki, along with maneuvering to exploit the vagueness of its organization to domainal advantage, became especially visible in two

86. *Fukuoka kenshi, Fukuoka han tsūshihen*, 1:525.
87. Nakamura, "Sakokusei no kakuritsu to Fukuoka han," p. 16.

incidents following Okubo's death: the *Return* incident of 1673 and the *São Paulo* incident of 1685.

The British ship *Return* sailed into Nagasaki harbor requesting commercial relations in the summer of 1673, departing within two months without incident. Although the *Return* was a merchant ship, domain officials knew from the captain's declaration that a sister vessel was due to arrive from Taiwan, putting them on edge as they awaited directives from Edo.[88] Two days after the ship's arrival, Kuroda Mitsuyuki, the lord of Fukuoka (the on-duty domain), received instructions from the Nagasaki magistrate, Okano Sadaaki, to leave for Nagasaki. As he prepared to depart, a second messenger brought new orders for Kuroda to remain in his castle town since the ship was just a merchant vessel (and thus apparently not threatening).[89]

Unsatisfied with the retraction, Mitsuyuki crafted a pretext to travel to Nagasaki. Because Mitsuyuki had succeeded his father as daimyo seven years after the arrival of the Portuguese ships in 1647 and had lived in Edo until that point, he had never seen a European ship other than that of the Dutch. He appeared determined to travel to Nagasaki while the *Return* was in port, apparently motivated by a combined sense of responsibility to his Nagasaki charge and his own curiosity. As the on-duty lord, Mitsuyuki still had to receive explicit permission from the magistrate before traveling to Nagasaki. Although Okano ordered him to remain in Fukuoka, Mitsuyuki soon found a pretense for pressing his case with the magistrate. According to precedent, in the sixth month of each year, the lord of the on-duty domain rushed to Nagasaki to greet the new factor—the chief of the Dutch East India Company's trading post on Dejima in Nagasaki harbor—as soon as news of his arrival reached the castle town. A week after the *Return* dropped anchor, a Dutch merchant vessel entered Nagasaki harbor, offering Mitsuyuki the opportunity he awaited.[90]

The incident makes clear that, even in times of emergency, the on-duty daimyo had to receive explicit permission from the magistrate before traveling to Nagasaki. But the lord had leeway in establishing a

88. The Fukuoka *kikiyaku* seemingly shared this information with Mitsuyuki just after he arrived in Nagasaki. Kawazoe and Fukuoka komonjo o yomu kai, *Shintei Kuroda kafu*, vol. 2, "Mitsuyuki ki," p. 362.

89. Ibid., 2:363.

90. Ibid., 2:364.

legitimate purpose for the trip. Mitsuyuki petitioned Okano for permission to travel with the arrival of this Dutch trading vessel, even though the factor was not aboard, since the presence of the *Return* presented unusual circumstances. But Okano declined to meet with Fukuoka officials, ostensibly because of other official business, and continually avoided a response. Finally, after nine days of deliberation, the magistrate permitted both Mitsuyuki and his heir, Kuroda Tsunayuki, to travel to Nagasaki. Still, Okano ordered them not to remain there awaiting the arrival of the factor's ship (a departure from protocol, Fukuoka officials noted, that would require special explanation in Edo).[91]

We can only speculate about each actor's motivations. There is no reason to conclude that the magistrate delayed his decision merely to ascertain if Mitsuyuki's presence was truly necessary, because in fact the daimyo's role was largely ceremonial and his subordinates made the critical military decisions in a crisis. It seems more likely that the magistrate equivocated to prevent the lord and his entourage from competing with him for symbolic control of the British presence during the first few days of the *Return*'s arrival. Mitsuyuki may have persisted purely out of curiosity, because of his eagerness to make an inaugural procession to Nagasaki as daimyo and parade his status before the magistrate, or perhaps because of the possibility of covert trade arrangements between his domain and the Dutch. But what is clear is that the military relationship between the magistrate and domains was sufficiently ambiguous to allow broadly differing interpretations of what justified the presence of the daimyo, and that the daimyo exploited this lack of clarity to exert his military authority over that of the magistrate.

During these first decades of duty, both Fukuoka and Saga domains seemed interested not only in establishing increasing military autonomy vis-à-vis the magistrate, but also in assuming exclusive control of the on-the-ground execution of responsibilities, barring the regular participation of other local domains. During the *Return* incident, the absence of the neighboring Ōmura daimyo from his domain resulted in the permanent concentration of additional defense power in the hands of Fukuoka and Saga. Since the beginning of Nagasaki harbor duty in 1641, Ōmura had been charged with providing guard boats to monitor the activities of foreign ships in the harbor. While the *Return* was in port, the magistrate requested that Ōmura provide boats as usual, but when

91. Ibid., 2:364–66.

the soldiers did not arrive, three small ships from Fukuoka domain replaced them. This substitution was later discussed with Nabeshima officials and, after consultation with Edo, became an additional responsibility of the on-duty domain. Ōmura domain, however, did not accept being edged out without a fight. It challenged this incremental concentration of the minutia of Nagasaki defense responsibility in the hands of these two domains with the arrival of the Portuguese frigate the *São Paulo* just over a decade later.[92]

In the sixth month of 1685 a Portuguese frigate named the *São Paulo* arrived in Nagasaki from Macau, ostensibly to return twelve Japanese sailors blown adrift.[93] It remained in port not quite two months and departed without incident. Upon its arrival, Ōmura domain requested to send guard boats, the duty it had been unable to fill in the earlier *Return* incident. Not surprisingly, Fukuoka officials argued that having supplied guard vessels in 1647, they should again be the ones to furnish boats for the *São Paulo*. Why Fukuoka officials were so adamant about supplying these boats is unclear, especially since three of the five vessels assigned were dispatched, along with their sailors, from Fukuoka, meaning additional expense for the domain. Perhaps this demand was a second, and hopefully decisive, attempt to push Ōmura from participation in harbor defense, concentrating the port's security even further in the hands of Fukuoka and Saga domains. Maybe it was a measure taken to ensure that potential illicit trade with these foreign ships could be more effectively monopolized by these two domains. Perhaps this was a way for the domain to take a larger role in an incident that, from repeated mention in Kuroda records, seemed safe and benign.[94] The motivation for the

92. Ibid., 2:366; Hayashi, *Tsūkō ichiran*, 6:356.

93. Most histories treat the *Return* as the last European ship to arrive in Nagasaki in the seventeenth century. See, for example, Nakamura, "Sakokusei no kakuritsu to Fukuoka han," pp. 17–18. Nakamura does mention this incident, but his discussion highlights how the *São Paulo* set precedent for village officials coming to retrieve repatriated castaways instead of venturing conclusions more specific to the role of Fukuoka in Nagasaki defense.

94. Although Minagi Kuroda, the branch house elder who served as head of defense, stayed in Nagasaki until the *São Paolo* set sail, Fukuoka confidence in a peaceful departure is most evident from the fact that the next rotation of battery guards, which was close to the normal date of departure from the castle town, waited until the end of the sixth month to travel to Nagasaki instead of leaving earlier to serve as reinforcements. Kawazoe and Fukuoka komonjo o yomu kai, *Shintei Kuroda kafu*, vol. 2, "Mitsuyuki ki," p. 471.

dispute may always remain hidden, but we do know that on receiving news that Fukuoka had been granted this role, the Fukuoka battery commanders visited the office of the Nagasaki magistrate to express gratitude for this privilege. Defense of the harbor was now decisively concentrated in the hands of two domains, Fukuoka and Saga.

Conclusion

Between 1641 and 1685, the shogunate identified the Nagasaki system as the cornerstone of Tokugawa maritime defense. With the successful management of the *Return* incident in the 1680s, the Fukuoka and Saga two-domain model ended its probationary period in Nagasaki as a new generation of Kuroda and Nabeshima lords established their fitness to ensure the harbor's protection. The Nagasaki system was now permanent. At this same juncture, the harbor's battery artillery also reached the apex of its firepower under Tokugawa rule to that point. Roughly twenty-four cannon and twenty smaller firearms—weapons technologically similar to those used in contemporary Europe—lined the harbor's shores. Fortress Nagasaki was at its highest state of emergency preparedness in terms of organization, infrastructure, and weaponry. The most significant consequence of the Nagasaki model for future defense efforts, however, was the development of a local culture of trans-domainal collaboration.

As we have seen, the expansion of the fortified area of Nagasaki Bay to stretch more than ten miles to the tip of the Nomo promontory made this maritime space a site of contested political authority on multiple levels. In both the *Return* and *São Paulo* incidents, Fukuoka domain was interested in establishing even a minimal naval presence with armed vessels to ward off attack, to the exclusion of domains other than Saga, such as Ōmura. The command of harbor waters had become an important proving ground for establishing military authority in the larger port. Yet, while the Fukuoka and Saga daimyo were assertive in expanding their military agency vis-à-vis the magistrate, they were singularly cooperative in alternating command of the seven main shoreline batteries, even when these garrisons fell in the territories of private domains instead of shogunal lands, as did five of the seven primary batteries in Nagasaki (map 3).

Domains participating in the larger defense of Nagasaki Bay recognized that at the water's edge, the security of discrete, sovereign domainal

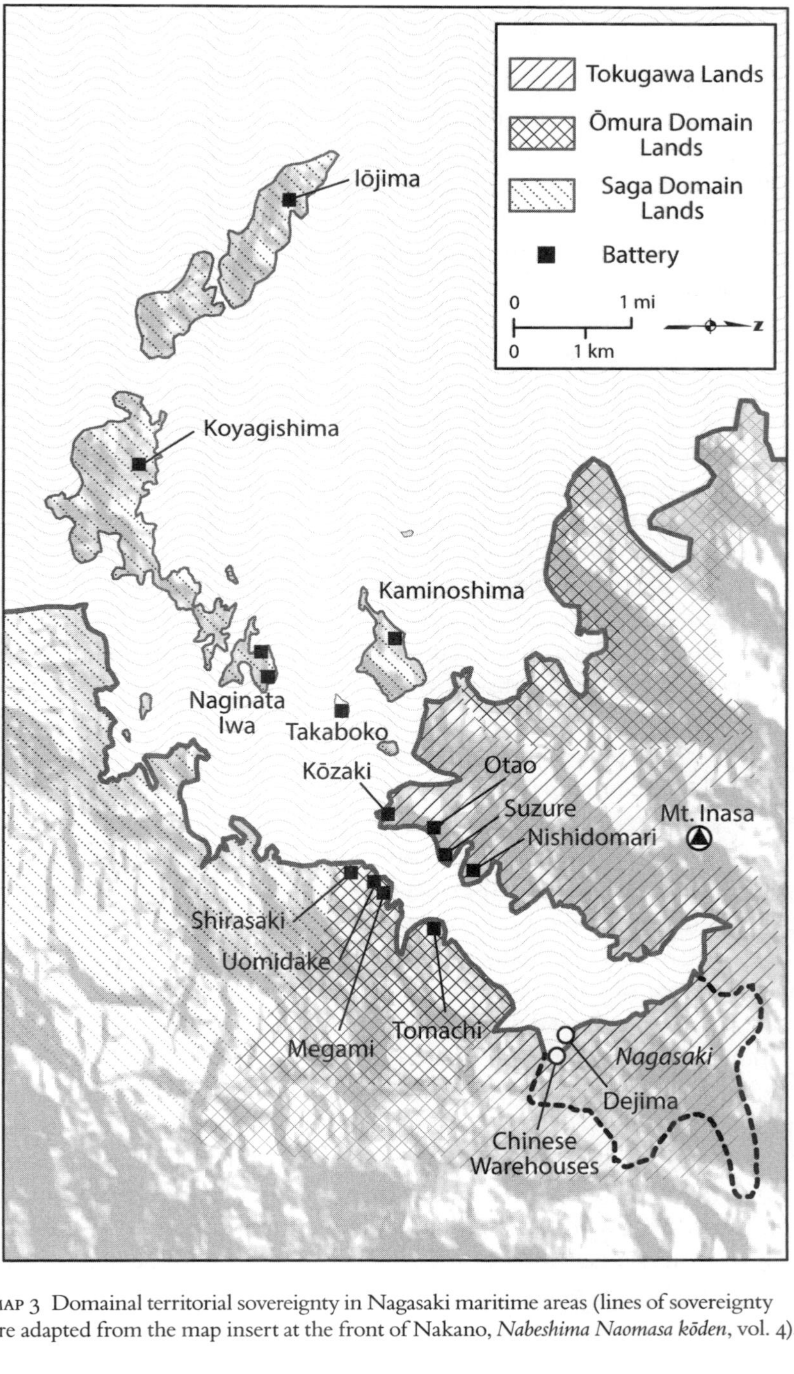

MAP 3 Domainal territorial sovereignty in Nagasaki maritime areas (lines of sovereignty are adapted from the map insert at the front of Nakano, *Nabeshima Naomasa kōden*, vol. 4).

territories was intertwined with that of both neighboring daimyo lands and those of the shogunate (*tenryō*). One of the three inner-harbor posts (assigned to the on-duty domain), Takaboko, and two of the outer-harbor posts (assigned to the off-duty domain), Kage no O and Naginata Iwa, were located in Saga territory. Fukuoka posted hundreds of soldiers at both garrisons in alternating years. But we find no evidence that Saga protested the presence of Fukuoka samurai in its lands, or that Fukuoka complained about guarding the territory of another domain. Similarly, two of the outer-harbor posts, Shirasaki and Megami, were built on Ōmura-domain territory, but neither Saga nor Fukuoka nor Ōmura appears to have balked at, or complained about, these assignments as an encroachment on domainal sovereignty. So why did sovereignty disputes (as occurred in Northern Kyūshū only decades later) not arise with this configuration? Perhaps the specter of Western attack prompted these domains to ignore what otherwise might have been interpreted as contentious and provocative trespassing on domainal prerogatives. Ōmura, as the domain charged with protection of the city proper, might have overlooked the mobilization of other domainal troops on its territory as welcome backup should a massive uprising occur in Nagasaki. What each of the domains recognized was that trans-domainal collaboration was critical to control disturbances in the water before destruction reached land.

But a still vaguely defined concept of water spaces as an extension of land-based domainal sovereignty also facilitated cooperation. During this period, no clear understanding of water space as sovereign domain territory (beyond fishing rights) had emerged. This still terracentric domainal mind-set allowed the shogunate to declare management of all floating, foreign traffic as a shogunal responsibility. Although protecting the Tokugawa territory surrounding Nagasaki, and its water access, was the root goal of Nagasaki defenses, foreign ships entering the harbor from the open sea passed through water bordering multiple domains. Thus, stationing troops at shoreline batteries in private, domainal lands lining the harbor was necessary for the protection of Tokugawa lands near the city and the water spaces in which foreign vessels operated. Even though the shogunate employed domainal forces to extend its authority into maritime spaces vis-à-vis foreign ships, the domains involved did not interpret their participation in this shogunal agenda as an intrusion into sovereign territorial spaces of local daimyo. In the following century, they would not be so agreeable.

With the waning concern about foreign attack in the late seventeenth century, and the concomitant rejection of naval power as necessary to preserve Tokugawa sovereignty, the Fukuoka and Saga domainal military responsibilities in Nagasaki became primarily surveillance of the Chinese and Dutch trading vessels. This shift to focus on curtailing smuggling activities at sea underscored that the purpose of the garrisons was not just protecting the city against attack but also enforcing Tokugawa commercial authority in proximate waters.

The most important result of the breathing space created by the absence of importunate European vessels in the late seventeenth century was the repurposing of Fukuoka and Saga's Nagasaki guard responsibilities to curb smuggling in the Genkai Sea, bordering Fukuoka to the northwest of Nagasaki. The departure of the *São Paulo* in 1685 is often framed as the conclusion of the first "European phase" of Nagasaki defense since no European vessels would threaten the harbor until the early nineteenth century. Analyzed from such Western perspectives, this episode initiates a century-long lull in the interest of Western powers in reengaging Tokugawa Japan in broader commercial relations. Yet, the 1680s began a fifty-year period of anti-smuggling efforts, in which the target of Nagasaki coastal defense shifted from Europeans to Chinese as the maritime implications of the Ming-Qing dynastic transition reached coastal Japan. We turn to examine this second developmental stage of the Nagasaki system in chapter 2.

CHAPTER TWO

Smuggling and the Chinese Interim of Coastal Defense

In the late seventeenth century, Tokugawa Japan reconfigured its maritime security to prioritize the extermination of smuggling as domestic economic upheaval made regulating the outflow of precious metals more critical than guarding against Western attack. The new fiscal threat prompted the shogunate to cast illegal Chinese traders as violent pirates, rather than as merely profit-motivated entrepreneurs, in order to legitimize the use of armed troops to repel them. This discursive transformation empowered new domains (including not only Fukuoka, but now also Kokura and Chōshū) along the Genkai Sea in Northern Kyūshū, where Chinese smugglers gathered, with the authority to use lethal force against foreign nationals.[1] The shogunate, in its desperation to suppress Chinese smugglers, ultimately solicited domainal input in larger maritime defense policy discussions in Edo, for the first time making domains architects of the policies they implemented on the ground. Instead of cementing the domains' wholesale cooperation, however, their inclusion in the highest levels of shogunal decision making further advanced their autonomy by allowing them to promote their own interests under the guise of collaboration. The shift of primary coastal defense efforts to a new location (the Genkai Sea), with a new object (Chinese smugglers) revealed how aggrandized local military agency outside of Tokugawa lands (as was Nagasaki, treated in the previous chapter) sparked new political tensions between the shogunate and domains over who was

1. Chōshū domain here refers to the territory of the Mōri daimyo and is also known as Hagi domain, drawing on the name of its castle town and capital city.

the primary executor of territorial sovereignty in proximate water spaces.

Writ large, this "Chinese interim" encompassed the fifty years between 1680 and 1730, when the greatest perceived threat to national security shifted from military invasion to evasion of trading laws, and thus from European gunboats to regional smuggling ships.[2] Fukuoka domain records in particular, along with those of Kokura and Chōshū, allow us to reconstruct maritime defense policy toward smugglers in this period, including debate over the first "shoot to destroy" (*uchitsubushi*) law in Tokugawa Japan. The emergence of Chinese sailors in Northern Kyūshū as a maritime threat reveals how localized smuggling imperiled the national economy, a fiscal crisis whose resolution ultimately integrated officials as far away as the Osaka magistrate into Kyūshū's coastal defense oversight. Yet, coalition domainal assaults on these smugglers were only marginally successful because the domains prioritized successful attacks in their own sovereign waters over effective policing of the trans-domainal maritime region of the Genkai Sea, where smugglers gathered. These mixed results underscored the challenges of domainal collaboration in guarding proximate water spaces outside of shogunal lands and lacking a Western presence.

From the beginning of Tokugawa coastal defense efforts, the shogunate had perceived foreign attack and infiltration by Christian missionaries as the direst threats to internal stability. From the 1680s, however, following the peaceful departure of the Portuguese vessel *São Paolo*, the greatest catalyst of Tokugawa insecurity was domestic. A shortage of precious metals, due to declining output from mines, combined with an increase in demand for currency in a growing economy to produce monetary debasement and inflation. Although the fiscal consequences of this shortfall were domestic, one of the primary obstacles to resolving this monetary crisis was foreign: an upsurge in Chinese smugglers who flouted new regulations designed to limit the outflow of precious metals. Although new policies decreased the outflow of silver by 90 percent, they did not eliminate smuggling, which continued unabated until the

2. The years between the 1685 departure of the *São Paolo* and the 1792 arrival of Russian empress Catherine the Great's representative, Adam Laxman, in Ezo have traditionally been a black hole in studies of Tokugawa defense because no European vessels, other than the expected Dutch merchants, landed in Japan.

shogunate mobilized coastal samurai to repel the Chinese with military force beginning in 1714.[3] The use of domainal troops to squelch smuggling had begun decades earlier in Nagasaki, however, as harbor guards assisted the magistrate in enforcing Tokugawa trade regulations, constituting the second function of coastal defense following decades of focus on Western attack. Soon their efforts shifted more than 100 miles north to the Genkai area, granting them heightened independence from magistrate oversight because of the increased distance from Nagasaki, even as the shogunate appointed a special inspector to coordinate domainal military collaboration. We turn first to examine the Nagasaki origins of this economic function of coastal defense, before then considering its consequences for domainal military autonomy in the expanding network of defended coastline in early eighteenth-century Japan.

Fukuoka and the Prosecution of Japanese Smugglers

With the turn toward enforcing trade restrictions to protect the national economy in late seventeenth-century Japan, defining offenses and exacting appropriate punishments for smugglers soon drew on the manpower of the Nagasaki defense system.[4] Shogunal decrees newly specified penalties for an array of offenses more generally characterized as smuggling. Now moneylenders financing the transactions, rowers, and even shipwrights involved in repairing the implicated vessels could be tried by association. The increased number of individuals prosecuted in

3. Previous studies of shogunal responses to smuggling and the currency crisis have focused on policy innovations, such as the development of commodity trading as an alternative to the exchange of metals and the creation of the Nagasaki import-export office, rather than military initiatives. Representative examples include Nakai, *Shogunal Politics*, pp. 97–114, and Bodart-Bailey, "Economic Plight."

4. Rather than explore the implications of these incidents for harbor defense, previous studies of these cases emphasized their legal significance, particularly their role in the development of standardized, yet differentiated, punishment for various smuggling offenses under Tokugawa law. While the Itō incident first codified sentencing standards for smugglers, the Suetsugu hearings were the first test case to consult, and then apply, these penalties. Nishimura, "Edo bakufu no nukeni torishimari rei," pp. 15–17; Harafuji, "Nukeni tsumi zakkō," p. 179.

smuggling incidents required that the domains originally charged with providing defense now also fulfill military duties during criminal hearings for smugglers.

Domainal military contributions to Tokugawa anti-smuggling efforts emerged in the late seventeenth century when Fukuoka's Nagasaki harbor guards first assisted in prosecuting homegrown smugglers in two criminal cases. In both the 1667 Itō and 1676 Suetsugu smuggling incidents, Kuroda troops and domain officials helped the Nagasaki magistrate convict Japanese smugglers who were accused of conducting illegal overseas trade. Since Nagasaki defenses had by this time performed successfully for more than two decades, local actors and the shogunate alike considered the harbor defense system to be complete. With the port's physical sovereignty deemed secure, Nagasaki defense efforts turned to focus on enforcing trade regulations. Military power, however, remained key. The ability of the Nagasaki magistrate to adjudicate smuggling cases depended on the presence of Fukuoka domain troops posted in Nagasaki to guard the accused and to maintain order at judicial hearings. This military reliance, an inescapable legacy of the early Tokugawa political settlement that allowed the *hatamoto* magistrate only minimal guards at his personal command, was a public reminder of the way the delegation of martial responsibilities, or "mediated" governance, could empower the domains.[5] Although the magistrate managed an extended bureaucracy of local commoner officials, including the administrator of Nagasaki lands beyond the city proper (*daikan*) and city elders (*machidoshiyori*), as individuals of nonwarrior status, none of these men had soldiers at his disposal to contribute to magistrate police duties. In other words, although shogunal law entrenched the juridical authority of the magistrate, resident domain troops with superior military capabilities circumscribed central power while embracing these new roles.

The first incident in which domains discharged military duties to help prosecute a smuggling case occurred in 1667, when the Nagasaki magistrate accused Kuroda domain merchant Itō Kozaemon of smuggling weapons to Korea.[6] As official purveyor to the Fukuoka lord, from

5. Berry, *Japan in Print*, p. 231.

6. Itō reveals his agenda in a letter sent to another Hakata merchant and colleague, Nishimura Kyūemon, specifying how Nishimura was to handle shipments of iron. For a transcription of the original letter, see Takeno, *Hakata no gōshō*, pp. 148–51.

his commercial base in Nagasaki, Itō had furnished military supplies to Kuroda harbor troops during the 1647 arrival of the two Portuguese ships. For his industrious contributions, the Kuroda awarded him a generous fifty-person allotment of rice and the magistrate treated him to banquets.[7] According to rumors heard by the Dutch factor at the time, Itō benefited so handsomely through these official dealings that he held assets worth more than 7,000 *kan* silver, placing him among the wealthiest of merchants in Nagasaki.[8] Kuroda patronage and impressive financial success did not prevent the temptation to acquire more, however, and placed the domain in the awkward position of helping prosecute one of its own residents who had facilitated the domain's Nagasaki military service.

The Itō case is particularly significant because following its resolution, Fukuoka domain's police role in Nagasaki became standard protocol during its years on duty as head of harbor defenses. From the inception of the legal proceedings against Itō, the magistrate strategically involved both the Fukuoka lord, Mitsuyuki, and his Nagasaki troops in the investigation. Although the Nagasaki magistrate, Kawano Michisada, first indicted Itō in the third month of 1667, he postponed arresting him until he met with Mitusyuki during the Fukuoka lord's visit to Nagasaki three months later for his customary inspection of the harbor garrisons. Only after informing Mitusyuki in person that Itō had been accused of selling arms and saddlery to Korea in 1663 and 1664 did the magistrate arrest Itō and place him under Fukuoka guard at the Kuroda detached residence in the Mizunoura section of Nagasaki.[9] Since numerous individuals less prominent than Itō had been accused of related charges and already detained for three months, the magistrate knew of Itō's involvement but waited for a face-to-face meeting with Mitsuyuki to announce the charges. Placing Itō in Fukuoka custody might have been a gesture of courtesy to Mitsuyuki since Itō was a favored merchant of the Kuroda. Itō's profits were widely thought to have benefited the Kuroda house. Even two months after his smuggling operations had been

7. Ibid., p. 147.

8. Factor's diary quoted in Takeno, *Hakata no gōshō*, p. 147.

9. Kawazoe and Fukuoka komonjo o yomu kai, *Shintei Kuroda kafu*, vol. 2, "Mitsuyuki ki," p. 314. The testimonies of two defendants state that the voyages in question occurred in 1662 and 1665, so perhaps the initial details the magistrate shared with Mitsuyuki were in error: "Mitsuyuki ki," pp. 315, 318–19.

exposed, Mitsuyuki had invited Itō to greet the Tokugawa roving inspectors (*junkenshi*) as they passed through Hakata.[10] This decision also reflected the magistrate's interest in delegating the expenses of supervising more than ninety suspects in custody through a system of "daimyo retainer guards" (*kerai azukari*), as Yasutaka Hiroaki has argued.[11] From the first indictments of the case in the sixth month until Itō's execution in the eleventh month, Fukuoka soldiers discharged a wide range of police and public peace duties, not only to guard Itō, but also to manage his extended family and servants.

The solicitation of Kuroda military guards revealed not only the incremental integration of domainal troops into new roles in Nagasaki, but also the unprecedented scale of Itō's smuggling operation. The Nagasaki magistrate's court prosecuted ninety-three individuals in this case, the largest number given in its court records for the seventeenth century. Of these, forty were executed (five crucified and thirty-five beheaded), two imprisoned, forty-one banished, and ten granted amnesty. Itō's collaborators included twenty-nine men from the Kuroda domain, along with eighteen from Nagasaki, sixteen from Tsushima, and others from as far away as Osaka and Sakai.[12] Despite Itō's unwavering protests of innocence, claiming that he had no knowledge of these dealings and attributing sole responsibility to his underlings, he was crucified with his son, Saburō, at the end of the eleventh month.

The Itō case revealed two important developments in Nagasaki maritime defense responsibilities that created a foundation for broadening domain agency in port. First, the domain on duty not only would keep watch over the activities of foreign boats in the harbor, but also provided soldiers to guard Japanese subjects in a police role when necessary. Second, the participation of domainal troops not just as jail guards, but also as witnesses at the interrogations, revealed that Fukuoka's military presence in Nagasaki was a significant tool for legitimizing and enforcing the judicial decisions of the magistrate.

Although Itō's operations resulted in forty executions, the prospect of capital punishment was not severe enough to discourage smuggling, and the magistrate called on Kuroda military forces within the decade to help prosecute another prominent smuggler with Fukuoka ties. In

10. Ibid., p. 312.
11. Yasutaka, *Kinsei Nagasaki shihō seido*, p. 323.
12. Morinaga, *Hankachō*, 1:2–12.

1676, the magistrate, Ushigome Katsutaka, accused Suetsugu Heizō Shigetomo (the Nagasaki *daikan*, or administrator of Tokugawa lands surrounding Nagasaki city proper, yet another descendant of a well-known Hakata merchant named Suetsugu Kōzen [1546–1630]), of purchasing a Thai vessel to transport weapons to Cambodia.[13] Signaling both his interest in avoiding the immense cost of maintaining a leading official in house arrest, and his generosity in sequestering a local elite with sympathetic custodians, the magistrate confined Suetsugu, his oldest son, Heibei, and his son-in-law, Heizaemon, in the Kuroda Nagasaki residence for the duration of the trial.[14]

Yet this solicitation of Fukuoka assistance was not only because of Suetsugu's ties to the domain, but also because the magistrate needed domainal police support for the trial. That year, 1676, was an on-duty harbor defense year for Fukuoka domain, as had been the case during the Itō incident in 1667, so the magistrate assigned Fukuoka troops already stationed in Nagasaki to guard the accused.[15] Ushigome notified Mitsuyuki of the charges against Suetsugu at the beginning of the year and within a month called the Fukuoka officer in charge of the main Nishidomari battery as well as Yoshida Tarōzaemon, the retainer overseeing the Kuroda Nagasaki residence, to notify them that Suetsugu would be placed in custody of Fukuoka samurai from the harbor guards.[16] Three days later, a Kuroda house elder departed Fukuoka with three high-ranking officials and men under their command to assist with guarding the prisoners. Ultimately more than fifty men were dispatched from the castle town to provide security for the proceedings.[17] When the magistrate finally sentenced Heizō, his son, and his son-in-law to exile on the Oki Islands, he called the three Fukuoka guard commanders to his residence as witnesses.

13. Harafuji, "Nukeni tsumi zakkō," p. 179.

14. Yamawaki Teijirō's analysis of this incident mentions that the Suetsugu men were sequestered in the principal Nagasaki residence of the Kuroda house, but he does not explain why. Kuroda sources answer this question by revealing that Fukuoka domain was on duty as harbor guard until the fourth month of 1676, when Saga took over, and thus served this police function as part of its larger harbor duties. Yamawaki, *Nukeni*, pp. 29, 48–49.

15. Kawazoe and Fukuoka komonjo o yomu kai, *Shintei Kuroda kafu*, vol. 2, "Mitsuyuki ki," pp. 388–89, 392.

16. Ibid., 2:389.

17. Ibid., 2:390–91.

Fukuoka's police duties did not end with the trial. Fukuoka samurai later escorted the sentenced individuals to the Kuroda residence before accompanying them to the Kokura domain border, where they departed for exile to the remote islands off the coast of modern-day Shimane prefecture in the Sea of Japan.[18] Fukuoka soldiers had originally been scheduled to return to the castle town in the early spring when Saga troops assumed responsibility for the harbor guard. Instead, they remained in Nagasaki to finish their job (until Heizō and his family had departed), only later returning to Fukuoka to be greeted by rewards and a celebratory banquet acknowledging their special service.[19]

Fukuoka's participation in the Suetsugu trial sheds light on the widening of domainal roles related to maritime defense at the end of the seventeenth century. First, the incident confirmed that domainal responsibility for harbor security was not limited to the defense of coastal waters, but also required ensuring the port city's public peace during the prosecution of crimes against Tokugawa foreign trade policy. Second, it demonstrated the limitations of the magistrate's juridical and military powers: without the police support of domainal troops, he could not enforce shogunal law. The magistrate deliberately kept Mitsuyuki informed about the Suetsugu case from the start. In an early letter to the Fukuoka lord, the magistrate assured Mitsuyuki that he could rest at ease because all matters related to the case would be discussed with Kuroda retainers serving in Nagasaki.[20] Including Mitsuyuki in the magistrate's inner circle of advisers might have also been a strategy to ensure that Mitsuyuki would feel duty bound to cooperate with the magistrate in a defensive emergency. At the same time, the presence of Fukuoka officers at the sentencing suggests that obtaining Kuroda affirmation of judgments was significant in securing the magistrate's juridical legitimacy.

These two episodes illustrate how domainal troops exposed the military limits of the magistrate's authority in new ways, even when no belligerent foreign ships threatened Nagasaki. Domainal contributions to managing these two trials redefined the greatest threats to political stability at the turn of the eighteenth century as economic rather than military. The use of domainal forces to eradicate smuggling began to shift from Nagasaki to Northern Kyūshū soon after the Suetsugu trial. Just

18. Ibid., 2:391, 394–95.
19. Ibid., 2:398–99.
20. Ibid., 2:390.

weeks before Suetsugu and his collaborators were sentenced, Kuroda officials ordered an increase in the number of lookout guards at six islands dotting the domain's coastline in the Genkai Sea because of the emergence of Chinese smugglers there.[21] Coastal defense operations to combat Chinese traders along this maritime region in northwest Kyūshū soon trumped the need for Fukuoka troops to act as a domestic police force for the magistrate in Nagasaki.

The Emergence of the Chinese Interim

By the 1680s, the decade after the Suetsugu trial, Western ships (apart from the Dutch) had ceased calling at Nagasaki to petition for trading rights because they were embroiled in a series of wars at home, such as the War of the League of Augsburg (1688–97), the War of the Spanish Succession (1701–14), and the Seven Years' War (1756–63). Of European insularity in this period, naval historian Andrew Lambert has observed that "by 1713, Britain was the strongest seapower, but her power was restricted to the European theatre."[22] Because of this European continental preoccupation, which meant the last non-Dutch Western ship of the seventeenth century to call at Nagasaki was the Portuguese vessel *São Paolo* in 1685, the most significant domainal maritime defense efforts shifted to focus on Chinese sailors. Qing traders, newly allowed to base operations in coastal China after the Manchu court had consolidated its rule, plied the Genkai Sea coast where it met with the Shimonoseki Straits to funnel water traffic to the Japanese Inland Sea. The domains of Fukuoka, Kokura, and Chōshū bordering this region extracted a new scale of military agency by executing maritime defense, against foreign nationals, in the service of Tokugawa economic policy.

The "Chinese interim" of coastal defense (roughly 1680–1730), in which suppressing Chinese smugglers became the priority of domainal maritime security activities, emerged in Northern Kyūshū because of a confluence of three factors: geography, the revision of Qing commercial regulations, and new Tokugawa trade restrictions. The Genkai Sea coastline where Chinese smuggling flourished was the Japanese territory

21. Ibid., 2:387. These islands were Iwaya, Chijima, Oshima, Ainoshima, Genkaishima, and Himejima.

22. Lambert, *War at Sea*, p. 104.

closest to the continental Qing Empire. Chinese ships without official trading privileges in Nagasaki, or vessels en route to Nagasaki for legitimate commerce but carrying excess cargo, found these shores a convenient location to rendezvous with enterprising Japanese traders plying the western circuit sea route between the Sea of Japan and the Inland Sea, entrepreneurs who had connections to the Osaka markets and beyond. Similar to the smuggling havens of Kent and Sussex, the English counties closest to France, the three domains of Fukuoka, Kokura, and Chōshū were the Tokugawa territories nearest to the southeast China ports of Shanghai, Ningpo, Amoy, and Canton, which were home to the majority of Chinese merchants trading in Japan.[23]

Heightening the importance of geographical proximity in bringing smugglers to these specific domains' shores was new legislation issued in both Qing China and Tokugawa Japan. In 1685, the Qing court repealed a domestic edict that had prevented its subjects from inhabiting the southeastern shore of the Chinese mainland since 1661, when an anti-Manchu rebel named Cheng Ching (known in Japanese as Coxinga) seized control of Taiwan. To deny Cheng's forces continental sources of manpower, food, and trading silk, the Qing government forced coastal populations to move inland at least ten miles, behind a guarded barrier.[24] It was just two years after the Manchu court finally gained control of Taiwan in 1683, cementing their control of imperial rule, that the transplanted coastal residents were allowed to return home to maritime regions. Their repatriation prompted renewed Chinese coastal activity and use of the Nagasaki markets, suddenly placing increased pressure on the Japanese metallic system to pay for imported Chinese goods. In 1685, the year following Qing repeal of the edict, eighty-five Chinese merchant vessels entered Nagasaki harbor. Compared with twenty-four ships the previous year, this marked a dramatic jump (roughly 250 percent) in the number of Chinese vessels seeking trade in Japan. Many of these vessels sailed to the Genkai region to unload surplus cargo.[25]

23. Nichols, *Honest Thieves*, p. 2. For ports of origin, see Iwao, "Kinsei nisshi bōeki," pp. 12–13.

24. Fairbank, *China: Tradition and Transformation*, p. 217; Zhao, *The Qing Opening to the Ocean*, pp. 79–98.

25. Yamawaki, *Nagasaki no Tōjin bōeki*, p. 50, cited in Nakai, *Shogunal Politics*, p. 108n32.

The domestic element compounding Chinese catalysts for smuggling was the imposition of new Tokugawa trade restrictions also beginning in 1685, the year after the Qing rescinded their edict. In this year, Edo limited the annual volume of both Dutch and Chinese trade so the shogunate could retain greater quantities of the metals critical for backing and minting its own currency, particularly silver. Three major objectives emerged as the new restrictions developed. First, the shogunate limited the maximum value of goods that merchants could bring in each year. Second, from 1688, Edo restricted the number of Chinese boats allowed to trade to seventy vessels annually, although this number varied slightly in subsequent years. Third, officials encouraged the development of "commodity exports," such as marine products and copper, to replace silver and created an import-export office to regulate trade. These measures reduced the outflow of silver to 10 percent of what it had been but sent home increasing numbers of Chinese ships denied permission to trade, vessels that often illegally unloaded their cargo along the northwest Kyūshū coastline.[26] In 1686, the first year the regulations were in effect, seventy-three ships traded at Nagasaki but another eleven were sent home. By 1688, when the Tokugawa restricted Chinese trade to seventy ships, another seventy-seven Chinese merchant ships were denied, meaning more ships were sent home than were allowed to trade in Nagasaki. From 1685 to 1731, Chinese ships full of unsold cargo were turned away in two years out of three. Those rejected had no alternative but to smuggle if they wanted to unload their goods. Over the previous nineteen years, dating back to 1666 (the earliest date for which records are available), only a total of five smuggling incidents had been prosecuted, an average of one every four years.[27] But during the forty-six-year period from 1685 to 1731, the Nagasaki magistrate's office heard 139 smuggling cases, an average of three per year. This average marked an increase of more than 1,000 percent, an escalation the shogunate charged domainal troops to help reverse.

As the magistrate tightened Nagasaki harbor security to respond to this increase in illicit trade, smugglers shifted their transactions to neighboring domainal waters where their exchanges were less aggressively discouraged. In 1688, the magistrate constructed a lookout post at Koseto, on

26. Nakai, *Shogunal Politics*, p. 108.

27. Arano, *Kinsei Nihon to higashi Ajia*, pp. 68–69.

the northern side of the Nagasaki harbor entrance, to monitor ships not visible from the post across the channel at Nomozaki.[28] Before this addition, smuggling had occurred close to shore in Nagasaki harbor, but afterward incidents shifted to more distant locations, such as Amakusa to the southeast and the Gotō Islands to the west, to escape detection. In addition to increasing harbor surveillance, the magistrate promulgated edicts to prevent Nagasaki citizens from leaving their homes at night and to prohibit foreign ships and local fishermen from setting sail after dark.[29] In 1690, the magistrate even attached guard boats with mounted guns to Chinese ships as they left Nagasaki. But these measures did not eradicate smuggling farther north.

From Amnesty to Mortal Force

As the menace of Chinese traders escalated northwest of Nagasaki, the shogunate promulgated multiple edicts encouraging domain officials there to watch for smugglers with greater vigilance and by 1714 granted domains permission to use mortal force in repelling them. By 1710, the shogunate had ordered western (Kyūshū) domains to install new lookout posts and to arrange guard boats to help prevent smuggling. Moreover, it restricted the sailing courses of Chinese ships in Japanese waters to areas free of sea islands. Any ships that strayed would have their trading permits in Nagasaki revoked.[30] By 1713, these domains were ordered to repair public signboards, particularly in coastal hamlets, in preparation for a new anti-smuggling campaign. The 1713 edict accounted for forty-six new placards on the Fukuoka domain coast, each of which read,

> We have heard that individuals are borrowing boats in various coastal towns and buying smuggled goods from foreign ships. Until recently, even if a ship's captain and sailors [boarded] a rented boat without knowing the purpose of its use, they were guilty of the same crime as the organizer of the smuggling. As has been previously communicated, if sailors and captains

28. Ibid., pp. 72–73, 86.

29. Kaempfer, *Kaempfer's Japan*, p. 394.

30. Hayashi, *Tsūkō ichiran*, 4:447. Cited in Nishimura, *Kinsei Nagasaki bōeki,* pp. 143–44.

> of seaside villages in any domain become involved with someone engaged in smuggling, they are to report this to the nearest official.[31]

Anyone reporting information on a smuggler that led to arrest not only would be pardoned from prosecution but would also receive a reward.[32] This amnesty policy reflected the desperation of officials, whose tighter trade regulations had restricted the verifiable outflow of silver from Nagasaki but had proven ineffective in halting the smuggling that thrived on Genkai shores. When this approach yielded few results, however, the next stage of action was to specifically target the Chinese, and with domainal troops.

The decision to combat Chinese smugglers took on a new level of seriousness as the shogunate granted domains permission to use mortal force against them (see fig. 2.1). Although convicted Japanese smugglers could be executed, the shogunate could only expel Chinese and Dutch expatriates suspected of illegal trading.[33] From the time of Tokugawa Ieyasu, the shogunate had entrusted the punishment of foreigners to their countries of origin, as international protocol dictated. Since the Tokugawa wanted to continue profitable relations with Chinese traders, Edo hesitated to present the Qing government with a request that they more tightly regulate their merchants.[34] But taking such a position and relying on a lighter sentence (expulsion, instead of various capital punishments or exile, the customary punishment for Japanese smugglers) left open the possibility that expelled violators of foreign nationality might return

31. Kawazoe and Fukuoka komonjo o yomu kai, *Shintei Kuroda kafu*, vol. 3, "Nobumasa ki," pp. 358–59.

32. Ibid., p. 359. Harafuji argues, from analysis of a report sent to the Nagasaki magistrate, that Fukuoka was not given permission to grant amnesty until 1720, but the 1713 edict suggests that the domain had been delegated that authority some seven years earlier. Harafuji, "Nukeni tsumi zakkō," p. 214.

33. Kaempfer, *Kaempfer's Japan*, p. 394. For Chinese, see notes of Dutch factor Joan Aouwer in October of 1718: "The Chinese (smugglers) will be sent home but if they ever return to Japan, they will be executed on the spot." At the beginning of 1715, Aouwer's predecessor, Nicolaas J. van Hoorn, recorded that the shogunate had notified Chinese sailors to tell Qing officials that future Chinese smugglers in Japan would be "punished according to Japanese law." But the 1718 mention above of expulsion suggests that this harsher punitive response was not implemented. Van der Velde and Bachofner, *Deshima Diaries, Marginalia, 1700–1740*, pp. 182, 228.

34. Arano, *Kinsei Nihon to higashi Ajia*, p. 83.

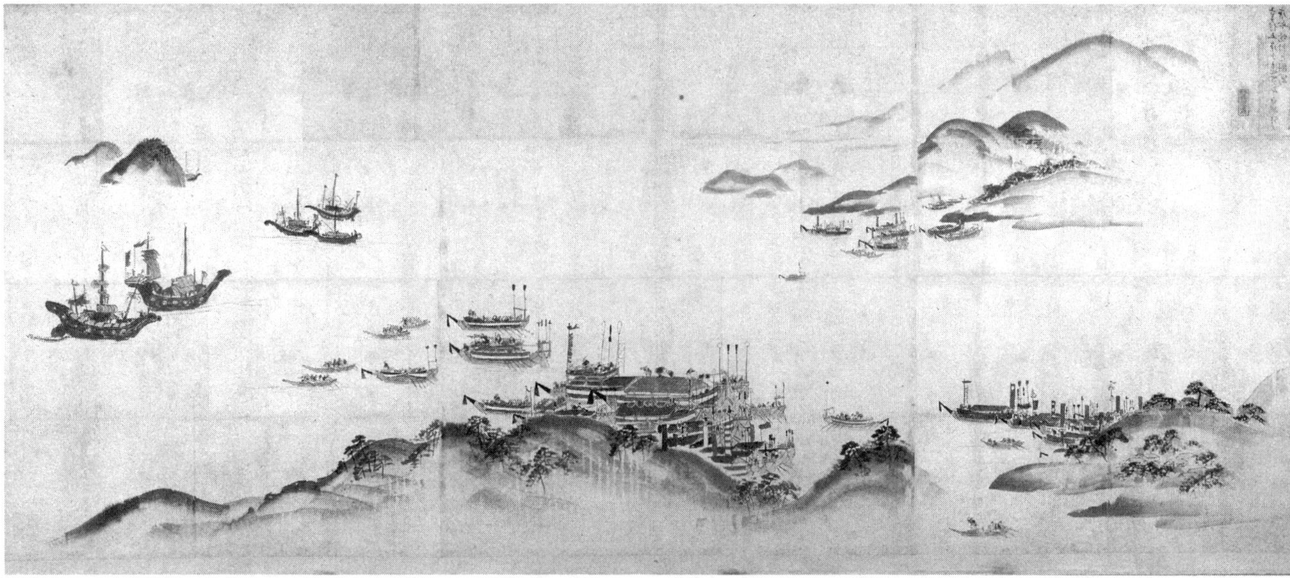

FIGURE 2.1 Fukuoka forces firing on Chinese ships near Shirajima. *Mitsubōekisen uchiharai zu byōbu*, folding screen, ca. 1730. Itami collection no. 510. Courtesy of the Fukuoka City Library.

to Japan. The logic of Tokugawa officials now ventured that Chinese smugglers would be less likely to chance shoreline trade if they were risking the possibility of death from attack.

By mid-1714, the shogunate first extended domainal troops permission to cut down suspected Chinese smugglers with bladed weapons when the senior councillor Inoue Masamine issued two edicts regarding Chinese smuggling to the Fukuoka house elder in Edo. The first read as follows:

> In recent times, the Chinese ships that trade in Nagasaki have increasingly engaged in selling goods through private connections, changed their route of sail, or have [tried to evade] by tacking. As well, we have no idea of the destination of many Chinese ships that come into sight. We hear that they go ashore at will, fetch water and cut trees, take the catch of fishermen's nets and the seaweed collected by women and children. When locals fight back, they pull out weapons, and when guard boats approach, they fire guns. . . . So from here forward when these ships approach, you are to seize them, cutting down all those aboard, and then quickly send notice. If Japanese ships approach a Chinese vessel, you are to seize those aboard and quickly send notice. If a Chinese ship drifts in after meeting with a storm, send notice as previously instructed and then escort the vessel to Nagasaki.[35]

Although this document did not specifically grant local soldiers permission to fire on the Chinese, it was the first edict that granted permission to use mortal force. This command extended the right for samurai to board suspicious ships and kill the Chinese sailors with bladed weapons, as the characters for the term "cut down" (*kirisuteru*) reveal. At the time, Fukuoka domain did not possess lightweight, portable firearms like the pistols used in Europe, so a sword was a samurai's best option for attacking Chinese at sea.

In order to justify adopting a policy of mortal force, this document identified Chinese smugglers as universally violent, a generalization that emerged out of incidents confined to Matsuura domain, just south of the Genkai area in northwest Kyūshū.[36] As historian Matsuo Shin'ichi observes, by emphasizing the belligerence of the Chinese, the Tokugawa

35. Takayanagi and Ishii, *Ofuregaki Kampō shūsei*, pp. 972–74; Kawazoe and Fukuoka komonjo o yomu kai, *Shintei Kuroda kafu*, vol. 3, "Nobumasa ki," pp. 371–72.

36. Matsuo Shin'ichi identifies this connection to Matsuura domain in "Shōtoku–Kyōhō ki karasen mondai," later published in slightly revised form as *Edo bakufu no taigai seisaku*, pp. 221–24.

may well have been trying to cast them as dangerous enemies so local residents would be less likely to view them as potential business partners. The image of Chinese smugglers as potential marauders who might physically threaten the Japanese had begun to circulate among shogunal officials a few months earlier, in the spring of 1714, when Matsuura domain reported smuggling along its shoreline to the Nagasaki magistrate. Matsuura recorded that since the end of the previous year, numerous Chinese ships had floated off their coastline, often dropping anchor and menacing the local residents.[37] Indeed, Inoue's edict of 1714 was a close paraphrase of the Matsuura text, as would be the account recorded in the autobiography of shogunal adviser Arai Hakuseki three years later.[38] Depictions of the Chinese as pirates continued to circulate in subsequent shogunal edicts to the domains. This characterization effectively transformed them, as Robert Hellyer has described of smugglers a century later, from smugglers whose "activities violate the law . . . by circumvent[ing] established commercial channels" to marauders "who use violence or the threat of violence to commandeer ships or to attack coastal settlements."[39] The shogunate's discursive manipulation turned the illicit Chinese trader into a pirate.

This recasting, which justified new levels of domainal military aggression, made an important distinction between Chinese outlaws and law-abiding Qing subjects in order to avoid endangering diplomatic relations with the Qing court.[40] A directive from the shogunal senior councillor Kuze Shigeyuki underscored that although some Chinese sailors had brandished weapons to intimidate coastal residents, these individuals were likely Chinese criminals who had fled to Japanese waters after the threat of capture and execution by Qing authorities. The document further distinguished between pirates (*kaizoku*), whom the Qing were attempting to subjugate or expel, and legitimate Qing subjects (*daichin no tōjin*), who would surely be familiar with Tokugawa laws.

37. Ibid.

38. Arai, *Oritaku Shiba no ki,* p. 236; Arai, *Told Round a Brushwood Fire,* p. 244.

39. This distinction comes from Hellyer, "The Missing Pirate and the Pervasive Smuggler," p. 5. Alan Karras offers a similar definition, although one that emphasizes the interest of smugglers in "elud[ing] discovery." Chinese smugglers operating off the Genkai coast seemed less concerned about discovery than about capture. Karras, *Smuggling: Contraband and Corruption*, p. 20.

40. "Shōtoku yon kinoeuma doshi Edo yori osewatasare omomuki on kakitsuke mittsū ontōrai no koto," in *Dai Nihon kinsei shiryō: Tōtsūji kaisho kichiroku, Tōtsūji kaisho nichiroku,* 7:86–88, quoted in Matsuo, *Edo bakufu no taigai seisaku*, p. 228, previously published as " 'Tōjin' 'karasen' mondai no suii," pp. 27–28.

As the anti-smuggling campaign continued, shogunal adviser Hakuseki later offered renewed support for firing against smugglers and pirates alike, but with a twist of his own. He asserted that Chinese were generally belligerent due to a long-standing Japanese culture of conciliation: "The reason why the Chinese and others behave like this is probably because of the lenient way foreigners were treated in the Jōkyō and Genroku eras (1684–1704). Our people were enjoined not to be hostile to foreigners, and when the lower officials of the Bugyōsho [Nagasaki magistrate's office] were threatened by the Chinese, and drew their swords and wounded them slightly, they were dismissed on the spot. In consequence, foreigners developed a bad habit of doing what they liked."[41] This critique implied that the shogunate had no recourse but to adopt more stringent measures to combat illicit trade. For Hakuseki, an aggressive response to the Chinese was necessary not only for the immediate, practical purpose of protecting Japanese residents and enforcing trade regulations, but also to defend the Tokugawa's significant tradition of military prowess. As he lamented, "Our country has from ancient days been famous as one that surpassed all others in its martial qualities, and it is quite intolerable that it should be thus insulted by these foreign merchants."[42] Following this logic, Hakuseki drafted orders to the daimyo of western Japan and the Chugoku region, commanding that when Chinese appeared in coastal waters and disembarked, "the people must burn their boats and kill those who came in them."[43] Edicts such as these codified the shogunate's newly aggressive stance, which Fukuoka domain first began to implement as its primary maritime defense duties shifted from Nagasaki to its own shores.

Expanding "Nagasaki Duty" to Combat Chinese Smugglers

This perceived aggressiveness of Chinese smugglers was a central reason that the famous Shōtoku Reforms of 1715 codified the expanded use of domainal troops posted to Nagasaki harbor in new anti-smuggling roles. Although the economic consequences for trade of the Shōtoku edicts generally receive greatest attention from historians, the documents

41. Arai, *Oritaku Shiba no ki*, pp. 396–97; Arai, *Told Round a Brushwood Fire,* p. 245.
42. Ibid.
43. Arai, *Oritaku Shiba no ki*, pp. 297–98.

outlining these details also contained specific provisions for the use of military forces to implement them. The Nagasaki magistrate could not possibly administer a host of new restrictions with his existing staff. Domainal guards would be critical for enforcement.

The new restrictions on foreign trade began precisely at the time the government restored national currency to its original standard, 80 percent pure Kyōhō silver, after decades of debasement. Even if officials did not wholly believe the demonized portrait of Chinese traders, the need to support currency restoration by stemming the outflow of silver through illegal channels legitimated harsh measures. The central problem impeding restoration, which began in 1714, was that no new ore was being mined. This made limiting the amount of silver exported imperative. The shogunate, therefore, issued further commercial regulations in 1715 to accomplish this, which collectively became known as the Shōtoku trade reforms.

These reforms regulated Chinese commerce through a tally system of permits for Chinese ships and new quotas limiting the total value of commerce allowed each year. They also targeted the number of permitted vessels, reducing Chinese boats from seventy to thirty. While maintaining the ceiling on silver exports at 6,000 *kanme*, the restrictions also limited the amount of copper the Chinese could take out of Japan. The first section of the document outlining the reforms, which specified new responsibilities of the Nagasaki magistrate in enforcing these changes, acknowledged that the twenty men under his direct command were insufficient for managing his many new duties. The magistrate was thus allowed to call on Fukuoka and Saga troops from the main batteries of Nagasaki harbor at Nishidomari and Tomachi when necessary.[44] Additional articles limited to twenty the number of men the magistrate could borrow from other Nagasaki administrative offices but did not restrict the number of harbor guards he could requisition. The ability of the magistrate to enlist these garrison troops, without limitations, suggests that military attack (the original, seventeenth-century motive for their dispatch to Nagasaki) was now not perceived as imminent. Ensuring economic stability now trumped preventing armed assault as the linchpin of national security.[45]

44. *Shōtoku shinrei* quoted in Suzuki, *Nagasaki bugyō no kenkyū*, pp. 10–11.

45. Shogunate-centered studies of the Shōtoku Reforms have praised them for creating "an effective framework of enforcing the regulations," yet study of Fukuoka documents suggests otherwise. See Nakai's interpretation in *Shogunal Politics*, p. 111.

Although the Nagasaki reforms granted the magistrate permission to assign domainal harbor guards to new, unspecified duties, the shogunate directly instructed the domains to prioritize vigilance of Chinese ships. The first article of this early 1715 edict read, "Initially, at the Nishodomari and Tomachi outposts in Nagasaki, the Nabeshima and Kuroda houses were ordered to stand guard against Portuguese (*nanban*) ships. However, from here forward, when Chinese ships arrive, and the Magistrate's inspector issues an order to mobilize men, the troops guarding the outposts shall be divided and [some portion] sent to the office of the Magistrate."[46] Domain troops originally assigned to protect against European military attack were now ordered to serve a new purpose as illegal Chinese trading became a more pressing threat than potential assault by Western powers.

The second article described specific measures the guards should take to counteract this illicit commerce. They were to watch not only for Chinese smugglers, but also for their entrepreneurial Japanese counterparts: "When Chinese ships enter port and depart, there are periods when they drift at sea along domain shores and you should be especially vigilant at these times. If you see Japanese ships approaching them alongside, you should quickly pursue them. Seaside lookout posts in the domains should be especially vigilant, and those in disrepair should be restored."[47] Although the first article was specific to Nagasaki, the second one extended to the waters of nearby coastal domains, including those of Saga and Fukuoka, thus expanding the geographic reach of shogunal interest in coastal defense.

The extent of Tokugawa concern became clear in instructions issued to officers of the Nagasaki guard in the third month of the following year, 1716: "As for Chinese ships, when, according to the instructions of the Nagasaki Magistrate and his chief inspector, men and boats from the two main batteries are dispatched, everyone down to the last foot soldier and sailor shall treat [the Chinese ships] with nothing less than the strict

---

Fred Notehelfer argues that shogunal efforts to control trade "further aggravated the smuggling problem," although he gives domainal responses only a cursory overview. Notehelfer, "Notes on Kyōhō Smuggling," pp. 11–12. My thanks to Adam Clulow for bringing this essay to my attention.

46. Kawazoe and Fukuoka komonjo o yomu kai, *Shintei Kuroda kafu*, vol. 3, "Nobumasa ki," p. 385.

47. Ibid.

vigilance accorded Portuguese ships (*nanban sen*)."[48] This string of edicts revealed an all-out effort to stop Chinese smuggling, with the shogunate even commanding Fukuoka soldiers to burn down Chinese ships with fireboats if necessary. The overt comparison with the Portuguese implied that Chinese smugglers were as critical a threat as Europeans had been in the 1640s. Within only a few months, domainal forces would have permission to attack them not only with bladed weapons, but with firearms as well, as the Genkai Sea, instead of Nagasaki, became the most critical arena of maritime defense in the Tokugawa realm.

Coastal Defense in the Genkai

Notwithstanding this repurposing of Fukuoka domain troops, by the spring of 1717, an exasperated shogunate abandoned the strategy of domains individually repelling Chinese ships. For the first time, it ordered a specific tri-domainal coalition attack on these vessels in the Genkai Sea. In spite of long-standing, coordinated domainal military efforts in Nagasaki, the shogunate anticipated barriers to the success of a coalition assault along a shoreline that did not encompass Tokugawa lands. Edo officials quickly excused the alternate attendance duties of the Kokura lord, Ogasawara Tadao, so that he could oversee a local response. His leadership was critical since the Fukuoka lord, Tsunamasa, was ill in Edo, and the Chōshū lord, Mōri Motonori, was only thirteen years old.[49] (Ogasawara's status as a *fudai* lord also augmented his suitability since the supreme military commanders [*tandai shoku*] of mid-seventeenth-century Nagasaki had been *fudai* daimyo.) These adjacent domains were to supply the troops of the tri-domainal composite force.

Fukuoka might have been expected to embrace a coordinated military response since it controlled the largest swath of shoreline affected. Shogunal officials could easily blame the persistence of smugglers in the larger maritime region on that domain's inability to manage the Chinese problem. Fukuoka domainal officials, however, hesitated to collaborate for a variety of political reasons. Fukuoka domain elder Yoshida Harutoshi complained that Chōshū and Kokura domains had not contributed sufficient ships to repel the Chinese, suggesting that Fukuoka shouldered

48. Ibid., 3:389.
49. Ibid., 3:17.

a disproportionately heavy burden and that contributions should be more equitable among the three domains. He declared that Fukuoka would not participate in a group effort until Edo issued a direct order for collaboration.[50] This justification implied that Fukuoka was concerned about being censured by the shogunate for mobilizing troops across domainal borders without permission from Edo. Perhaps, in addition, the domain remained interested in maintaining illegal trade because of local benefit. We have scattered evidence of the nighttime landing of Chinese on Fukuoka shores during this period, reportedly to acquire drinking water, that the domain did not report to shogunal officials or to the Nagasaki magistrate.[51]

Local samurai officials often embraced the rare opportunities, such as this anti-smuggling initiative, which endorsed the use of mortal force, to demonstrate their military prowess, but these authorities had to balance martial ambition with the internal stability of the larger domain. Commoners providing labor and materials for these maritime attacks generally lacked the enthusiasm of warrior-class participants, and resentment could escalate into rebellion. Peasants in the Fukuoka-Kokura border regions of Wakamatsu in particular, where tri-domainal troops gathered in the protected inlet to launch assaults, shouldered the heaviest burden of human and animal labor for transporting defense-related goods. In this area, for a single deployment the following year, district officials would mobilize more than 1,000 peasants to serve for eighty days.[52] As well, since 1695, Fukuoka domain had assessed a sailor/rower levy on the commoner population of coastal villages, requiring that 962 men be ready to serve the Kuroda lord's alternate attendance procession by sea, the reception of Korean envoys, or Nagasaki defense duty. This corvée labor tax was undoubtedly invoked as officials of the Fukuoka castle town shipped barges of goods and hundreds of boats northward to Wakamatsu in the early 1700s.[53] Chōshū domain coastal residents in southern Honshū also submitted concerns about their corvée burdens to local officials during the Chinese smuggling crisis.[54] Thus a domain's decision to mount seaside defenses did not hinge exclusively on the avail-

50. Higaki, *Yoshida kadenroku*, 2:396–97.
51. Ibid., 2:441.
52. Yao, "Sakoku ka no Fukuoka han," p. 274.
53. *Fukuoka kenshi, Fukuoka han tsūshihen*, 2:688.
54. Yamamoto, "Karasen uchiharai taisei," p. 484n46.

ability and receptivity of its warrior base, but also calculated the cost of potential peasant discontent due to requests for labor contributions perceived as onerous, and the perceived burden of time away from livelihood activities such as fishing, gathering seaweed, or farming. Concerns about peasant uprisings related to defense service would emerge roughly a century later as shogunal officials discussed, and then rejected, a large-scale mobilization of peasant militia to respond to Western pressure.

The Nagasaki magistrate, Ishikawa Masasato, could have helped consolidate a trans-domainal response, but he hesitated to issue instructions to Kokura and Fukuoka officials when they first approached him for advice in early 1717. At that time, he had yet to receive specific guidance from the shogunate on how to respond to the northward movement of Chinese smuggling operations.[55] Although previous edicts stated that Fukuoka forces stationed in Nagasaki for harbor defense could be reassigned to the Genkai area for anti-smuggling efforts, these documents did not clarify if those relocated forces, stationed in their home domain, would remain under magistrate oversight. The magistrate seemingly surmised they would be organized and deployed by the domains, as internal troops responding to internal domain affairs rather than those of the shogunate. The magistrate's unwillingness, or bureaucratic inability, to manage a coalition response outside of the shogunal lands of Nagasaki, combined with the resistance of Fukuoka to joining a collaboration, nearly deadlocked the effort.

Acknowledging these multiple local obstacles to an effective response, by the spring of 1717 the shogunate issued a five-point order to neutralize the continuing reluctance of domains to cooperate in areas where their maritime borders merged.[56] From the perspective of Edo officials, domainal disputes over military autonomy in water spaces where multiple domains claimed sovereignty constituted the major impediment to effective coalition attacks. Thus, this directive instructed Kokura, Fukuoka, and Chōshū to coordinate in the tri-domainal border region encompassing the myriad small sea islands where smugglers were most likely to flee and most difficult to capture (map 4). Outside of this specific, limited zone at the entrance to the Shimonoseki Straits, where lines

55. Miyake, *Tōsen hyōryūki,* p. 11; Kawazoe and Fukuoka komonjo o yomu kai, *Shintei Kuroda kafu*, vol. 4, "Tsugutaka ki," p. 16.

56. Kawazoe and Fukuoka komonjo o yomu kai, *Shintei Kuroda kafu,* vol. 4, "Tsugutaka ki," pp. 17–18.

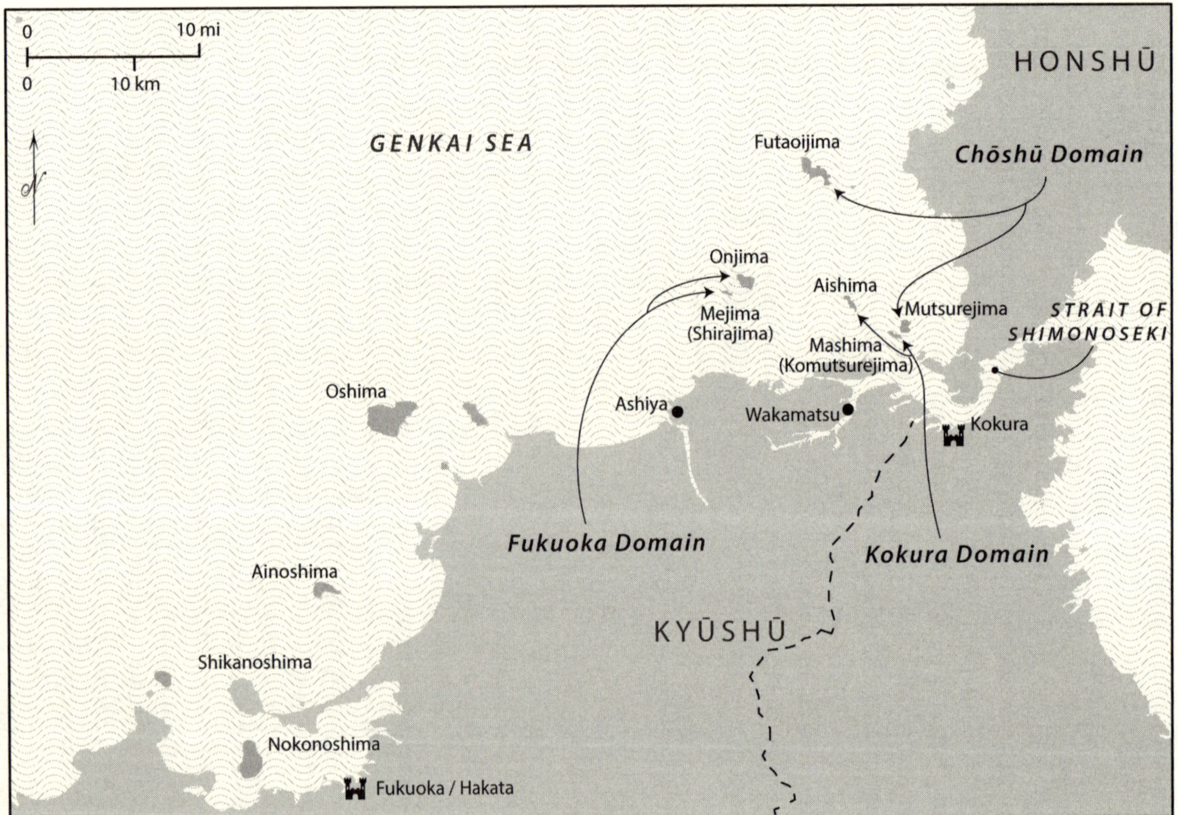

MAP 4 Sea islands and domainal sovereignty in the Genkai Sea, early eighteenth century (adapted from Miyake, *Tōsen hyōryūki*, ii).

of maritime sovereignty were difficult to define, however, the shogunate recognized the sovereignty of domainal waters: domainal boats were to stop at their maritime boundaries and stand on guard when the smugglers fled from one domain's bailiwick to another's. The mistaken assumptions behind this perspective were that local maritime boundaries were clearly defined (they were not) and that domains could clearly communicate about the transfer of armed pursuit (they could not). In practice, Chinese ships often fled with impunity from one domain's territorial waters to those of another to escape attack.

An additional article of the edict addressed Fukuoka's concerns about Kokura domain shouldering oversight command while contributing fewer troops and vessels than Kuroda forces. This section of the shogunal directive ordered domains to confer about the number of boats and men to contribute. Although it did not specify the arbiter of this discussion, Kokura, as local overseer of the coalition, emerged as the mediator of these figures. As a concession to Fukuoka's ongoing concerns about encroachment on its domainal authority, Kokura officials instructed Fukuoka domain to send the numbers of forces it found appropriate (instead of imposing a specific number of troops and boats). This accommodation set a precedent for interpreting the article about "conferring" on the details of each domain's contributions to mean that domains could participate as they saw fit.[57] Although these self-determined offerings may have been of a smaller scale than ideal numbers, they proved effective in the short run. Early in the fifth month, coalition forces consisting of roughly 2,100 men and 109 boats repelled seven Chinese ships from the Shimonoseki border region.[58] A domain-regulated response seemed promising.

With inconsistent success over the fall of 1717, however, by the end of the year Edo contemplated adopting a more hard-line stance, "shoot to destroy" (*uchitsubushi*), which required the domains now to marshal not only troops and ships, but also firearms for coalition attacks.[59] In the twelfth month, shogunal councillor Inoue Masamine convened the Edo liaison officers of all three domains to gather their opinions on the feasibility

57. Miyake, *Tōsen hyōryūki*, p. 18.

58. Kawazoe and Fukuoka komonjo o yomu kai, *Shintei Kuroda kafu,* vol. 4, "Tsugutaka ki," p. 19.

59. Yamawaki, *Nukeni*, p. 82; Kawazoe and Fukuoka komonjo o yomu kai, *Shintei Kuroda kafu*, vol. 4, "Tsugutaka ki," pp. 16–18; Higaki, *Yoshida kadenroku,* 2:407–8.

of this more aggressive response. Previously, domainal troops had merely chased smugglers away without firing on them. Now they would shoot to both sink vessels and potentially kill those aboard. In these collective decisions, domains became not only executors, but also architects, of maritime security.

To elicit local, on-the-ground knowledge, Inoue first surveyed domainal opinions on the feasibility of a "shoot to destroy" policy. The initial Fukuoka response emphasized the material challenges to execution: (1) the difficulty small domainal armed (and heavy) boats faced maneuvering in high seas and (2) a shortage of firearms because the domain had transferred extra weapons to Nagasaki for its harbor defense duties.[60] Yet Inoue remained content to allow domains to resolve these details of weaponry and transportation. Instead, he focused the conversation on the overarching policy question of whether the Tokugawa should realistically adopt and implement a policy of "shoot to destroy" regarding the Chinese. The collective conclusion was yes. No longer would Japanese ships merely pursue Chinese ships to repel them; they would now fire to kill. This outcome was important because it marked the first time on record that the shogunate had formally solicited, and implemented, domain input on defense policy in Edo. Tokugawa officials may have invited this unusual collaboration because they recognized that domains would be more likely to subject their samurai to a potential exchange of live fire if domainal officers were parties in crafting a position in common. Moreover, shogunal councillors may have been concerned that Genkai Sea domains would hesitate to kill foreign nationals, for fear of retribution, if they were not integrated into policy decision making.

Yet, the shogunate recognized the challenge of coordinating on-the-ground efforts among domains accustomed to relative military independence within their own territories. Adopting the precisely defined goal of shooting to destroy, which required more intricate teamwork to achieve than simply chasing smugglers from shore, called for a new scale of collaboration. To facilitate this, three days after these domain officials endorsed the fire-and-destroy stance, the shogunate appointed Watanabe Geki as special inspector for overseeing Northern Kyūshū's coastal

60. Kawazoe and Fukuoka komonjo o yomu kai, *Shintei Kuroda kafu*, vol. 4, "Tsugutaka ki," p. 24.

defense.[61] He departed Edo in early 1718 to establish his headquarters in Kokura domain.[62] Although the text of his appointment explicitly targeted Fukuoka shores, Kokura, the domain just north of Fukuoka, became Geki's center of operations for two reasons. First, it was the geographical heart of the targeted shoreline, which stretched from northwest Kyūshū to the southwest corner of Honshū. Second, the borders of Kokura domain extended from the Genkai Sea eastward through the entire Shimonoseki Straits, where merchants from the Inland Sea and Osaka lingered to trade with the Chinese. Even though his primary residence in Northern Kyūshū fell in the Ogasawara domain, high-ranking Kuroda domain officials escorted Geki from Osaka to Kyūshū through the Inland Sea, a journey made aboard Fukuoka ships. This partitioning of domainal duties, though perhaps a division dictated by the shogunate to distribute the expenses of hosting a Tokugawa deputy, reflected latent rivalries between Fukuoka and Kokura in claiming leadership in the coalition effort.

To encourage the domains to accept Geki's arbitration, the shogunate couched his oversight authority as situation dependent. Geki alternated his time between Kokura and Nagasaki, home of the magistrate, Geki's immediate superior, from where communication with the domains took roughly two days by express messenger. During the first several months of his service, when the Chinese smugglers were most ubiquitous, Geki resided in Kokura only about three weeks out of every two months and spent the majority of his time in Nagasaki, as befitted traditional inspectors. This frequent absence from the Genkai area facilitated domainal independence by allowing domains to fire on Chinese ships without express permission from Geki. Before Geki's departure from Edo, shogunal officials had issued an unusually precise description of his authority in Northern Kyūshū, specifying that domains were to halt pursuit of Chinese ships until his arrival. Yet a conflicting directive permitted the same domains to chase these ships away as had been customary. Once Geki arrived in Kyūshū, this outline of his oversight power ordered domains to send notice of Chinese smugglers to Geki in Nagasaki during his periods of residence there and to hold their fire until they received his permission or he personally returned. But this same article

61. Kuroita, *Tokugawa jikki*, 45:102.

62. Arano, *Kinsei Nihon to higashi Ajia*, p. 95; Yamawaki, *Nukeni*, p. 84. Watanabe would later fill the post of Nagasaki magistrate between 1728 and 1730.

contained a concluding clause stating that if circumstances demanded, the domains could attack the Chinese ships without direct approval from Geki.[63] The shogunate acknowledged that independent decision making by domains was expected and even encouraged to respond to certain situations. Yet what it did not foresee was how domains would gradually usurp broader authority than had been delegated to them.

In practice, Edo granted domains discretion to address the Chinese smugglers in the way they saw fit, whether or not that method was objectively the most effective vehicle for exterminating illicit trade. The varying degrees of domainal autonomy likely reflected concern in Edo over who would be held responsible in the case of a failure. The greater the domainal agency, the more the shogunate could escape criticism for poor policy. Yet, permission for the domains to fire without waiting for approval from Nagasaki also reflected that multiday lags in communication could not be tolerated in a situation where the offending ships might disappear overnight. The shogunate wanted the policy to succeed, but the abovementioned caveats to Geki's role demonstrated that the Tokugawa were unwilling to mandate the specifics of the policy's execution on the ground, even as they dispatched a special overseer to monitor the anti-smuggling response. So why did the Tokugawa not grant Geki authority of supreme command and create mechanisms to enforce it, as they had done earlier, in pre-1670 Nagasaki, with the emergency military administration by the "Nagasaki commander"? The historical record offers only hints at an answer, but one consideration was that the cost of alienating domains and planting resistance to coalition forces in the future (in the case of Western attack) was perceived as greater than the benefits of exterminating the Chinese smugglers in the present.

Cognizant of the probability that domains would minimize Geki's authority of command, the shogunate explicitly ordered them to treat the inspector as if he were of the same status as the Nagasaki magistrate.[64] Yet everyone involved knew that this parity would develop only if the magistrate became ill and unable to execute his duties, in which case the inspector might temporarily replace him. Although the inspector maintained an office in the magistrate's Tateyama residence and enjoyed privileges of audience with daimyo in Nagasaki equal to those of

63. Higaki, *Yoshida kadenroku,* 2:450–52.

64. Suzuki, *Nagasaki bugyō no kenkyū*, p. 75.

the magistrate, he was still a subordinate of the magistrate, which compromised his oversight authority in Northern Kyūshū.

When Geki finally reached Kokura in the spring of 1718, coalition troops began assaults that resulted in the first Chinese deaths from shelling. Multiple domains, however, soon competed to establish responsibility. By the fifteenth of the fourth month, composite forces from Fukuoka, Chōshū, and Kokura had fired on suspected Chinese smuggling ships, sinking at least one vessel. Significantly, these were the first foreigners killed by Japanese in national defense since the Portuguese executions in 1640.[65] On the night in question, Fukuoka forces joined a large armada of sixty boats to assault just nine Chinese ships.[66] The Chinese quickly pulled anchor, but their efforts to flee were stymied by lack of wind. At least five or six were killed, and eight or nine seriously wounded.[67] In another incident just days later, Fukuoka forces fired 300 rounds on alleged smugglers, felling one or two Chinese in their boats.[68] The Chinese were unable to counter the onslaught since they lacked weapons of their own. As the Dutch factor at the time, Christiaen Van Vrijeberghe, remarked, "The smuggling trade must be very profitable since the Chinese do not seem to be afraid of Japanese musketballs."[69]

Because these incidents destroyed at least one Chinese ship and killed five or six Chinese sailors, both Fukuoka and Kokura claimed that the shelling took place in their waters, reflecting the continued contest for military leadership among domains. From the spring of 1718, Fukuoka was the on-duty domain in Nagasaki, and the reassertion of its agency there in this precise period may have prompted it to aggrandize its role in the Genkai area. For Kokura, collaborating with a domain such as Fukuoka, which had already established itself as a central military actor in Nagasaki when Kokura had no such experience, may have prompted the domain to aggressively assert its role in the Genkai area.

The altercation that occurred on the fifteenth day of the fourth month took place at night in the open sea, making the exact site of engagement

65. Bolitho, "The *Han*," p. 204, mentions the 1644 sinking of a presumably Chinese ship in Karatsu by five domains. This incident appears in *Karatsu shishi*, p. 570, but estimates of deaths are not provided there.

66. Yamawaki, *Nukeni*, pp. 84–85.

67. Miyake, *Tōsen hyōryūki*, p. 105.

68. Kawazoe and Fukuoka komonjo o yomu kai, *Shintei Kuroda kafu*, vol. 4, "Tsugutaka ki," pp. 30–31.

69. Van der Velde and Bachofner, *Deshima Diaries, Marginalia, 1700–1740*, p. 223.

difficult to pinpoint, ambiguity that allowed both domains to claim that the encounter had occurred in their waters. Fukuoka sources placed the confrontation at Ainoshima, a Fukuoka island with an illustrious history where the Tokugawa hosted Korean embassies. Kokura sources, on the other hand, conveniently suggested it was further north, within sight of their lord's view from a shoreline tower.[70] Claims that effective firing had occurred in one's own domainal waters were not only self-congratulatory, but also implicitly criticized the rival, neighboring domain's inability to destroy the vessel before it had fled its territory. Although neither side appears to have been wholly objective, Fukuoka sources were particularly biased. Despite providing the lengthiest treatment of the episode, Fukuoka documents omitted mention of the other two domains' contributions.[71] By contrast, Kokura records at least admitted that a composite armada had gathered at the protected Wakamatsu inlet, an unusually configured harbor located in Fukuoka domain, but immediately adjacent to the Kokura land border and opening into Kokura territorial waters. Despite this politically complicated geography, officials of both domains recognized that this was the most favorable spot for ships to gather undetected and take the Chinese ships by surprise.

The domains' success in these attacks depended less on the potency of Japanese weaponry than on the absence of return fire from the Chinese. The average quantity of ammunition per fatality was more than 200 rounds, using only the numbers from Fukuoka vessels. These figures suggest that even though local forces ultimately repelled the Chinese, the accuracy of gunners, and weapons, was poor. Firing shoulder cannons (*hōtsutsu*) from boats that were unbalanced by wave motion was certainly difficult. But at a distance of thirty to thirty-five feet (five to six *ken*) from the Chinese ships, these were still low percentages. In spite of the high shot-to-mortality ratio, however, shogunal officials considered these initial attacks effective. Geki summoned the Nagasaki liaison officers of the three domains to commend their soldiers for the attacks, and the senior councillor Mizuno Tadayuki summoned the Fukuoka house officer,

70. Yamawaki, *Nukeni*, pp. 84–85; Kanai, *Nagasaki sōsho*, pp. 167–70; for Kokura claims, Miyake, *Tōsen hyōryūki*, p. 105.

71. Kawazoe and Fukuoka komonjo o yomu kai, *Shintei Kuroda kafu,* vol. 4, "Tsugutaka ki," pp. 27–32.

Nagaoka Shichidayu, to recognize his domain for their contributions to the same assault.

Coalition domainal shelling was destructive enough that successive Chinese ships calling at Nagasaki mentioned the attacks, and contrary to Factor Van Vrijeberghe's sense of things, at least one of their reports claimed Chinese merchants would no longer sail off Fukuoka shores.[72] A Chinese ship from Shanghai entering Nagasaki in the tenth month of 1718 confirmed that two Chinese ships had been attacked in Kokura Bay that spring. By the time these vessels limped back to Amoy, several among the crew were dead or wounded. This destruction was enough for the captain to claim that Chinese ships would no longer sail to the Genkai area.[73] At the same time, however, Chinese merchants appear to have had new commercial prospects. Not merely the threat of death diverted them from Northern Kyūshū; the same report reveals that in the seventh month, a Qing imperial edict had restored permission for Chinese sailors to trade in the South Pacific.[74]

These initial successes did not keep Geki from working to refine coalition tactics, although he remained wary of encroaching on the domains' tradition of relative autonomy in executing maritime defense. Thus instead of consulting one of the Genkai domains about material improvements, he first approached neighboring Saga domain artillery officials in early 1719 for advice on selecting the most effective weapons to sink Chinese ships in the Genkai Sea.[75] Saga troops were not posted

72. One of these ships fled to the island of Iki after the attack, and its captain, Ri Kafu, after fabricating a story about meeting a terrible storm, was sent to Hirado and then Nagasaki. From questioning, officials of the Nagasaki magistrate learned that after the attack, ten of his fifty-three crew members had died and several more had been wounded. See Yamawaki, *Nukeni*, pp. 85–86, and Kanai, *Nagasaki sōsho*, p. 169. A Nanking registered ship entering Nagasaki from Shanghai in the sixth month reported that ships fleeing from the Genkai area had sailed to Ningbo and Saho with several sailors wounded or killed. See Hayashi, *Kai hentai,* 2:2802. The Dutch factor at the time, Van Vrijeberghe, also recorded that a Chinese junk with ten dead men aboard had landed at Hirado, claiming that the men were killed in a storm. He questioned their explanation, however, hypothesizing that the junk had been fired on in Kokura. Van der Velde and Bachofner, *Deshima Diaries, Marginalia, 1700–1740*, p. 222.

73. Hayashi, *Kai hentai,* 2:2816.

74. Ibid., 2:2816–17.

75. This request for Saga input likely reflected Geki's recognition that the domain's Edo liaison had informed the senior councillor Abe Masataka in mid-1718 that the domain did not consider the Genkai Sea smuggling efforts as an extension of

to the Northern Kyūshū shores, but the domain had long performed maritime duty in Nagasaki harbor. Hara Jirōbei, one of the Saga battery officers Geki interviewed, knew from having accompanied the Nabeshima lord on tours of Dutch vessels that Dutch hulls were roughly two feet thick. Chinese ship hulls were much thinner, and from these calculations, he ultimately suggested a light cannon (which used ammunition of one *kanme*, or roughly 8.7 pounds) on grounds that it would penetrate Chinese hulls and be relatively easy to maneuver in strong seas. Hara knew from domainal firing tests at the Megami battery in Nagasaki that rounds of this diameter had penetrated rock to a depth of two feet after being fired from a distance of almost half a mile. Certainly this would be sufficient to pierce the wooden beams of Chinese junks.[76] Extant records do not specify what weapons were used in attacks during the spring of the following year, but perhaps they were the category recommended by Hara, because an attack in the fifth month became the deadliest assault of the "Chinese interim."

Final Assaults

The following decade (1720–30) saw both the most lethal attack on the Chinese and a return to domain-specific shelling instead of composite-force assaults, signaling the irreconcilable divisiveness of tensions over domainal military autonomy in the Genkai area. The return to single-domain offensives meant that the shogunate did not replace the inspector Geki with an overseer of Northern Kyūshū maritime defense, leaving the domains to sort out their maritime military differences without an arbiter. In the fifth month of 1720, just after returning from Edo, the newly appointed Fukuoka lord Tsugutaka ordered local forces to shoot

---

its Nagasaki service (as a 1715 edict had in fact declared), but rather a concern specific to Fukuoka, Kokura, and Chōshū domains. This declaration apparently developed from discussions about transporting Nagasaki-based weapons (including those owned by Saga) to other domains were a nearby maritime emergency to develop. *Saga ken kinsei shiryō*, vol. 1, no. 5, pp. 167–68.

76. Ibid., pp. 183, 188. While Geki might have solicited this same information from similarly experienced Fukuoka artillery experts, he was an ambitious bureaucrat. Within a decade he would be appointed Nagasaki magistrate and perhaps had foreseen the political utility of cultivating Saga's favor as preparation for a successful tenure overseeing Nagasaki defenses.

Chinese vessels on sight as part of a reinvigorated shogunal anti-smuggling campaign. This shogunal charge was delivered to Kokura and Chōshū domains also, although it did not specify a coordinated response.[77] Following these instructions, Fukuoka soon sent fourteen gunners to Wakamatsu, and another sixteen boats and 256 men to Oshima Island, where a Chinese ship had been drifting. The head guard at Oshima, Kojima Gozaemon, approached the vessel and asked to view its Nagasaki trade permit, but the seal on the document handed over was not clear. Over the next few days the ship retreated when pursued and then returned when the guard boats withdrew. When finally a Japanese ship from Hyūga passed and skirted advances by the Chinese ship to engage in trade, shore guards had no doubt the sailors were smugglers.[78] The destruction of their vessel would be the bloodiest incident of the "Chinese interim."

Why did the shogunate find it necessary to reissue its hard-line stance against the smugglers? Even though Edo had rewarded individual domains for their efforts over the past two years under Geki's supervision, smuggling had not been eradicated, and by the summer of 1719, the shogunal senior councillor Inoue criticized the efforts of western (Kyūshū) domains as "ineffectual" (*mueki*).[79] The shogunate then temporarily relaxed instructions to fire on Chinese ships so that they could more easily approach the shores, allowing local officials to apprehend Japanese smugglers trading with these vessels. Though this approach skirted the persistent problem of domainal maritime sovereignty, the new legal strategy failed. In the spring of 1720, the shogunate issued new orders to destroy the smugglers' ships and kill the Chinese.

A summary of this deadly attack following the reinstatement of aggressive measures is instructive because we know more details about the offending vessel and its crew and captain than we do about the details of any other shelling incident of this campaign. On the night of the twenty-second of the sixth month, armed Fukuoka boats entered the water at Oshima Island, northwest of the castle town. At daybreak, Fukuoka vessels made their way to the Chinese ship and began firing when they were about fifty feet away. Chinese appeared on deck asking for mercy,

77. Kawazoe and Fukuoka komonjo o yomu kai, *Shintei Kuroda kafu*, vol. 4, "Tsugutaka ki," p. 33.

78. Ibid., p. 37.

79. Higaki, *Yoshida kadenroku*, 2:574; Yao, "Sakoku ka no Fukuoka han," p. 284.

but according to Kuroda records, domainal soldiers continued discharging, partly out of concern that the Chinese had weapons aboard.[80] When the firing finally stopped, all men on board the domainal boats, from the ships' captains to the rowers, grabbed their halberds and boarded the ship to inspect. They did find weapons—two rifles, one shoulder cannon, and two boxes of ammunition—but not nearly the kind of firepower that would have posed a serious threat to Fukuoka forces, which had fired 700 rounds of ammunition that day. After boarding the ship, Fukuoka soldiers shot or speared nineteen more Chinese. Countless others died in the spreading ship fire or drowned as they jumped overboard. A final three were found hanging by a rope to the rudder as the still burning hull was pulled to shore. In accordance with the instructions of the magistrate, all dead bodies were thrown into the sea and the boat entirely burned. As the ship disappeared into the sea, a local samurai, Katō Naoemon, noted the words "Songjiang province Shanghai ship number five" on the stern and bow, confirming its Chinese provenance.[81]

From interrogating a Japanese smuggler, Fukuoka officials discovered that the captain was probably a Chinese merchant named Ling Suyan (Jap. Ryō Sogen).[82] Although Ryō had seemingly set sail with a permit to trade in Nagasaki (which provided an alibi for being in these waters), he had previously sold cargo illegally around Amakusa and the Gotō Islands and had sailed this time for the Genkai coast after hearing he could unload goods on local smugglers. His cargo was worth approximately 1,000 *kan* silver, one-sixth of the total annual value of trade allowed to all Chinese merchants in Nagasaki. Domainal records seemingly overstated the number of Chinese sailors aboard this ship at eighty to ninety men to aggrandize the scale of their accomplishment, when only thirty-four men were reported to the shogunate. What seems certain, however, is that the entire crew perished, making this the deadliest engagement with a foreign ship since Hideyoshi's attack on Korea a century before.[83] The obliteration of the ship and its crew was considered a

80. Kawazoe and Fukuoka komonjo o yomu kai, *Shintei Kuroda kafu*, vol. 4, "Tsugutaka ki," p. 37.

81. This was located in southeast Jiangsu Province, just southwest of present-day Shanghai.

82. Arano, *Kinsei Nihon to higashi Ajia*, pp. 95–96.

83. Yamawaki, *Nukeni*, pp. 84–86. The document describing this incident to the *rōjū* in Edo, dated the sixth month, revealed that thirty-four crew had been counted.

great service to both shogunate and domain, and in the coming months men were rewarded in both Edo and Fukuoka. On the twenty-first of the eighth month, the senior councillor Inoue called the Fukuoka liaison officers to the castle to present them with four robes and thirty pieces of silver to distribute to subordinates involved in the attacks. After returning to Fukuoka, these two officers also had their stipends increased from 100 to 200 *koku* and were presented with gold pieces for their performance. All other men involved, down to the foot soldiers and rowers, were presented with small coins or rice.

Despite the accolades, no wave of similar incidents followed. Previous scholarship suggests that a 1727 petition to the magistrate from Chinese merchants halted the mortal force policy.[84] Fukuoka sources, however, reveal that domains retained the authority to shell Chinese vessels through the 1750s, even though this privilege was seldom invoked. The continuation of an aggressive stance toward Genkai smuggling was most evident in the appointment of Watanabe Geki (the inspector who had organized a trans-domainal response to Genkai smuggling) as Nagasaki magistrate in 1727.[85] Since 1724, the post of inspector in charge of Genkai defenses had been vacant, returning oversight of smuggling to the magistrate's purview. Perhaps in an attempt to reassert further magistrate command of Northern Kyūshū's coastal defense, Watanabe met with Fukuoka lord Tsugutaka on his way to Nagasaki from Edo to emphasize continuation of the shelling policy. He also requested that the domain forward him a list of Fukuoka soldiers with a superlative performance in shelling the Chinese.[86]

After Watanabe's appointment, Fukuoka records do not mention Chinese smuggling again until 1730. In the spring of that year, a Chinese ship was spotted for several days off of Oshima but ultimately withdrew.

Two corpses had been noticed, and the report speculated that the remainder had burned or washed out to sea.

84. Ibid., p. 88. According to Yamawaki, a petition from a Chinese merchant in 1727 led to the cessation of shelling. The petition is reprinted in Hayashi, *Tsūkō ichiran*, 5:255–56.

85. This upswing occurred primarily because of the lifting of a Qing ban (first imposed in 1717) on Chinese seaborne trade with Asia. Hall, "Notes on Early Ch'ing Copper Trade," p. 456n40.

86. Takayanagi and Ishii, *Ofuregaki Kampō shūsei,* p. 978. Incident briefly noted in Kawazoe and Fukuoka komonjo o yomu kai, *Shintei Kuroda kafu*, vol. 4, "Tsugutaka ki," pp. 92–93, 99.

In spite of this apparent inactivity, the Nagasaki magistrate, Miyake Yasutaka, issued yet another edict five months later. Now even if Chinese ships that carried a trading permit were found to have left their normal sailing route, shore gunners should have no qualms about shooting to destroy.[87] Local soldiers might fire to destroy even if a ship carried legitimate trading papers. In a period of rare sightings of Chinese vessels along the Genkai coast, however, this edict seemed designed as much to project the authority of the magistrate during an era of diminished smuggling as to respond to a resurgent threat. In 1753, after more than two quiet decades along Fukuoka shores, the magistrate issued a final edict urging the use of shelling if necessary against Chinese ships. But would-be smugglers seem to have been diverted by the rumors of loss of life and destruction of cargo, as well as by the promise of new markets.

Conclusion

These Chinese smuggling episodes might have sparked an incremental transition from littoral zones as primarily domainal-administered waters to maritime space where Tokugawa central authority prevailed. Yet, during the period of fiscal and commercial reform in the early eighteenth century, the potential political costs to the shogunate of waging this battle with domains did not seem worth the benefits. In the long run, the profitability of the Nagasaki trade, as Bettina Gramlich-Oka persuasively argues, was the shogunate's priority in the administration of Kyūshū.[88] Diverting resources and manpower from this international port to more definitively squelch the Chinese smuggling problem, which Edo optimists wagered was temporary, was not an enticing remunerative or stabilizing strategy. Neither did domains see that adjudicating their maritime border disputes through the shogunal court system was attractive, since suits could take decades and the Chinese nuisance might be short-lived. In addition, as Luke Roberts has explored in his analysis of late seventeenth-century Shikoku territorial disputes, daimyo could not officially pursue cross-domainal border disputes, but rather had to rely on commoners to file the petitions with Edo courts.[89] In the Genkai case,

87. Kawazoe and Fukuoka komonjo o yomu kai, *Shintei Kuroda kafu*, vol. 4, "Tsugutaka ki," pp. 139–40.

88. Gramlich-Oka, "Thorn in the Eye of the Shogunate."

89. Roberts, *Performing the Great Peace*, p. 105.

the maritime territories of disputed military responsibilities were further removed from shore than the areas acknowledged as proprietary fishing grounds, so fishermen (who were of commoner status) would have little legitimate reason to be involved. What remains clear is that the domainal maritime "cooperative system" of defense (*kyōroku taisei*) that historian Kamishiraishi Minoru suggests emerged in the early nineteenth century was far from present.[90] The shogunate's acknowledgment of this persistent domainal self-interest in an area far removed from its capital, and thus challenging to control, contributed to its reassertion of authority in Nagasaki commerce, a sphere it could more realistically dominate.

These fundamental tensions between the shogunate and domains over maritime sovereignty in Northern Kyūshū stand in stark contrast to the more collaborative control of sea spaces in mid-seventeenth-century Nagasaki, examined in chapter 1, where Saga and Fukuoka domains alternated responsibility for guarding the port. Since Nagasaki harbor was some ten miles long but only a mile or two wide, fixed cannon could hit vessels from either side. As well, the mountainous topography of the shoreline there prevented strong ocean winds from entering the bay and deprived sailing ships of the ability to move quickly within the harbor.[91] Yet the most important distinctions between domainal collaboration in seventeenth-century Nagasaki and lack of it along the early eighteenth century Genkai Sea area were not geographical but rather differences of political economy: (1) the semipermanent presence of Western vessels in Nagasaki, which prompted greater collaboration than against Chinese ships because of their larger perceived threat, (2) the political classification of the shoreline lands: largely shogunal lands (*tenryō*) in Nagasaki but domain-managed lands in the Genkai area, and (3) a reconfiguration of the duties of the Nagasaki magistrate. To recap how this "Chinese interim" informs our understanding of Tokugawa state formation during the early eighteenth century, the second two points are most important.

The use of lethal force to repel Chinese smugglers, who multiplied due to Qing political consolidation, reflected an emerging Tokugawa understanding of sovereignty based on economic security, but a sovereignty

90. Kamishiraishi, *Bakumatsuki taigai kankei*, p. 273.

91. The relative stillness of the air is a defining characteristic of many contemporary prints of Nagasaki harbor, which depict Dutch sailing ships being towed to Dejima by Japanese oared vessels because of the absence of wind in the inner bay.

that could be ensured only with the continued devolution of military authority to the domains. As Anne Pérotin-Dumon has observed of catalysts for European piracy and its suppression between 1450 and 1850, so, too, in East Asian waters, the motivations for smuggling were economic, but the dynamic that regulated it was political.[92] The political configuration of authority in Northern Kyūshū—where the three domains of Fukuoka, Kokura, and Chōshū shared imprecisely defined maritime borders in the area they were charged to regulate—proved especially contentious because the Genkai waters did not border Tokugawa lands (as did Nagasaki), which would have encouraged timely resolution of these disagreements.[93] All three domains tended to prioritize successful attacks by domainal troops in their own territorial waters over effective policing of the trans-border maritime region. Early rewards, in fact, for participation in assaults seem to have been an encouragement to continue collaboration rather than commendation for a concrete act. Part of the problem lay in the custom of defining midsea water boundaries by islands, which was inherently imprecise and rife with possibility for dispute.

A final element augmenting domainal agency in the smuggling crisis was the change in 1715 from a system of four Nagasaki magistrates to a system of two, with only one at a time residing in Nagasaki. A single magistrate, in this period of complex administrative overhaul following the Shōtoku commercial reforms, did not have time to oversee the minutiae of smuggling issues outside of Nagasaki proper. Instead, responsibility for managing events in greater Kyūshū was delegated to the newly created office of Nagasaki inspector Although the shogunate granted this individual an administrative office in the magistrate's residence and directed him to cosign official documents issued by the magistrate, he was a subordinate of the "*bugyō*."[94] In one sense, the move to fewer magistrates may seem incongruous with implementing new and expanded commercial regulations, which required greater manpower. Yet under this streamlined command structure of one inspector

92. Pérotin-Dumon, "The Pirate and the Emperor," pp. 197–98.

93. Miyake, *Tōsen hyōryūki*, pp. 57, 61. Ruddle and Tomoyama underscore the way the angle at which maritime boundaries were extended from land boundaries could cause friction in "Sea Tenure in Japan," p. 341.

94. Suzuki, *Nagasaki bugyō no kenkyū*, p. 72. A list of rights and privileges is on pp. 68–69.

assisting one magistrate, the hierarchy of authority was more clearly defined. Still, coordination of the Genkai smuggling response by the inspector, an official of lesser rank than the magistrate, granted the domains greater discretion in their maritime defense duties than they had enjoyed under the previous structure.

Previous scholarship generally situates the military response to Chinese smuggling in the Genkai Sea as an anomaly, a departure from the "more significant" historical development of maritime defense centered on Nagasaki and potential European adversaries. But analyzed through the lens of coastal defense, this interim is an instructive transitional phase that foreshadows important developments in a more comprehensive national security paradigm. The period 1680 to 1730 offered the shogunate two critical lessons for maritime defense policy. First, the expansion of Fukuoka's Nagasaki duty to focus on Chinese revealed that foreign nations outside of Western Europe could imperil Tokugawa security. Officials in Nagasaki were not seriously concerned about a Qing invasion of Kyūshū, but the shift of harbor guard troops to combat smugglers in the Genkai conceptually prepared the shogunate for the diplomatic and economic pressure from new directions such as Eastern Europe, specifically Russia, that surfaced in Ezo sixty years later. This spatial transfer of adversaries (to China) and garrisoned coastline (to the Genkai Sea) proved that national security could no longer be guaranteed through permanently fortifying a single port (Nagasaki). Second, the mobilization of the three domains of Fukuoka, Kokura, and Chōshū along the Genkai Sea provided a second model (after that of Fukuoka and Saga in Nagasaki) of the synergy, and limitations, of composite military forces in combating external threats. Although this Genkai coalition was temporary and achieved only modest results, the shogunate applied yet another adaptation of the "Nagasaki model" of maritime defense in Ezo, and later the Kantō region, in the late 1700s as the region of greatest perceived external threat shifted from the East China Sea to the North Pacific. To appreciate that transformation, however, we must first examine the third and final incarnation of the "Nagasaki system" of defense: its custodianship and protection of Dutch traders, examined in the next chapter.

CHAPTER THREE

Defending Dejima

Although the tiny Dutch merchant island of Dejima is well known as the crown jewel of Tokugawa foreign trade, historians have been slow to explore how its security shaped the defensive arrangements of Nagasaki harbor and of the broader Tokugawa realm. Following the diminution of shogunal concern about Portuguese pressure and Chinese smuggling, discussed in the previous two chapters, by the mid-eighteenth century, guarding a distinct foreign presence, Dutch traders stationed at Dejima, became the centerpiece of maritime defense efforts. Between 1720 and 1844, even as Russian envoys in the 1790s and then Anglo-American whalers in the early nineteenth century began to intermittently probe Tokugawa receptivity to expanded foreign relations, the most constant and persistent object of coastal defense activities were the Dutch in Nagasaki. Their numbers were small, with often fewer than twenty men remaining at Dejima during the winter season, but their consequences for coastal defense efforts were profound. Dutch acquiescence to shogunal orders to relinquish all gunpowder, ammunition, and firearms while in port reflected their subordination to the Tokugawa monopoly on violence, a martial order enforced by the domainal troops guarding these European guests. In the second half of the eighteenth century, a period of relative quietude along the Japanese coastline when no alarming ships arrived, domainal forces in Nagasaki focused their military energies on cultivating social networks of reciprocity with the Dutch to facilitate communication in a defensive emergency. As this chapter reveals, these contacts produced long-term military and economic benefits for all involved, particularly the domains whose Dutch relationships later placed them at the vanguard of defensive reform. By 1844, the long domainal custom of guarding the Dutch in Nagasaki, which granted Saga lord Nabeshima Naomasa the unprecedented privilege of inspecting the Dutch flagship *Palembang*'s armaments, newly arrived to protect King Willem II's trade emissary, catapulted an outside daimyo to national prominence as the primary architect of a new generation of maritime defense.

The most significant material result of domainal responsibility for Dutch security to shape national defense was Naomasa's tour of the *Palembang* in 1844. Yet a long history of interaction undergirded that single event. Domainal protection of the Dutch had emerged in the 1640s, immediately after the relocation of the Dutch trading compound from nearby Hirado to Nagasaki. Following this transfer, newly assigned domainal harbor forces began to verify that Dutch trading vessels had indeed turned over all weapons to Japanese authorities, as shogunal law required when they entered the harbor, and then served as guards for these unarmed guests. Over the centuries, these vessel inspections, initially conducted to confirm the absence of weapons, transformed into ritual pleasure outings in which the attending daimyo (ostensibly in port to review his shoreline troops) cultivated social relationships with the Dutch trading chief. Responsibility for Dutch security precipitated some of the most significant military reforms of the early nineteenth century, including those following the infamous 1808 *Phaeton* incident, when local domains began to shift from a maritime defense strategy based on mobilizing thousands of troops to one centered on the maintenance of reliable artillery. By the 1840s, the threatening geopolitical environment of the North Pacific, following China's capitulation to Britain in the First Opium War, made the shogunate receptive not only to patronizing Dutch weapons' technology, but also to delegating these initiatives to daimyo. Following the *Palembang*'s departure in 1844, guarding the Dutch, and the attendant political stature it granted domains as intermediaries in foreign affairs, provided Saga domain more agency in executing the monopoly on violence than any local actor had possessed since the beginning of the Tokugawa period.

The present chapter explores how Fukuoka and Saga domains' function as protector of the Dutch trade mission in Japan aggrandized their political and military status within the Tokugawa order by privileging them with safeguarding foreign nationals rather than simply defending the port and its native citizens. This perspective provides an important corrective to the predominant understanding of domainal-Dutch relations, generally focused on interactions in Edo following the late eighteenth-century rise of the Dutch studies (*rangaku*) movement.[1] Executing this responsibility of "military custodian" of Dutch traders comprised the third function of the "Nagasaki system" of maritime security, following defense against attack (treated in chapter 1) and enforcement of trade regulations (treated in chapter 2). As with these previous two dimensions, guarding the Dutch also served as a battleground for the magistrates and daimyo to contest authority in port, with daimyo often besting the Tokugawa deputy not only in military matters, but also in larger foreign affairs. To explore how custodianship of the Dutch influenced broader Tokugawa state formation, the first section of this chapter outlines how the Dutch merchant season determined the calendar of domainal troop rotations, and then analyzes the evolution of the Kuroda and Nabeshima daimyo interaction with the Dutch, giving particular emphasis to the eighteenth century, when cultivating Dutch relations became the centerpiece of Nagasaki military service. The second section compares the two seminal incidents testing the Dutch-Tokugawa security relationship to explore how their resolution shaped larger maritime defense policy. The first, the 1808 *Phaeton* incident, during which Nagasaki domainal troops failed to prevent British seizure of two Dutch hostages, prompted a shift in maritime defense strategy from an emphasis on mobilizing increased manpower to prioritizing artillery improvements. The second, the 1844 survey of the Dutch warship *Palembang* by Saga lord Nabeshima Naomasa, revealed how the long history of the daimyo-Dutch military custodianship positioned him, an outside lord, as an unprecedented leader in crafting national maritime defense policy.

1. Previous studies of domainal-Dutch relations have generally focused on interaction with Hirado in the early seventeenth century, or followed the emergence of the *rangaku* movement in the late eighteenth century. For representative examples of the former, see Adam Clulow, "From Global Entrepôt to Early Modern Domain," and Chaiklin, *Cultural Commerce and Dutch Commercial Culture*, pp. 62–63. Terrence Jackson suggests that the formative years of daimyo interest in cultivating relations with the Dutch began in the 1770s and, similar to Grant Goodman's analysis, emphasizes the development of these ties through domainal contact with the Dutch in Edo rather than through interaction in Nagasaki. Jackson, "Socialized Intellect"; Goodman, *Japan and the Dutch*. This chapter complicates and expands these perspectives by exploring the relationship between the Dutch and their daimyo defenders across the mid-Tokugawa period. It argues that critical preconditions for Dutch relationships with Kyūshū daimyo began in the mid-seventeenth century—in Kyūshū—rather than in the Tokugawa capital.

Origins of Domainal Defense of the Dutch

Throughout the Tokugawa period, the Nagasaki military service of domains, which the shogunate had implemented in 1641, revolved around the Dutch trading season (lasting from roughly August to October) to provide a secure commercial environment for these vessels. Dutch ships generally arrived in late summer due to the favorable trade winds and currents flowing northward from the Dutch East Indies during this season. Barring bad weather or an equipment malfunction, they departed by early October (the twentieth of the ninth month according to the lunar-solar calendar in use by the Tokugawa) as mandated by shogunal law of 1633. During the intervening three months, Dutch vessels anchored in port to unload items such as silk and deerskins or to await the arrival of camphor and copper from other parts of Japan to carry to Batavia, center of operations of the Dutch East India Company (VOC) in Asia. The size of the fleet varied over time, from as many as ten ships in the early seventeenth century to as few as one or two at the turn of the nineteenth century, when the VOC hired neutral Danish and American ships to transport their cargo during the Napoleonic Wars in order to avoid attack by British vessels.

Although the Tokugawa profit from Chinese trade generally surpassed that from the Dutch, the shogunate offered special protection to its European guests because Edo prized Dutch cargo for its value as prestige goods. Moreover, the official reports submitted by Dutch captains comprised the most important source of intelligence about the outside world. In the mid-seventeenth century, the shogunate had mandated high defensive vigilance during the short three-month Dutch trading season because of the passing concern that the Dutch might launch a military assault. In the long term, however, the Tokugawa most feared that rival Western merchants might attack the unarmed Dutch in port.[2] As a result, the Dutch trading cycle dictated the schedules of the domains providing Nagasaki harbor troops in three areas: alternate attendance of the daimyo, troop deployment, and harbor inspection tours.

As early as 1648, only six years after the creation of what would become the permanent Nagasaki defense system, the shogunate scheduled the period of the two harbor defenders' alternate attendance for only three months, instead of the more typical twelve, to allow the Saga and

2. Innes, "The Door Ajar," pp. 408–10.

Fukuoka lords to be present in their domains on standby defense duty for most of the year. The off-duty lord departed for his abbreviated alternate attendance duties in Edo in the tenth or eleventh month, immediately following the departure of the Dutch on the twentieth of the ninth month. He generally returned to his castle town no later than the fourth month of the following year to accept responsibility as the new on-duty domain and to begin preparations for the summer arrival of Dutch merchant vessels.[3] The total length of these Edo trips for both Fukuoka and Saga was roughly five months, with the journey from Northern Kyūshū to Edo taking about a month each way. This schedule allowed both daimyo to be at home for seven months throughout the year, ready to oversee troop mobilization in the event of an attack in Nagasaki.

Because the presence of Dutch trading vessels, and their expensive cargo, sparked the greatest concern about potential attack by a foreign marauding gunboat, the Dutch trading season also determined the rhythms of deploying domainal troops to Nagasaki shore batteries.[4] During the period from the departure of the Dutch merchant vessels in the ninth month until their return the following summer, when only a skeleton crew of twelve to sixteen Dutchmen resided on Dejima, troop strength in Nagasaki was at its nadir of some 300 to 400 domainal samurai.[5] But this figure increased to roughly 1,000 when the trading ships returned, to ensure the safety of unarmed European merchants.[6]

Daimyo trips to Nagasaki (known as "inspection tours," or *daiba junsatsu*), usually three per year, followed a calendar similar to that of their troops' movement. Barring delays in travel from Edo, illness, or other unusual circumstances, the first daimyo inspection occurred in the fourth month, following the return of the off-duty lord from Edo to resume duties as the on-duty domain. This trip marked the official transfer

3. Maruyama, "Nagasaki keibi to sankin kōtai," p. 994. Kuroda Tadayuki returned from alternate attendance in the fourth month for the first time in 1643, but this custom did not become regularized until the middle of Kuroda Mitsuyuki's reign, around 1661. For a comprehensive chart of the dates of Kuroda alternate attendance trips between 1612 and 1676, see Maruyama, "Sankin kōtaisei no keisei, kakuritsu katei," pp. 48–51.

4. Kawazoe and Fukuoka komonjo o yomu kai, *Shintei Kuroda kafu*, vol. 2, "Mitsuyuki ki," p. 249.

5. Huibert, "De Coningh on Deshima," p. 359.

6. *Kiyō gundan*, pp. 25–27. For additional figures on numbers of troops, see Nakamura and Takano, "Nagasaki keibi to zaisei," pp. 503–4.

of security responsibilities between Fukuoka and Saga domains and the beginning of preparations for the Dutch trading season. The second trip characteristically occurred in the seventh month, following the arrival of the Dutch trading vessels. The final trip was made in the ninth month, timed to coincide with the departure of the Dutch on the twentieth, so that the on-duty lord could personally oversee the loaded vessels' security as they exited the harbor.[7] Further revealing the centrality of Dutch trade to the defensive calendar, for the majority of the Tokugawa period, the fall replacement for the on-duty magistrate in Nagasaki arrived from Edo several days before the Dutch vessels departed, with the outgoing magistrate remaining in the port until the Dutch sails had disappeared. Requiring that not only one but rather two direct Tokugawa deputies be present to monitor the safe departure of the Dutch vessels projected an extra measure of respect and goodwill for the Dutch from the Tokugawa.

For Dutch ships scheduled to depart on the twentieth of the ninth month, the date decreed by shogunal edict and generally observed, the on-duty lord invariably visited Nagasaki for the departure. Daimyo could rarely arrange to be in Nagasaki precisely when the Dutch vessels arrived, since this date varied anywhere from the sixth to the eighth month, and there was no effective means for the captains to communicate changes in travel time.[8] Departures were a different matter. Departing Dutch ships left Dejima and then anchored in the shelter of Takaboko Island awaiting favorable winds before setting sail for the open sea. Since the mouth of the harbor was some ten miles from the wharf area, the attending lord did not actually view the moment when the sails disappeared. Instead, the report of a lookout stationed at the Nomozaki promontory, that the white sails had disappeared on the horizon, was official evidence that the Dutch had left Tokugawa protective oversight. Since the daimyo was a military figurehead rather than a de facto, on-the-ground commander, as numerous defensive emergencies in the seventeenth century had demonstrated, his presence in Nagasaki was not critical for protecting the Dutch. What seems to have been most

7. Nakamura, "Shimabara no ran to sakoku," pp. 236–37. If ships arrived later than normal, they were allowed to stay beyond this date, provided they departed within fifty days of their arrival.

8. Kawazoe and Fukuoka komonjo o yomu kai, *Shintei Kuroda kafu*, vol. 2, "Mitsuyuki ki," pp. 275, 380.

important for the attending lord was the public opportunity to display his privilege of protecting the Tokugawa's most important foreign guests. Daimyo journeys to oversee the Dutch provided an opportunity for the Kuroda and Nabeshima lords to remind the magistrate of his dependence on domainal troops to secure the most important foreigners in the country.

The shogunate had originally assigned domainal guards to Dutch merchants in the 1640s as a courtesy to unarmed traders, but also because Edo officials did not completely trust their loyalty. Until the early 1650s, the Tokugawa suspected that the Dutch East India Company supported Portuguese efforts to reestablish trade ties with Japan (as chapter 1 details), a development the shogunate resolutely opposed. The discovery by Edo officials that the Dutch had provided a pilot to Goncalo De Siquiera de Souza, the ultimately rebuffed 1647 Portuguese ambassador to Japan, confirmed this mistrust.[9] Although concerns about Dutch duplicity diminished over time, continued restrictions on their presence in port (including constant oversight by domainal guards and strict limitations on their movement outside of the small island compound of Dejima) publicly demonstrated Tokugawa mastery of a Western power. Officials of the Nagasaki magistrate confiscated gunpowder, ammunition, and swords from the Dutch when they entered the harbor, and dismantled even the heaviest cannons and rudders.[10] Given these early misgivings about Dutch fidelity, and their inferior status as barbarian merchants within the Tokugawa Confucian social order, guarding the Dutch, even with the attendant cultural access it provided, did not transform from a burden into a prerogative of the domains until the late seventeenth century.[11]

Lingering concerns about Dutch diplomatic allegiance had not stopped the Edo elite from developing an interest in broader Dutch culture as a window into European habits during the late seventeenth century. One indication of growing shogunal appreciation for the Dutch presence in Japan, and new prestige for their domainal handlers, was the elevation of the rank of the Nagasaki magistrate during the 1690s. By

9. Hesselink, *Prisoners from Nambu*, p. 159; Blussé, "The Grand Inquisitor Inoue Chikugo no kami Masashige," p. 40.

10. The Japanese discontinued removing these latter two items over time because, according to Dutch physician Engelbert Kaempfer, stationed at Dejima in the 1690s, it became "unnecessary." Kaempfer, *Kaempfer's Japan*, p. 213.

11. Goodman, *Japan and the Dutch*, p. 24.

1699, he received the place of highest honor among all the "distant magistrates" (*ongoku bugyō*) seated in the Lotus Hall (Fuyō no ma) space of Edo Castle, including the esteemed post of Kyoto magistrate.[12] A second sign of increased regard for Dejima culture was the new courtesies that Shogun Tsunayoshi (r. 1680–1709) extended to the Dutch during the Genroku (1688–1703) and Shōtoku (1711–15) periods. For example, Tsunayoshi increased shogunal audiences with the annual Dutch missions to Edo from one to two meetings, and his Confucian adviser Arai Hakuseki met with the Dutch in Edo on at least four different occasions.[13] Tsunayoshi was also the first shogun to summon Dejima interpreters, men of comparatively humble social status, to demonstrate their linguistic skills to him.[14] The heightened esteem for things Dutch in Edo prompted a concomitant interest among Kyūshū lords in cultivating relationships with Dejima, site of the only Dutch residential compound in Japan. Because of their frequent interaction with the Dutch factor (head of the trade mission in Japan), the lords of Nagasaki harbor forces were uniquely positioned to leverage this spreading appreciation for Dutch culture among Tokugawa elite to their own military and political benefit.

Although in retrospect, the constant Dutch presence throughout the Tokugawa period is often considered an inevitable given, tensions over whether or not to maintain a commercial relationship with the Dutch lingered throughout the first century of Tokugawa rule. Until the early eighteenth century, frequent discussions had erupted in Edo over the continued desirability of Dutch trade because it drained Tokugawa precious metal reserves. But the eighth shogun, Yoshimune (r. 1716–45), demonstrated his commitment to continuing Japan's relationship with the Dutch when his 1717 audience with Dutch factor Joan Aouwer lasted an "unprecedented six hours."[15] Moreover, the perceived value of the Dutch was not limited to the shoguns' inner circles. Daimyo Kuroda Tsunamasa, who oversaw Fukuoka domain's Nagasaki defense duty between 1688 and 1711, repeatedly offered gifts such as snipe and geese to the Dutch factor while also making ritual inquiries about his health.[16]

12. Suzuki, *Nagasaki bugyō no kenkyū*, p. 306.
13. Goodman, *Japan and the Dutch*, p. 46.
14. For this shift, see van der Velde, "The Interpreter Interpreted."
15. Ibid., p. 55.
16. In three successive years of alternate attendance duty at the beginning of the eighteenth century (1705, 1707, and 1709) Tsunamasa sent special gifts or

Although these courtesy gestures were an established element of the Tokugawa culture of ritual gift exchange, their extension to the Dutch represented a special effort to integrate the factor into the defender daimyo's social networks. Renewed domainal military attention to Dutch security soon followed this heightened cultural exchange. The case of Fukuoka provides a particularly telling example.

After the waning of the Genkai Sea smuggling crisis in the 1720s (treated in chapter 2), which had shifted Fukuoka's military priority to Northern Kyūshū, the domain refocused defensive efforts on guardianship of the Dutch by reassigning domainal troops and equipment back to Nagasaki. Yoshida Harutoshi, Kuroda domain elder in charge of Nagasaki defense, commented on this retooling of military duties to once again privilege relationships with the Dutch in his diary entries of these years. At the height of the smuggling crisis—between 1713 and 1720—Harutoshi had recorded the arrival and departure of Dutch merchant vessels in Nagasaki, but those notations included only a perfunctory line or two of text.[17] By contrast, he devoted nearly 100 pages during that same period to detailing the role of Fukuoka troops in quelling Chinese smugglers in the Genkai Sea.[18] But just as quickly as interest had turned away from the Dutch, with the final major attack on Chinese smugglers in 1720, it turned back again. Later that year, Harutoshi provided an extended narrative of the visit of the Fukuoka lord Tsugutaka to oversee the Dutch ships' departure. He even enumerated the various dignitaries who were notified when Tsugutaka left Nagasaki to return to his castle town, including other Kyūshū lords (such as those of Saga, Kokura, Yanagawa, Hirado, Karatsu, and Ōmura domains) and shogunal proxies (such as the Kyoto deputy [*shoshidai*], keeper of Osaka Castle [*jōdai*], Kyoto City magistrate [Kyoto *machibugyō*], Osaka City magistrate [Osaka *machibugyō*], and Fushimi magistrate [Fushimi *bugyō*]).[19] Recording this unusually extensive list of political elites kept apprised of Tsugutaka's movements reflected the domain's new priorities. First,

---

delivered greetings, or both, to the factor while the two men were in Edo or on the return journey to Kyūshū. In 1705, the "lord of Chikuzen" sent "two common snipes," in 1707 "two geese which were labeled as sweets," and in 1709 the "lord of Chikuzen inquired after our [the Dutch factor's] well being [in Osaka]." Van der Velde and Bachofner, *Deshima Diaries, Marginalia, 1700–1740*, pp. 65, 86, 110.

17. Higaki, *Yoshida kadenroku,* 2:432–33.

18. Ibid., 2:141–221.

19. Ibid., 2:724–25.

the notifications served to remind both local and shogunal actors of Tsugutaka's command of Nagasaki defenses, since he had become daimyo only the year before. Second, it affirmed the commitment of domain elders, such as Harutoshi, to the larger domain's reengagement with security in Nagasaki, particularly the Dutch compound, after a decade of prioritizing the Genkai Sea coast.[20]

Entrenching Reciprocity: The Dutch and Their Daimyo Defenders

For most of the eighteenth century, domainal protection of the Dutch centered on the exchange of ritual gifts and other material favors since no serious harbor emergencies required military coordination, save an occasional warehouse fire. These seemingly frivolous interactions, however, were not merely a substitute for a more consequential martial relationship. They produced substantial political and economic benefits for both parties, particularly the domains.

From 1730 to the 1790s, the journals of the Dutch factors consistently noted more visits to Dejima per year by the Fukuoka and Saga daimyo than by any other lords, attesting to the special access these domains acquired because of their military responsibilities.[21] Local domainal elites came to know Dejima residents well because many Dutchmen served multiple commercial tours in Japan. As historian Willem Remmelink has observed, of the twenty-four Dutch factors posted to Dejima between 1740 and 1800, "only four served for just one year and had had no prior Japan experience." Another three men served only once as factor but had substantial experience in lower positions at Dejima. Although another five factors had no prior background in Japan, they served three to five times as factor. Hendrik Romberg was the "champion," with five appointments to factor and more than twenty total years in Japan. Numerous colleagues shared similarly long tenures

20. Ibid., 2:721–24.

21. The examples in this section pull from English translations of the "marginalia," or margin notes, written by the Dutch factors to serve as a guide to the lengthier entries of the factor diaries themselves. Yet, the two volumes cited here, both edited by Paul van der Velde, contain amplified and contextualized versions of the sparse original notes, which, as Derek Massarella observes, "enables the sources to stand as a source in their own right." Massarella, "Review of *The Deshima Dagregisters*," p. 553.

on Dejima in a variety of positions.[22] Daimyo visits to Dejima to watch a game of billiards, sample Dutch confections, listen to the violin, try European liquors, view the harbor from a telescope, or watch "black boys" climbing the flagpole created the opportunity to entrench these domainal elites as allies of the Dutch. More militarily consequential, however, these courtesy calls provided occasion for local lords to parade domainal retinues, as large as 1,500 men, throughout Nagasaki—another means of asserting the military authority of these daimyo as superior to that of the magistrate, the local Tokugawa proxy.[23] The largest recorded domainal retinue (1,500 strong) to visit Dejima, in June of 1731, included the 300-man personal bodyguard of then Saga lord Nabeshima Muneshige.[24] As the Dutch factor Pieter Boockesteijn observed in his journal, Muneshige's security detail for this social call consisted of twenty-four riflemen, twenty-four pikemen, and twenty-four bowmen, a special weapons' corps whose appearance must have been particularly impressive to merit this precise description. Yet this subgroup, which comprised less than 5 percent of Muneshige's overall retinue, was larger than the entire complement of personal retainers under the Nagasaki magistrate's direct command.

In spite of the daimyo defenders' insistence on accentuating the military nature of their Nagasaki duty, the Dutch had long recognized the growing technological gap between Tokugawa and European firearms. Even surface comparisons of the weapons posted at harbor fortifications with those aboard Dutch merchant ships (which were, in turn, of markedly lesser firepower than the arms of European gunboats) revealed that the domainal guards could not realistically defend the Dutch in an attack. As early as the 1690s, Kaempfer recounted in his memoirs of Nagasaki that fortifications were flimsy: "The harbor has a number of water gates to allow for the mounting of cannons (which do not exist). Also, on each side of the harbor, about half a mile from the city, is an open, unfortified guard station."[25] He later continued, "The guard posts have no fortifications, entrenchments, or cannons and are merely housed in

22. Remmelink, "Introduction," in Blussé and Remmelink, *Deshima Diaries, Marginalia, 1740–1800*, p. x.

23. Van der Velde and Bachofner, *Deshima Diaries, Marginalia, 1700–1740*, p. 382 (June 1, 1731).

24. Ibid.

25. Kaempfer, *Kaempfer's Japan*, p. 138.

wooden buildings. For decoration, the surrounding courtyard is enclosed with military awnings when ships arrive and enter the harbor, and each must be honored with a special gun salute."[26] Yet, VOC officials had long recognized that the economic advantages of residency in Japan outweighed any security risk. Thus, even after observing that domainal troops could not plausibly protect Dejima, Dutch merchants continued to treat Fukuoka and Saga domains with special hospitality because their military presence offered additional avenues to court favor with Tokugawa officials. Cultivating the goodwill of daimyo resulted in not only gifts of interesting local delicacies and materials for ship repair, but also the possibility of an ally in Edo for instituting more favorable trade policies. The factors labored to convert these local lords into supporters of Dutch commercial interests by plying them with Spanish wines, Dutch meats, Lisbon oil, saffron, Peruvian balsam, and pistachio nuts, as well as easy access to the clandestine trade of prestige goods. To cultivate relationships of reciprocity, the Dutch also regularly obliged requests from these same daimyo. When the Saga lord Nabeshima Yoshishige asked the factor, Nicolaas Joan Van Hoorn, to provide a derrick that could "pull heavy objects up a mountain" in 1715, Van Hoorn readily agreed. He pointedly asked his carpenter to produce a model "in the hope that it will improve our relations [with the Saga daimyo]."[27] The Dutch also facilitated the export of Hizen porcelain, produced under the patronage of Saga lords and prized by European aristocrats.[28] As Leonard Blussé has observed, "All kinds of symbolic interaction and activities took place to create a favourable atmosphere for the sales and purchases."[29] These examples suggest that across the Tokugawa period, the factors deliberately leveraged what was ostensibly a military relationship with the domains to promote their own commercial advantage.

Fukuoka and Saga domains were equally aware that the heightened political stature gained from participating in these rituals of external relations (an unintended diplomatic role accorded no other domains in the realm except for Tsushima, Satsuma, and Matsumae in their management of foreign trade) surpassed the at times onerous financial obligations

26. Ibid., p. 153.

27. Van der Velde and Bachofner, *Deshima Diaries, Marginalia, 1700–1740*, p. 187.

28. Blussé and Remmelink, *Deshima Diaries, Marginalia, 1740–1800*, p. 531; Cobbing, *Kyushu: Gateway to Japan*, pp. 206–7.

29. Blussé, "A Glimpse Behind the Screens."

of providing troops to the port. These domains embraced public opportunities in Edo to make their familiarity with the factors known to a broader audience of daimyo. As Factor Cornelis Lardijin noted, in an antechamber of Edo Castle in 1712, several daimyo had glanced at him, but only the "Lord of Chikuzen," Fukuoka daimyo Kuroda Nobumasa, greeted him.[30] Back in Kyūshū, the provision of special foodstuffs and forest products to the Dutch often reflected the particular interest of individual lords in Dutch culture. Yet the extension of these courtesies over successive centuries revealed not only habits of custom, but also more long-term, strategic interest in establishing the domains as brokers of European cosmopolitanism. Dejima residents received a wide variety of foodstuffs from the surrounding lords, such as wild geese, sea bream, oysters, seaweed, sake, dried cuttlefish, snipes, and melon, and on one occasion the Saga lord provided ten specially selected trees to serve as masts for damaged Dutch ships.[31] In 1733, Saga domain provided 180 porters to carry the goods of the Dutch during their journey to Edo. The factor at the time, Hendrik van der Bel, surmised that the shogun had directed the domain to supply this labor, an order with which the Saga would have certainly complied. Since the Dutch compensated the porters, however, it was not a financially onerous duty, and merely further cemented the relationship between the two parties.[32]

From 1792, as the specter of a Russian attack in the north, and potentially on Nagasaki, became a serious threat to the Tokugawa following Adam Laxman's request in Ezo for trade on behalf of Russian empress Catherine the Great, domainal interest in projecting military power through spectacle in Nagasaki escalated. Daimyo "inspection tours" of the harbor, which summarily examined shore batteries before paying respects at Dejima, were the most frequent vehicles for these displays. Already in September of 1788, Factor J. F. Van Reede Tot De Parkeler had commented on the military pageantry that characterized the harbor tour of Saga lord Nabeshima Harushige. According to Parkeler, Harushige conducted his tour of the harbor fortifications in September of 1788 with "a lot of pomp."[33] By 1794, Factor Gijsbert Hemmij observed that daimyo tours of Nagasaki emphasized the pageantry of processions over

30. Van der Velde and Bachofner, *Deshima Diaries, Marginalia, 1700–1740*, p. 145.
31. Ibid., p. 731.
32. Ibid., p. 406.
33. Ibid., p. 581.

any probing inspection of fortifications: "The cannon has been fired in the presence of the first secretary of Chikuzen [Fukuoka domain]. He sailed here in full state in a yacht arrayed in all its glory with all insignia and banners. He was accompanied by several other smaller vessels which were all decorated with pennants and the Lord's banners."[34] As these remarks suggest, domains were often as interested in the display of military regalia, which allowed them to visibly project their clan's martial heritage, as in the efficacy of the defense of their European guests. This domainal discretion to respect the "form" of duty to the Tokugawa, even if it did not carry out the intended "content," was but one example of the built-in safety valves that prevented daimyo resentment of shogunal obligations from escalating to insurrection. As Luke Roberts has observed of this important safeguard within Tokugawa political culture, "The ability to command this *performance* of duty—in the thespian sense when actual performance of duty might be lacking—was a crucial tool of Tokugawa power that effectively worked toward preserving peace in the realm."[35] While this theatricality may have served to distract the Dutch from the growing inefficacy of domainal weaponry were it to face European attackers, it also projected to the domestic Japanese audience the unique privilege of these domains to parade their military forces through this international, shogunal city.

This lack of military rigor, and the absence of Dutch concern about their security at the end of the eighteenth century, was understandable since no belligerent vessel had ever attacked the Dutch while in port. During each successive decade without incident, the prospect of attack on the Dutch in Nagasaki harbor seemed increasingly remote. Even after Adam Laxman's disconcerting 1792 request for trade at Ezo, Dutch factor Hemmij, writing again in 1794, privately doubted that the Russians would travel as far south as Nagasaki. He "encouraged" shogunal officials to fear them, however, because he wanted to prevent rival merchants from joining the Nagasaki trade.[36] He did not express concern for the safety of his trading mission and, even were Russian ships to arrive, assumed that these vessels would enter port merely to reprovision.[37] Hemmij must have watched with amusement as growing concern

34. Blussé and Remmelink, *Deshima Diaries, Marginalia, 1740–1800*, p. 677.
35. Roberts, *Performing the Great Peace*, p. 3.
36. Blussé and Remmelink, *Deshima Diaries, Marginalia, 1740–1800*, p. 680.
37. Ibid.

among Nagasaki officials about the expected arrival of Russians created a defensive stir. In the spring of 1794, Hemmij noted the construction of an additional battery on the southeastern side of the harbor within range of the customary entry into port near the island known to the Dutch as Papenbang. He attributed this project to Tokugawa disquiet about the expected arrival of a Russian ship.[38] Following Laxman's request, the shogunate had instructed all domains to inspect any foreign ships approaching their shores and granted permission to fire and sink the vessels if they refused this interrogation. The new 1794 garrison in Nagasaki was part of the infrastructure to ensure that domainal troops could execute this directive.

With this project, material improvements in Nagasaki first substantially intersected with an increasingly national maritime defense initiative, stretching the length of the Japanese archipelago. Yet this new and daring vision of a more comprehensive coastal defense system including not only Ezo and Nagasaki, but also the Tōhoku region and the Kantō, was primarily the brainchild of shogunal senior councillor Matsudaira Sadanobu. With his resignation in 1793, attributed by many historians to skepticism among his colleagues about an overzealous (and inordinately expensive) coastal defense project, this grand vision stagnated for a decade, until the arrival of Rezanov in Nagasaki in 1804.

Aware that Edo was newly receptive to strengthening ties with its Dutch guests given their utility as conduits of information from Europe about Russian interests in Japan, from the 1790s, factors cultivated social relationships with domainal defenders not merely to receive material privileges, but also to leverage local ties for political and economic advantage in the shogun's capital. Factors understood the wider political structure and flows of power in the Tokugawa polity. Local daimyo families had direct blood connections to the Tokugawa, and factors were aware that special kindness to these individuals might be recognized as hospitality to the shogun's extended family. In 1793, the factor Hemmij received notice that the current shogun's (Ienari) third-born son (Hitotsubashi Naritaka) had been adopted by the lord of Fukuoka (Kuroda Harutaka) as his heir. Naritaka's familial links to the reigning shogun

38. Ibid., p. 677. Known to the Japanese as Takabokojima, the Dutch term meant "Catholic's island." It supposedly gained this name because Christians in the previous century had been thrown to their death in the ocean from the island's peaks.

made his announced visit to the Dutch trading compound an important event. To prepare for his arrival, the Nagasaki magistrate instructed Hemmij to cover the floors of the rooms Naritaka would enter with new mats and to offer all food and drink in new vessels. As Hemmij noted, the visit of Naritaka was propitious because a shogunal doctor preceded him, allowing the factor to "invoke his recommendation of the Company [VOC] at Court." During this visit, the Dutch staff indulged Naritaka in all the usual requests of Japanese visitors: "Next he asked to see Dutch being written. I immediately had the scribe perform this, bent over the floor. The lord chose to have his fan inscribed with the words 'hemel,' 'aarde,' 'vuur,' and 'water,' and those of the doctors and secretaries with gardens, cranes, tortoises, tigers, and other such things with propitious meanings. He amused himself with all this and viewed the whole bay with the telescope."[39] Naritaka's amusements might have been easy to oblige, but the context revealed how a complicated political calculus—including the extension of Dutch favors to daimyo as a tool for gaining favor in Edo—often undergirded Dutch engagement with these domains. This favored treatment of domainal elites, however, did not go unnoticed by the Nagasaki magistrate. He was acutely aware of the cumulative political and economic advantages to the domains of this long history of special courtesies by the Dutch and had already taken steps to minimize them.

"Dutch Custodianship" and the Negotiation of Port Authority

From the beginning of their Dejima tenure, the Dutch recognized that the spectacle of domainal defense duty was not primarily an attempt to impress foreign guests, but rather a manifestation of the competition between the daimyo and magistrate for military authority in the port (fig. 3.1). As early as the 1690s, Kaempfer noted that when a new magistrate arrived in Nagasaki from Edo, the local daimyo would often come to congratulate him on his safe journey as a "gesture of respect toward the shogun." Although the lord would assume an inferior position when inquiring about the health of the shogun, after the perfunctory greetings ended,

39. Blussé and Remmelink, *Deshima Diaries, Marginalia, 1740–1800*, pp. 668–69.

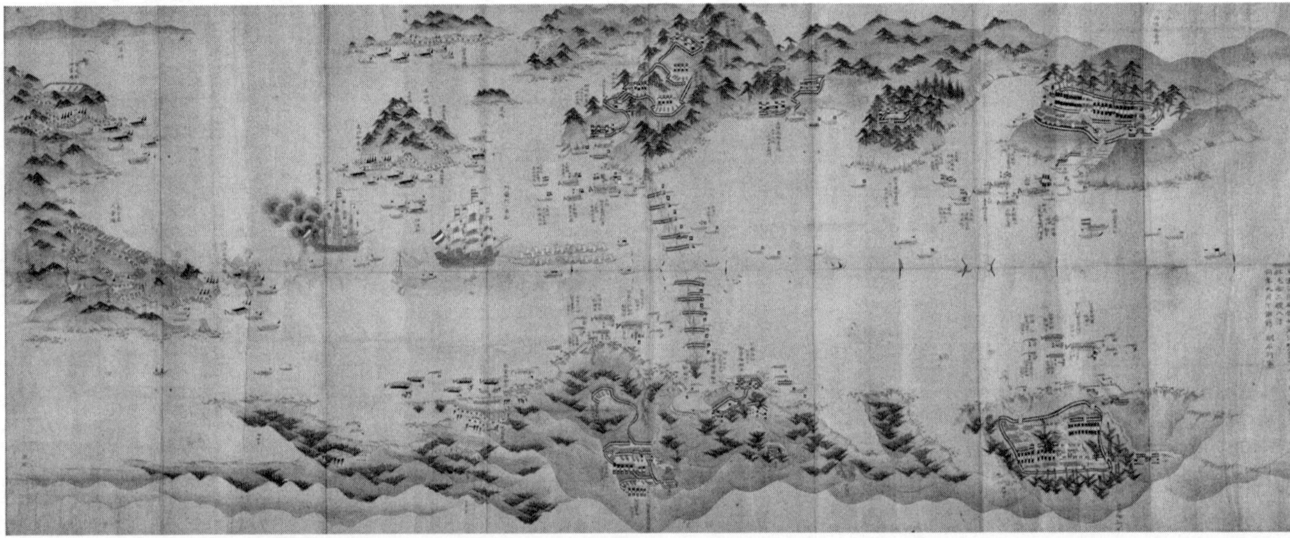

FIGURE 3.1 Fukuoka domain's guard ships secure the harbor entrance as an approaching Dutch vessel fires a ritual cannon salute. The armed rowboat line between the central shore batteries was a last desperate line of defense should the approaching vessel be in fact that of an enemy masquerading as Dutch. *Nagasaki keiei zu*, folding screen, 1813. Courtesy of the Fukuoka City Museum.

the lord again "assume[d] his superior rank."[40] Some two decades later, during an unspecified 1709 dispute between Nagasaki magistrate Sakuma Nobunari and then Fukuoka lord Kuroda Tsunamasa, Sakuma forbade the Dutch factor to entertain the Fukuoka daimyo's secretary with the normal hospitality.[41] Because of the very status that managing foreign guests began to confer during this period at the turn of the eighteenth century, the Tokugawa-Dutch relationship became a central site for the harbor guard domains and the magistrate to negotiate their agency in executing coastal defense. This jockeying between magistrate and daimyo for military authority in Nagasaki was not necessarily evidence of dysfunction within the Tokugawa political order, but rather a widely apparent characteristic of a quintessential early modern state in which power was "ambiguously allocated." In his analysis of the political history of early modern Europe, James Allen Vann observed how this "maneuvering" in the Duchy of Württemberg, within the Holy Roman Empire, occurred in "the effort to achieve increased status through skillful exploitation of . . . conspicuous consumption and lavish military and cultural patronage."[42] The interaction of Nagasaki elites with the Dutch involved similar calculations.

Maneuvering for public stature between the magistrate and daimyo as they negotiated access to the Dutch reflected how military capabilities shaped status politics in Tokugawa Japan. Because of their special standing as hereditary defenders of Nagasaki, Fukuoka and Saga had the most frequent domainal interaction with Dutch officials across the early modern period, and the magistrate notified them before any other domains when Dutch vessels arrived.[43] Yet, to counteract their growing stature in port, in 1765, the magistrate codified the details of access to Dejima to establish a textual basis for his superiority among local elites. The specific architect of these new regulations is not clear from the historical record, but given that Nagasaki magistrate Ishigaya Kiyomasa engineered a broad series of reforms between 1763 and 1766 to increase shogunal income through tighter control of foreign trade in Nagasaki, it is likely that he also authored these new rules to strengthen Tokugawa authority in Dutch-domainal relations.[44] While Bettina Gramlich-Oka's

40. Kaempfer, *Kaempfer's Japan*, pp. 395–96.
41. Van der Velde and Bachofner, *Deshima Diaries, Marginalia, 1700–1740*, p. 114.
42. Vann, *The Making of a State*, pp. 17, 21.
43. "Nyūtsu no koto," in *Sakoku jidai: Taigai ōsetsu kankei shiryō*, p. 47.
44. Gramlich-Oka, "Thorn in the Eye of the Shogunate," pp. 64–69 passim.

recent analysis of Kiyomasa's tenure suggests that he succeeded in augmenting the shogunate's coffers, he was not as successful in reasserting Tokugawa control of daimyo-Dejima relations.

In explicitly restricting Dejima access to domains with forces stationed in Nagasaki, the magistrate's 1765 handbook was the first document to definitively frame custodianship of the Dutch as a subset of larger Nagasaki defense, even though the calendar of troop rotations had reflected this relationship in practice since the 1640s. This document granted specific permission to visit Dejima and board Dutch merchant ships to fourteen western daimyo, including not only those of Fukuoka and Saga but also Satsuma, Kumamoto, Tsushima, Kokura, Yanagawa, Shimabara, Hirado, Karatsu, Chōfu, Ōmura, Gotō, and Hyūga.[45] It ordered these same domains to post notices announcing the arrival and departure of Dutch vessels, a practice designed to avoid the circulation of rumors about an uninvited, belligerent vessel that might prompt panic. With the exception of Hyūga, these were the exact domains that, in the 1640s, had been ordered to post "intelligence liaisons" in their Nagasaki residences to help mobilize troops in time of an external military threat. These fourteen domains bore the costs of maintaining special residences in Nagasaki that would serve as command centers in time of defensive emergency. In partial compensation, they gained privileged access to Dejima and its curios of European culture. This arrangement proved particularly beneficial for Fukuoka and Saga domains, which shouldered the bulk of the defensive burden.

Shrewd maneuvering on the part of both magistrate and daimyo over these handbook regulations was yet another example of how the competition for military authority in port centered on interactions with the Dutch during the long eighteenth century when no belligerent ships entered the harbor. Sections of the 1765 document that restricted daimyo access to Dejima also provided the Nagasaki magistrate, a *hatamoto* official inferior in social status to any lord petitioning him, a means to display his local authority. The new regulations required that lords from "nearby provinces" petition the magistrate's office to schedule visits to Dejima and to obtain written approval for exchanging ritual gifts of wine and fish with the factor. They also specified the types of dress and number of magistrate officials that must accompany each domainal delegation

45. *Sakoku jidai: Taigai ōsetsu kankei shiryō*, "Oranda sen nyūtsu narabi kiho no migiri reinen ryōdo urafure no koto," p. 43.

to Dejima.[46] As chief representative of Tokugawa interests in Nagasaki, the magistrate appropriated the right to use higher-ranking attendants than the daimyo during these visits, even though the domainal lords were his social superiors. The handbook instructed a city administrator (*machidoshi yori*) to accompany the magistrate on visits to Dejima. But only a ward headman (*otona*, an official of lesser status than the city administrator) would escort daimyo unless they requested the presence of the city administrator. Dutch records indicate, however, that in numerous instances after 1765, Fukuoka and Saga lords arrived on Dejima accompanied by the presiding city administrator (*rapporteur burgemeester*) or city administrator (*stadsburgemeester*), suggesting that at least the daimyo of these two domains ignored the 1765 edict or insisted on ceremonial parity.[47] In the end, these precisely articulated restrictions seem to have backfired, providing the domains with a more concrete method of using interaction with the Dutch to challenge the authority of the magistrate, even if only the Nagasaki elite were aware of these transgressions. Although the magistrate's attempt to reassert his authority with these restrictions largely failed, the regulations established for the first time in text the centrality of Dejima's protection to domainal defense duty.

Contests for Military Authority in the *Phaeton* Incident

These tensions of port military authority persisted into early nineteenth-century Nagasaki, erupting most dramatically in the two defensive emergencies centered on the Dutch: the infamous *Phaeton* incident of 1808 and the arrival of Dutch king Willem's embassy of 1844 aboard the gunship *Palembang*. The new emphasis on material improvements that followed these episodes marked the beginning of a shift in national maritime defense strategy across the first half of the nineteenth century from one based on mobilizing thousands of soldiers, generally armed with bladed

46. Ibid., "Oranda sen nyūtsu yori shuppo made gyōji chō," pp. 64–65.

47. Blussé and Remmelink, *Deshima Diaries, Marginalia, 1740–1800*, p. 405 (May 22, 1777); p. 478 (Dec. 2, 1783); p. 661 (Oct. 14, 1792); *commissaris burgemeester* (senior *machidoshi yori* who served simultaneously as either commissioner of foreigners or commissioner of the Nagasaki *kaisho*), p. 667 (May 1, 1793); *rapporteur burgemeester*, p. 685 (Sept. 23, 1794); *opperrapporteur burgemeester* (variant of *rapporteur burgemeester*), p. 732 (May 13, 1799).

weapons, to one centered on building shoreline fortifications and providing workable artillery. Even as these attempts, which constituted the most significant coastal defense improvements since the inception of the Nagasaki system in 1641, fell short of Western technological standards, once again, domains were both architects and executors of these "public works" projects undertaken to avoid future embarrassment. This focus on material upgrades, instead of on more clearly defining the right of supreme military command in Nagasaki, provided the first important intimations of the shogunate's debilitating inability, or refusal, to implement central oversight of maritime defense. By midcentury, this organizational shortcoming would produce grave questions about Tokugawa political legitimacy, namely, how a shogunate that based its claim to authority on military supremacy could justifiably rule if it was unable to orchestrate and manage the critical security of its ocean borders.

The 1804 appearance of Russian ambassador Nikolai Rezanov in Nagasaki had not sparked significant defensive changes because he arrived with the permit for entry acquired in 1792 by Adam Laxman, professing the goal of negotiating trade rights. The magistrate was confident of Rezanov's peaceful intent and refrained from mobilizing an obvious buildup of domainal troops. Both domains and the magistrate considered their defensive response successful because Rezanov left without aggression, even after the shogunate rejected his request for trade. Only four years later, with the 1808 *Phaeton* incident, in which a British frigate sailed into Nagasaki harbor disguised as a Dutch trading vessel and kidnapped two Dejima secretaries, did both domains and the magistrate question the adequacy of Dutch security and raise the need for fundamental reforms to the harbor defense system. Yet the changes that followed emphasized upgrading infrastructure and weapons and more carefully guarding secret Dutch flag signals, instead of clarifying the hierarchy of military authority in port.

Survey histories of nineteenth-century Japan often characterize the historical significance of the 1808 *Phaeton* incident as evidence of the failure of the Tokugawa regime to embrace the weapons revolution long under way in contemporary Europe. Yet for understanding the nineteenth-century trajectory of the Tokugawa monopoly on violence, the most important consequence of this 1808 episode had less to do with firearms and more with the rejection of a centrally controlled military command structure. The *Phaeton*, a British vessel in search of Dutch plunder at the height of the Napoleonic Wars, was in port for only three days and released the final hostage Dutch secretary, Gerrit Schimmel, unharmed after receiving supplies, which included water, four cows, and two sheep. The suicide of the magistrate, Matsudaira Yasuhira, and then punishment of Saga domain for their collective inability to protect their Dutch guests revealed how military responsibilities for protecting Dejima were inextricably intertwined with guarding against Western attack. This would be the only case during the entire Tokugawa period in which the Nagasaki magistrate took his life for defense-related matters.

When the *Phaeton* arrived unexpectedly in port in the summer of 1808, magistrate officials immediately realized its superior armament. The gunship was armed with thirty-eight 18-pound cannon, eight 32-pound carronades, and two carronades of unspecified caliber, so harbor officials were roughly accurate in counting fifty cannon on board.[48] In the nearest Saga-manned shoreline battery, Takaboko, the largest of the seven firearms was a 12-pound cannon, and the smallest used ammunition of only 4 ounces.[49] Perhaps this intimidating firepower, which prompted subordinates of the magistrate to describe the *Phaeton* as a "small castle," led them to overestimate the length at 36 *kan*, or roughly 216 feet, when it was only 141 feet long, an exaggeration of some 53 percent.[50] These same observers recorded 350 crew on board, although British sources indicate that warships of this class carried approximately 280 men.[51] Even if the British crew were of this lesser figure, they would have still outnumbered the local Japanese troops by five to one. If the *Phaeton* chose to attack, the harbor troops faced almost inevitable defeat.

As galling as this visible inferiority of Japanese weaponry and the sudden capture of Dutch hostages may have been, the most embarrassing shortcoming for the magistrate was his inability to retaliate because of lack of forces. When the *Phaeton* came into view, Saga domain had only some 50 to 60 soldiers positioned at the shoreline garrisons, instead of the required 200 to 400 men. Yasuhira's death note, written shortly before

48. Carronades were generally lighter and had shorter muzzles than other cannons mounted on warships in this period. Gardiner, *The Heavy Frigate*, p. 101; Hayashi, *Tsūkō ichiran*, 6:418.

49. Kajiwara, "Kansei bunka ki no Nagasaki keibi," p. 16.

50. Hayashi, *Tsūkō ichiran*, 6:418; Gardiner, *The Heavy Frigate*, p. 101.

51. Hayashi, *Tsūkō ichiran*, 6:418; Gardiner, *The Heavy Frigate*, p. 100.

he took his own life on the night before the *Phaeton* left, placed primary responsibility for the absence of adequate troops on Saga domain, rebuking its officials for both insubordination and general negligence. According to his analysis, they had not maintained the required minimum number of soldiers at the batteries, and, moreover, they had allowed troops to depart from the harbor fortifications without permission. The first criticism was unequivocally legitimate. The second critique, however, that reinforcements had (prematurely) withdrawn to the domain without his explicit permission, was less justified and revealed the persistent unclear hierarchy of authority in the military relationship between magistrate and daimyo regarding the Dutch.[52] Since no Dutch merchant ship had arrived in 1808, the Saga reinforcements returned to their home domain before the arrival of the *Phaeton* (which arrived on the fifteenth of the eighth month, well before the twentieth of the ninth month, when summer troops conventionally withdrew), as custom allowed.

Whether or not Saga withdrawal of summer troops, posted to guard Dutch merchant vessels, constituted a conscious dereliction of duty depends on whether or not precedent required the magistrate to grant them specific permission to return to their home province. The historical record suggests that in crisis situations, such as that of Rezanov in 1804, the magistrate directed the movement of emergency reinforcements. Records of the Rezanov incident—initially a period of defensive alert—reveal that the magistrate issued Kuroda reinforcements explicit permission to return home roughly two months after the arrival of the Russians, when the shogunate deemed the embassy innocuous.[53] Prior to the arrival of the *Phaeton*, as preparation against a rumored Russian attack, several extra troops from Saga domain had been dispatched to Fukahori, with supplementary Fukuoka soldiers stationed in guard boats, but they were all "recalled by the Nagasaki Magistrate's office so that not a single man was left."[54]

Normal yearly troop rotations, however, appear to have occurred without special permission. From the first decades of the annual departure of summer troops from Nagasaki in the 1640s, we do not find

52. Yasuhira's last will and testament is reproduced in Hayashi, *Tsūkō ichiran*, 6:443–44.

53. Kawazoe and Fukuoka komonjo o yomu kai, *Shintei Kuroda kafu*, vol. 5, "Narikiyo ki," p. 352.

54. Hayashi, *Tsūkō ichiran*, 6:413.

mention of explicit magistrate permission for withdrawal of summer forces. The return of Saga and Fukuoka forces to their domains, in periods without defensive emergency, was a customary movement of soldiers in the ninth month that followed the return of the on-duty lord to his castle town after having presided over the departure of the Dutch merchant vessels. One document relates that more than half of the Saga troops withdrew secretly (*nainai*), implying "inappropriately," but then continues to suggest that the Fukuoka reinforcements had also returned when no Dutch vessel appeared.[55] The departure of Saga troops in 1808 was one of those customary withdrawals given that a Dutch ship was not expected to come. The magistrate did not possess regular, supreme command of the movement of military forces in Nagasaki.

Aware that the magistrate had minimal control over domainal troops, even as he was theoretically the Tokugawa shogunate's chief proxy in Nagasaki, Yasuhira's death note argued for a prescient reform: an increase in the stature of the holder of the position of magistrate, not just to increase the number of forces under his direct command, but to acquire the social standing that would more effectively force domains to comply in deploying the minimum number of harbor troops required. This critique underscored the manpower constraints of the magistrate's *hatamoto* status, which Yasuhira contended had impeded his response to the *Phaeton*. As explored in chapter 1, the military limitations of Yasuhira's position were largely the result of his predecessor, Takenaka Shigeyoshi, the only other Nagasaki magistrate to commit suicide in office, whose misconduct had made daimyo ineligible for the post of magistrate. Because of Takenaka's transgressions in the early seventeenth century, at the time of the *Phaeton* incident, Yaushira held neither the position of daimyo nor the accompanying thousands of retainers at his command that would provide him both the status and the manpower to manage a military emergency. Yasuhira had an income of 3,000 *koku* and roughly twenty-five direct retainers at his disposal at the time of the incident. The average income of magistrates since the inception of Nagasaki guard duty in 1641 had been just under 1,600 *koku*, and the median income 1,450 *koku*, so Yasuhira's income placed him in the top quintile of his peers.[56] For an increase in status, as he suggested, to be effective,

55. Ibid., 6:426.

56. Figures calculated from income data for Nagasaki magistrates in *Nihonshi jiten*, pp. 1288–90.

the holder of the office of magistrate would have to be a daimyo in his own right. And to have troops at his instant disposal, Nagasaki would need to convert into a coastal castle town, similar to that of nearby Fukuoka domain, with a citadel surrounded by thousands of samurai residences.

Understanding why this arrangement did not unfold helps explain how responsibility for guarding the Dutch shaped magistrate-domain relations. Having two adjacent domains defend a direct Tokugawa territory, such as Nagasaki, was the least expensive way for the shogunate to protect its European guests, even if a permanent, residential samurai population would have provided more effective security. Even given the embarrassing *Phaeton* debacle, the existing system of domainal military responsibility in port had political advantages for the Tokugawa. As Constantine Vaporis and George Tsukahira have observed of the political utility of alternate attendance corteges, the annual daimyo processions to Nagasaki of lords discharging harbor defense duty were concrete expressions of fealty that also symbolically reaffirmed ties of allegiance between the Kuroda and Nabeshima houses and the Tokugawa.[57] From the shogunate's perspective, the political advantages of maintaining the Nagasaki defense system as is, with neighboring domains dispatching troops as needed, outweighed the potential military benefit of organizational restructuring that might grant the magistrate augmented command powers. Retaining the existing system, instead of implementing oversight reforms that amplified the magistrate's authority and clarified it as supreme to that of proximate daimyo, allowed domainal officials in Nagasaki to preserve their relative military autonomy.

In addition to these domestic political calculations, after realizing that the *Phaeton* incursion was the result of temporary hostilities of the Napoleonic Wars, the Tokugawa did not perceive a long-term external threat that demanded the scale of radical organizational change Yasuhira suggested. Given that the two most recent European gunboats (the *Pallada* of Rezanov in 1804 and the *Phaeton* of 1808) had brought only a few hundred men each, the shogunate likely did not embrace the necessity of thousands more troops. Neither did Saga domain, where seven military officials committed suicide and the daimyo, Narinao, suffered the ignominy of house arrest, push for a more demanding level of troop

57. Vaporis, *Tour of Duty*; Tsukahira, *Feudal Control in Tokugawa Japan*.

mobilization, or accountability, that might ensure sufficient forces were always present.[58] The apparent consensus domain and shogunal opinion on reform in the aftermath of the *Phaeton* incident was that the current manpower arrangements were adequate and would now be executed in good faith. Unlike the "military revolution" of early modern Europe, which included not only technological improvements but also major shifts in the organization of armies, domainal improvements to harbor defense involved only increases in buildings and weapons, with no discussion of clarifying the military relationship between the magistrate and domains. Material upgrades in weapons and fortifications became the keys to strengthening shoreline defense and guaranteeing the security of the Dutch, even as the technologies driving them lagged centuries behind those of their European adversaries. These infrastructure improvements included the five new garrisons built in Nagasaki by 1809, and the more than 100 additional firearms (although cast decades, if not centuries, before) in place there by 1813, reforms that revealed how domains were expected to be the executors of these material improvements.[59]

A temporary heightened vigilance, reflected in these artillery initiatives, persisted in Nagasaki through about 1815, but given the absence of further military attack following the *Phaeton* incursion and the Tokugawa knowledge of the end of the Napoleonic Wars, the activities of domainal harbor-duty officials in Nagasaki returned to the pre-1808 rituals of complacency.[60] Even as the magistrate ordered Fukuoka and Saga to double the amount of ammunition stockpiled for each of the firearms in the harbor batteries, the domains contributed not even half of the almost 5,000 units of shot ordered.[61] When the shogunate promulgated a nationwide "shell and repel" policy in 1825 following the British whaler episode at Mito, the sense of peril remained most acute in the Kantō region. Whereas most coastal areas started from a baseline of zero in constructing defenses to enforce this new 1825 policy, Nagasaki considered itself already prepared.

58. Saga kenshi hensan iinkai, *Saga kenshi,* 2:325; Nakano, *Nabeshima Naomasa kōden*, 1:153–56; Hayashi, *Tsūkō ichiran*, 6:453–55.

59. Kajiwara, "Feyton go jiken."

60. Ibid., p. 32.

61. Kawazoe and Fukuoka komonjo o yomu kai, *Shintei Kuroda kafu*, vol. 5, "Narikiyo ki," pp. 393–94.

Disproportionate domainal attention to their relationship with the Dutch, to the neglect of Nagasaki shoreline defenses, revealed the lack of concern about implementing this new "shell and repel" policy in Nagasaki. A series of Fukuoka domain diaries from the late 1820s and 1830s, entitled "Records of Seeing Off the Dutch Sails" (*Oranda sen hokage mikakushi no ki*), were officially kept to record the Kuroda lords' harbor defense inspections, but their most detailed entries regularly summarized extended visits to Dejima by domainal elites. One such diary from 1827, two years after the shogunate promulgated the "shell and repel" order, revealed how domainal calls to Dejima received much greater attention by scribes than scrutiny of the harbor garrisons.[62] According to the diary of that fall's harbor tour, the fortification inspection was a cursory glance of the exterior of the defensive compound, executed from the remove of boats in the water, and noted summarily in less than a page in the journals. In contrast, the diary described the subsequent Dejima visit in minute detail, including notes about a billiards game, European mirrors, and the sampling of Dutch sweet cakes (*kasutera*).[63] Conversation there included the mention of Dutch frictions with France, a rare glimpse into European political affairs that might actually inform domainal defensive precautions. Such seemingly desultory encounters may have been justifiable as important social lubricants to facilitate cooperation between Dutch and Japanese in another military emergency. Yet domainal surveys of defense capacity were perfunctory. In a diary of one of Fukuoka's fall inspections the following decade, in 1835, custom and precedent, rather than defensive efficacy, still dominated in the summary review of the harbor batteries.[64] The garrison inspection by Fukuoka officials in the tenth month was cursory, recorded as following "without alteration" the route of 1821 instead of planning an itinerary that gave particular attention to sites recently refurbished or of special concern in 1835.[65] The replication of a schedule from 1821, instead of the creation of a deliberate tour of installations specific to 1835, suggested that no significant military improvements had occurred in the intervening fourteen years (the precise years following the "shell and repel" law) that merited

62. *Bunsei jūnen chōgai ku gatsu Oranda sen hokage mikakushi no ki*, vol. 1 and vol. 2 (Akitsuki Kuroda ke monjo).

63. Ibid., 1:69–70.

64. *Tempō roku nen kugatsu Oranda sen hokage mikakushi no ki* (Akitsuki Kuroda ke monjo).

65. Ibid., p. 15.

evaluation. Yet responsibility for guarding the Dutch allowed the domains to continue to serve in Nagasaki with a sense of military purpose during these quiescent periods, without the arrival of uninvited foreign ships, when the utility of their military service might have been questioned.

The Warship *Palembang* and Nabeshima Naomasa

At the core of the disconnect between this comparatively carefree attitude among daimyo in Kyūshū and the siege mentality of Edo, which had resulted in the 1825 "shell and repel" law, was the long history of an established defense system in Nagasaki which, even with its shortcomings in the *Phaeton* incident, had modestly reformed, producing an idealistic confidence in the absence of renewed threats. The 1825 law is frequently cited as the critical Tokugawa proclamation of the early nineteenth century that precipitated the cultivation of an increasingly national defense system. Yet as the recent work of Kamishiraishi Minoru has suggested, the goal of the coastal defense network that this directive mandated was not to sink and destroy belligerent ships but rather to threaten them so that they would flee and abandon attempts to trade with coastal inhabitants.[66] Shogunal officials realized that whalers, the very vessels that had sparked this order, were not armed warships that might invade if fired upon. As the *Phaeton* incident had revealed, however, "intimidation capacity," which might suffice to scare away sailors in distress or entrepreneurial whalers, was not adequate capability at Nagasaki to secure the Dutch. By 1842, news of China's defeat by Britain in the First Opium War, and the expected appearance of a variety of Western gunboats in Tokugawa waters that might indeed attempt to invade, elevated the threshold of ideal defensive readiness to lethality instead of mere intimidation. The arrival of the Dutch king's flagship, *Palembang*, in 1844, to request expanded trade relations, and the Saga lord Nabeshima Naomasa's maneuvering to inspect its weapons, provided the most concrete military advantage yet to a daimyo in charge of harbor defense. Naomasa leveraged this visit, and his domain's tradition of guarding the Dutch, to develop artillery that would arm a new stage of maritime defense policy based on weapons instead of bodies.

66. Kamishiraishi, *Bakumatsuki taigai kankei*, p. 50.

When the imposing, thirty-eight-gun Dutch warship anchored at Nagasaki in August of 1844, the magistrate, Izawa Masayoshi, and Saga lord, Nabeshima Naomasa (who was in charge of harbor defenses that year), soon sparred over the legitimacy of Naomasa's unprecedented request to board a foreign gunboat, which Izawa granted only after lengthy negotiations. Since Naomasa was an outside (*tozama*) daimyo, he was excluded from the shogunate's highest-level decisions, particularly ones concerning external relations. Thus, his tour of a warship dispatched by a foreign head of state, with whom the Tokugawa did not hold a diplomatic relationship, was a destabilizing political event because it marked the first time any category of daimyo had inspected a warship sent by a foreign monarch. Most important, it introduced Naomasa to armaments on board a state-of-the-art European vessel that the very shogunal officials in Edo deliberating coastal defense reform in the wake of the First Opium War had not yet viewed.

Naomasa's appraisal of the superiority of the *Palembang*'s weapons technology catalyzed the reascendance of Tokugawa maritime security policy based on military preparedness.[67] Even with the knowledge of the First Opium War and China's capitulation to Western gunboats, many shogunal officials still defined coastal security with the modest goal of the 1825 "shell and repel" law, as the ability to scare off foreign ships. As well, however, the shogunate carefully restricted state-to-state diplomatic interaction to its own select officials and interpreted Naomasa's tour of an official envoy's flagship as an intrusion into Tokugawa external relations. That this envoy was unwelcome did not help matters. By contrast, Naomasa equated effective harbor security with military defense and thus justified the inspection of the *Palembang*'s technology as

67. Since the late seventeenth century, protecting economic sovereignty and maintaining the status quo in diplomatic relations had been the linchpins of maritime security for the shogunate. This book's perspective differs from the predominant interpretation of this incident, which emphasizes that its most significant result was Tokugawa confirmation of the existing diplomatic order, through its rejection of the Dutch request for broader commercial rights. Representative examples include Mitani, *Escape from Impasse*, pp. 52–55; Matsukata, "King Willem II's 1844 Letter to the Shogun," originally published as chapter 6 of *Oranda fūsetsugaki*; and McClain, *Japan: Modern History*, p. 134. A competing cultural interpretation is that of Martha Chaiklin, who suggests that the shogunate's acceptance of Dutch gifts, and then sending of reciprocal gifts with its reply, revealed "acceptance of diplomatic interaction." Chaiklin, "Monopolists to Middlemen," p. 256.

critical for updating his knowledge about recent artillery developments in Europe.

Ironically, Naomasa was able to leverage the *Palembang*'s visit to advance his own military reform agenda only because the shogunate's attempt to use the Dutch to broadcast changes in Tokugawa defense policy to European nations had backfired. In 1842, primarily as a response to news of Britain's defeat of China, the shogunate had revised, and softened, the aggressive 1825 "shell and repel" law to now provide food and water to foreign ships in distress. To inform the wider world of this more conciliatory stance, Tokugawa senior councillor Sanada Yukitsura asked the Dutch factor to spread news of this shift to Western powers. Sanada wanted European powers to approach Japan expecting hospitable treatment and spare the Tokugawa a hostile encounter with gunboats of superior firepower. The Dutch, however, were concerned that rival European powers would mistakenly interpret this revision as an indication that the Tokugawa were willing to consider commercial relationships with additional nations. Thus, the Dutch delayed disseminating the news and instead mounted their own campaign for expanded trade relations, resulting in King Willem's letter delivered aboard the *Palembang*.

The shogunate had revised maritime defense policy in 1842 specifically in response to reports from the Dutch that the British had declared they would wage war on Japan were they treated inhospitably when they arrived, as planned, to request trade.[68] Rumors had been circulating in Europe for some time that Japan was Britain's next target after China.[69] During his journey to Nagasaki, the new Dutch factor Pieter Albert Bik had landed briefly in Macau, where he heard British sailors remark that a war would break out if they were not treated well when they went to Japan. He then shared this news with the resident Dutch factor Eduard Grandisson in a private communication. The information reached the ears of Dutch interpreters, who then relayed it to Edo. The revision of the 1825 law a month later was a direct response to this news—and an attempt to avoid military confrontation with the British.[70] As historian Kamishiraishi has pointed out, the object of the 1825 "shell and repel" law had been whalers and merchant ships that the shogunate wanted to prevent from interacting with Japanese coastal residents, as had become

68. Fujita, *Bakuhansei kokka no seijishiteki kenkyū*, pp. 267–69.
69. Beasley, *Great Britain and the Opening of Japan*, pp. 42–43.
70. Fujita, *Bakuhansei kokka no seijishiteki kenkyū*, p. 269.

custom. These Western ships were not well armed, however, and the shogunate did not expect them to launch a retaliatory attack against shoreline firing. By 1842, however, the geopolitical environment in the North Pacific had changed in the wake of the First Opium War, and shogunal officials now feared that Western military vessels plying the East China Sea on missions to mainland China might also approach Japan. This shift in the categories of vessels likely to reach Tokugawa shores prompted revision of the 1825 law; Edo officials did not want to antagonize gunboats of superior firepower.

Edo officials remained committed to maintaining highly restricted state-to-state commercial and diplomatic interaction. Naomasa, on the other hand, viewed the *Palembang*'s visit as an opportunity to further Dutch ties with the aim of improving Nagasaki defenses. His interest in strengthening Nagasaki security through Dutch connections had been growing since he consolidated his position as daimyo in the mid-1830s. Most recently, during the spring preceding the *Palembang*'s arrival, he had launched several significant initiatives. In the fourth month of 1844, Naomasa pushed to install a cannon purchased from the Dutch at the Iōjima battery in Nagasaki harbor. The following month, he established the new office of intendant of firearms technology to advance technical knowledge of Western-style weapons.[71] Just days before news of the *Palembang*'s impending arrival reached Nagasaki, a 3-pound cannon, two 50-centimeter-diameter mortars, and a 62-centimeter-diameter howitzer had been cast in Saga, apparently from bronze.[72] These projects represented a watershed in the local evolution of maritime defense since no previous lord anywhere in Japan had directed this magnitude of patronage and investment toward coastal security efforts. Such daimyo commitment would become increasingly common over the following decade and foreshadows the shogunate/domain split that culminated in the Meiji Restoration.

Compounding the divide over shogunal and Nabeshima visions of the benefits of the *Palembang*'s visit was a continuing divergence of opinion, which had emerged in the late 1700s with concern about Russian attacks in Ezo, over which region of Japan was the highest defensive priority. Even after hearing the rumors of impending visits by British

71. Nakano, *Nabeshima Naomasa kōden*, 3:159; Kajiwara, "Bakumatsu Saga han ni okeru kajutsugumi."

72. Nakano, *Nabeshima Naomasa kōden*, index, "Nenpyō," p. 76.

vessels in the early 1840s to request trade, missions that would certainly include stops in Nagasaki, the shogunate had not shared this knowledge with Fukuoka and Saga domains, the very defenders of the port. Likely, Edo wanted to avoid requests to subsidize improvements to Nagasaki defenses so they could concentrate funds in the Kantō area and protect the Tokugawa capital. Under threat, the shogunate prioritized Edo over Nagasaki. On hearing of British victory in the First Opium War, in the summer of 1842, the shogunate had charged the Kantō domains of Kawagoe and Oshi with defense of Edo Bay. By the end of the year, it reinstated the position of Shimoda magistrate and created the new post of Haneda magistrate to oversee security of the Kantō area. The following year, the Tokugawa ordered construction of the Inbanuma waterway to create a new transport route for cargo boats to supply Edo from the Choshi promontory to the north of the city should belligerent vessels blockade Edo Bay. That one of the five principal domains assigned to this project was Akitsuki, a Kuroda branch domain contiguous to Fukuoka that had supplied considerable numbers of troops during harbor emergencies in Nagasaki, confirmed the growing shogunal emphasis on Edo security that had been building since the landing of British whalers on Mito shores in 1824.

The relative lack of shogunal attention to Nagasaki did not mean, however, that the domains assigned defense duties there followed suit. When a single Dutch merchant vessel entered Nagasaki and notified the magistrate that a ship carrying a request from the Dutch king would enter the harbor in about six weeks, the magistrate and domains began to mobilize. The next day, the Nagasaki magistrate, Izawa Masayoshi, communicated news of the Dutch embassy to the Nabeshima and Kuroda intelligence officers, as well as those of other neighboring domains. He also gave orders for the harbor garrisons to be specially fortified since the flagship *Palembang* would be accompanied by an imposing twenty-four-gun corvette, the *Boreas*. Further, the magistrate alerted the off-duty domain, Fukuoka, that it should be prepared to dispatch men and supplies from the home province at a moment's notice. Five hundred men departed Fukuoka within the week.[73]

Perhaps because of the newly issued and conciliatory "foreign ship" edict of 1842, Izawa seemed conflicted about how he should respond to

73. Kawazoe and Fukuoka komonjo o yomu kai, *Shintei Kuroda kafu*, vol. 6, *Nagahiro kōden*, vol. 1, p. 155.

this unprecedented arrival. Should he try to convey a sense of normalcy in the harbor and maintain troop levels as if the vessel were the standard Dutch trading ship (embracing the conciliatory approach of the 1842 revision), or prepare with reinforcements for a potential armed confrontation? Bearing in mind the disastrous 1808 *Phaeton* incident, he decided on the latter course.[74]

Since Saga domain was the on-duty military force in Nagasaki that year, it, too, prepared. More than a week before the ships' arrival, the domain had its baseline of 1,000 soldiers at the harbor batteries. An additional 1,000 men reinforced them while 5,000 more prepared to follow. Two hundred boats sat ready in the harbor for the embassy's arrival.[75] Saga's massive mobilization demonstrated Naomasa's desire to reestablish the domain's military credibility following the *Phaeton* debacle. His father, the on-duty daimyo at the time of the *Phaeton* incident, had supplied only paltry numbers of troops. His failure to take the threat seriously was highlighted by the fact that Fukuoka domain had dispatched more than 8,000 soldiers.[76]

Even though local officials expected a peaceful encounter, beyond Saga's initial dispatch, a composite force of more than 18,000 troops soon assembled in the harbor. Kumamoto had 3,000 troops on alert, and 200 boats awaited dispatch from Fukuoka. The magistrate also ordered thirteen surrounding domains—Satsuma, Higo, Kurume, Tsushima, Nagato, Yanagawa, Kokura, Gotō, Shimabara, Hirado, Karatsu, Ōmura, Nakatsu—to be ready to send troops. Fukuoka supplied more than 2,000 men, but Saga, as on-duty domain, ultimately dispatched roughly 13,000 soldiers, more than six times the contribution of Fukuoka.[77] Given the extraordinary numbers of resident military forces in 1844, the domains stationed troops not only at the harbor batteries, but also at the hillside temple grounds of Kofukuji and Daitokuji.[78] Contemporary reports recorded more than 10,000 boats ready in the harbor; bonfires on shore

74. A diary of this Fukuoka mobilization, *Tempō go nen shintatsu shichi gatsu itsuka hassoku Oranda honkoku sen tōrai no ki* (Akitsuki Kuroda ke monjo), p. 59 (twenty-sixth day of the seventh month), reveals that Kuroda officials also discussed the need to avoid an "embarrassment" like that of 1808.

75. Yanai, *Tsūkō ichiran zokushū*, 2:417.

76. Aston, "HMS Phaeton," p. 334.

77. Yanai, *Tsūkō ichiran zokushū*, 2:432.

78. Ibid., 2:430.

were so numerous it seemed as if the stars of the night sky had descended to earth.[79]

Even while prioritizing the military response, Naomasa was aware of the diplomatic complexities of the visit. Before the *Palembang* reached port, the magistrate and factor negotiated the specifics of protocol for receiving the embassy, taking care to demonstrate respect without showing excessive deference. Negotiations over Dutch requests for special diplomatic courtesies in Nagasaki finally concluded on the day after the *Palembang*'s arrival. Magistrate Izawa waited another four days, until consulting with the on-duty Saga lord Naomasa, to conclude that the Dutch acceptance of these limited concessions was sincere. With peace assured following the Dutch agreement, Izawa could safely order troop reinforcements to return to their home domains.[80] After overseeing the withdrawal of several thousand troops dispatched by his wealthiest vassals, Naomasa conducted a perfunctory tour of harbor installations, returning to his castle soon after. Shoreline troops of more than 10,000 seemed sufficient to the magistrate against warships carrying a few hundred men. Nonetheless, he did not take any chances; the shogunate excused Kuroda Nagahiro, daimyo of Fukuoka, from that year's alternate attendance duties to focus his attention on Nagasaki defenses.[81]

In spite of the magistrate's promises to sink the embassy ships were they to exhibit any prohibited behavior, the harbor garrisons would not likely have been able to repel an attack. While the thirty-eight cannon of the *Palembang* may not alone have seemed overpowering, its accompanying corvette, the twenty-four-gun *Boreas*, multiplied the possible threat.[82] Eyewitnesses also remarked that the sixty-plus Dutch cannons did not have any rust, indicating that they appeared immediately operable (unlike many Nagasaki harbor artillery pieces). Further, they recognized that the superiority of Dutch firepower was not limited to mounted deck weapons, but also included smaller, portable firearms.[83] Representatives of the magistrate who first boarded the vessel recorded seeing numerous weapons: about 800 firearms with a short barrel, 100

79. Ibid.
80. Nakano, *Nabeshima Naomasa kōden*, 3:169.
81. Ibid., 3:157.
82. Yanai, *Tsūkō ichiran zokushū*, 2:422.
83. Ibid., 2:421.

hatchets, 300 swords, and 6,000 to 7,000 firearms with blades attached.[84] Other accounts, by contrast, noted only fifty smaller firearms with fixed blades on board.[85] This discrepancy suggests that magistrate officials likely exaggerated their estimates to justify the troop mobilizations.

Naomasa first visited Nagasaki at the end of the sixth month, on hearing of the *Palembang*'s impending arrival, and traveled to Nagasaki five times while the warship was in port.[86] Surprisingly, during the first four of these visits, he did not tour any of the Dutch merchant vessels in port as was customary. Instead, he chose to leave this inspection privilege to his chief elder, Nabeshima Yasufusa.[87] In delegating this early ritual responsibility to Yasufusa, he enhanced his chances to board the gunboat *Palembang*. Naomasa would later argue that he needed to tour the ship because he had not inspected a vessel that fall as his habitual courtesies to the Dutch required. As the customary autumn date for Dutch departures neared, Naomasa finally petitioned the magistrate for permission to tour the *Palembang*.

Initially he justified his request by arguing that surveying the latest European firearms would benefit his capacity to defend Nagasaki harbor. Indeed, the military utility of such visits was long-standing.[88] In spite of this demonstrated defensive application, the magistrate, Izawa, a known opponent of Westernizing coastal defenses, stalled in issuing permission. When Izawa expressed concern about public outcry at a *tozama* daimyo boarding a foreign gunboat, Naomasa shifted tactics.[89] He claimed that personally welcoming Dutch vessels with an onboard visit was a customary responsibility of Nagasaki defense duty. The timing of the *Palembang*'s departure, scheduled for the same day as that of regular trading ships, helped Naomasa legitimate his visit as a necessary part of his expected harbor duty. Excluding the *Palembang* from this traditional show of hospitality granted to the less illustrious Dutch merchant vessels

84. Ibid., 2:422.

85. Ibid., 2:423.

86. Nakano, *Nabeshima Naomasa kōden*, 3:169.

87. Ibid., 3:116.

88. One such example was a tour of 1719. That inspection allowed Saga retainers to calculate the size of ammunition necessary to pierce the hulls of Chinese smuggling junks by estimating their thickness in comparison to that observed of Dutch vessels while touring them. *Saga ken kinsei shiryō*, vol. 1, no. 4, pp. 183, 332–33.

89. On Izawa's conservatism, see Matsukata, "King Willem II's 1844 Letter to the Shogun," p. 111n56.

might be interpreted as an affront to the king. It could even produce a belligerent response from the Dutch frigate. The magistrate needed to avoid such a possibility until he was certain of the *Palembang*'s intentions.

Naomasa's logic separated his defensive role specific to Nagasaki from larger national security priorities. His insistence on the visit as a routine part of a scheduled harbor survey revealed a problematic policy divide between Saga and Edo. Saga domain was committed to evaluating the technological strength of potential enemies. Yet the shogunate's priority was maintaining the status quo in trade relations and thus it did not want to offer a vessel representing a head of state special courtesies that might hint at Tokugawa receptivity to its request.[90] We can not be certain if the magistrate ultimately granted permission because the visible armaments of the ships convinced him of the benefit of evaluating the firearms more closely. He may have merely chosen to avoid alienating a daimyo whom Edo recognized as an important ally in buttressing Kantō-area defenses. What we do know is that the magistrate finally granted Naomasa permission; he toured the ship the day before it departed.

Doing so made him the first daimyo of any category to board a European warship since 1638, when Kyūshū lords had toured Dutch *fluyt* ships sent to subdue the Shimabara insurgents.[91] Seventy Saga retainers accompanied Naomasa aboard the *Palembang*. The survey began with a morning introduction to the layout of the ship, including a candlelight inspection of the cellar, where wine and beer barrels were stored, and then a demonstration of cannon firing, which was undoubtedly the product of elaborate negotiation since the magistrate's officials had repeatedly forbidden the Dutch to fire a twenty-one-gun salute when they initially entered the harbor.[92] Naomasa and his retinue then returned to their vessels for lunch before reboarding the Dutch ship that afternoon. In this session, the second-in-command of the ship instructed Saga samurai in how to discharge handheld firearms and larger cannon. This inspection had two main benefits for Naomasa. First, he had an opportunity to prevail over the magistrate's reluctance to allow him aboard the *Palembang* and to assert his military authority in port. Second, the tour cemented in his mind the necessity of large-scale improvements to

90. Nakano, *Nabeshima Naomasa kōden*, 3:173.

91. Geerts, "The Arima Rebellion," pp. 89, 99. My thanks to Adam Clulow for bringing this example to my attention.

92. Nakano, *Nabeshima Naomasa kōden*, 3:177.

harbor defenses for Saga to effectively execute its duty in Nagasaki. As the following chapter explores, within two years, these reforms would catapult him to national influence as he became a central consultant to defensive reform in the Kantō area and larger Japan.

In the wake of the *Palembang*'s departure, commendations from the shogunate helped Naomasa leverage his tour of the ship to advance defensive plans for Nagasaki. First, Naomasa received a letter from senior councillor Abe Masahiro in early 1845 excusing him from alternate attendance duty, a perquisite that allowed Naomasa to remain in his domain and continue discussions with local technicians and military experts about coastal defense reform. The reason given was his exemplary military service while the *Palembang* was in port.[93] This exemption, at least in part, was likely offered as recompense for the fiscal drain of the massive Saga troop mobilization when the *Palembang* first arrived. It also, however, may have been a precaution against possible Dutch retribution. The Tokugawa were about to give notice that they had rejected the Dutch request for expanded economic relations. Having Naomasa in residence near Nagasaki, instead of in Edo, might allow him to mobilize Saga forces more quickly in the event of a retaliatory attack.

As soon they notified the Dutch in mid-1845 that commercial arrangements would continue in their current state (rejecting the request for expanded trade), Edo officials turned inward to solicit Naomasa's suggestions for improving coastal defenses in the wake of the *Palembang*'s visit. The Dutch reaction to rebuff had been civil, if not warm, so shogunal officials did not anticipate military retribution and could once again focus on domestic affairs. Edo officials shared a slightly revised version of their reply to the Dutch with Naomasa, Fukuoka daimyo Kuroda Nagahiro, and Tokugawa Nariaki (lord of Mito and Abe confidant), demonstrating the unusual inclusion of two outer lords in the inner circle of Tokugawa intelligence.[94] This sharing of carefully guarded diplomatic documents with the Saga and Fukuoka daimyo was especially surprising, in spite of their military role in Nagasaki, since the shogunate had not provided copies of the Dutch correspondence regarding the *Palembang*'s visit, or even a list of tribute items, to the trusted Gosanke houses of Owari, Kii, and Mito. This singular courtesy to the Saga and Fukuoka lords suggested that the shogunate was eager to foster goodwill with the Nabeshima and Kuroda lords and to facilitate information exchange

93. Ibid., 3:191.
94. Sugitani, *Nabeshima kansō*, p. 22.

about maritime defense matters. But it also expected reciprocity, in other words, the supply of closely guarded details about anticipated overhauls to the weaponry and general military strategy in Nagasaki. This political calculus became evident when senior councillor Abe requested that the Nagasaki magistrate interview Fukuoka and Saga officials about planned upgrades for the Nagasaki fortifications. The implicit goal of these conversations, however, seemed to be less about confirming that Nagasaki would be well prepared for a potential military attack by gunboats armed with weapons similar to those of the *Palembang* and more about gleaning insight into how improvements to Nagasaski harbor security might be applied in the Kantō region.

Conclusion

The advent of the *Palembang* and recognition of the superior artillery capabilities of up-to-date European gunboats prompted an important shift in Tokugawa maritime defense tactics. Even if the reigning shogunal defense posture was conflict avoidance, as the tenor of the conciliatory 1842 law suggested, coastal installations now had to be updated with weaponry capable of defending against the most recent naval technology in Europe. Naomasa was the first daimyo to embrace this mind-set. He was able to begin casting cannon to implement it because of his historical responsibility for guarding the Dutch, which both facilitated permission to inspect the *Palembang*'s weapons and then expedited access to broader European weapons technology. Within a decade, Naomasa's Nagasaki strategy of securing the "potential to engage" in case "avoidance" failed became a national strategy. The prevailing local response to coastal defense orders during the early nineteenth century, even among domains on the Bōsō Peninsula where whaling ships frequently appeared, had been to mobilize troops, often in the form of farmer-soldiers, rather than outfit coastal garrisons with artillery.[95] The answer to threat was bodies, not weapons. The arguably inordinate mobilization of some 18,000 domainal troops to greet the 338 men aboard *Palembang* was but the most recent example of this approach.[96] The reverberatory furnace for casting cannon that Naomasa built with Dutch assistance in

95. Kamishiraishi, *Bakumatsu taigai kankei*, p. 78.

96. Yanai, *Tsūkō ichiran zokushū*, 2:421. This number included 320 sailors and 18 black servants.

the aftermath of the *Palembang*'s visit began to change this vision as greater quantities of higher-quality firearms became available.

Saga domain was able to insert itself as a leader in this shift of defensive strategy only because of its long-standing relationship with the Dutch, which had justified Naomasa's survey of European artillery aboard the Dutch flagship. The 200-year history of serving as military custodians of these European traders, which included inspections of their merchant vessels, provided the critical precedent to make this tour possible. But with this inspection also ended what had been an arguably idyllic century of defensive quietude in Nagasaki, where except for a short-lived concern about Russian belligerency and the *Phaeton* incident, the most extensively recorded activity of domainal military elites were social calls to Dejima. Guarding the Dutch had provided the domains with an ostensible military function in port even when concern about Western attack (chapter 1), and armed Chinese smugglers (chapter 2) had waned from the 1730s.

The enduring influence of the *Palembang*'s visit on Naomasa's thinking—and on larger national defense policy—was nowhere more evident than in his 1846 memorial to shogunal senior councillor Abe Masahiro, in which Naomasa recalled that "the mission's ship was heavily equipped with many cannon, and the total appearance was like that of a floating fortress."[97] Naomasa recognized that his Nagasaki fortifications would not have been able to repel an assault from warships of this firepower. Years later, in 1889, Meiji naval architect Katsu Kaishū claimed that the *Palembang*'s visit sparked interest in developing a navy, a movement that became "the cause of the political changes of succeeding years."[98] Although Katsu Kaishū may have overstated the case, Naomasa understood the need to meet this intimidating standard of military development. He would spend the next ten years cultivating the scientific expertise in his domain to achieve a maritime defense that was more reliant on updated artillery and less on the mobilization of massive quantities of troops. The following chapter examines how Naomasa envisioned and executed this agenda, in the process spreading Nagasaki defensive lessons to the Kantō region.

97. Hideshima, *Saga han kaigunshi*, pp. 27–28.
98. Katsu, *Kaigun rekishi*, vol. 1, leaf of second page.

PART II

Applying the Nagasaki System to the Realm

CHAPTER FOUR

Pan-Daimyo Collaboration and the Fortification of Edo Bay

The most critical impetus for shogunate-led coastal defense reform might have emerged not in 1853 with the arrival of Commodore Matthew Perry, but in the guise of another American commodore, James Biddle, when he appeared to request trading privileges in the summer of 1846. The disquieting arrival of this first-ever representative of a Western state to reach Edo Bay prompted unprecedented discussions of building a navy, in addition to the most extended consideration ever of mobilizing peasant militias and strengthening Kantō-area shoreline fortifications. Most shogunal officials, however, rejected these proposals and clung to a posture of conflict avoidance because of their fiscal conservatism or concern about retaliatory attack. Instead, precisely during this period, Saga lord Nabeshima Naomasa seized the defensive initiative and committed his domain to cultivating the capacity to repel Western ships with a new generation of firearms. During this era of frugality and inaction in Edo, Naomasa emerged as a key architect of late Tokugawa maritime defense both because he operated with relative autonomy as the defender of Nagasaki and because he cultivated a potent network of daimyo to support his visionary military reforms. By 1855 the shogunate had installed artillery from his Saga foundries at the Edo Bay batteries built following Perry's arrival. That firearms cast by daimyo retainers, instead of shogunal artisans, protected the Tokugawa capital as the crisis of Western pressure escalated eloquently revealed that shogunal projects were no longer the vanguard of military innovation. Though the pan-daimyo advocacy of Naomasa's foundry ultimately better prepared the realm to defend itself, the very emergence of these social networks undermined the Tokugawa regime's claim to control the devolution of the monopoly on violence.

Naomasa first began to acquire momentum to update Nagasaki artillery when, following the return of the Dutch warship *Palembang* in 1844 (treated in the previous chapter), newly appointed shogunal chief senior councillor Abe Masahiro solicited Fukuoka and Saga domains' opinions on coastal security. No high shogunal officer had approached domains for detailed advice on coastal defense policy since the Chinese smuggling crisis of 1717. Abe's request of two *tozama* lords, a category of daimyo generally excluded from official consultative bodies in the shogunate, revealed the desperation of a leadership consumed with concerns about national security but lacking promising policy ideas within its small circle of advisers. Thus, Abe approached these two lords not merely out of concerns about Nagasaki, but also out of curiosity about how the organization and infrastructure of that harbor's defense system might be replicated in the Kantō region. This gesture revealed that from the beginning of his appointment to the shogunate's top leadership post, years before his well-known 1853 survey of daimyo opinion about how to respond to Perry's demands, Abe foresaw the politically destabilizing potential of strong-minded lords and thus attempted to cultivate a political culture of consensus building. After four years of negotiations, Abe would reluctantly approve Naomasa's plans for strengthening Nagasaki defenses, including construction of a reverberatory furnace for producing cast-iron cannon. Whereas Naomasa had waited for official approval before beginning construction of his new foundry, Abe acquiesced because he saw smaller, and promising, elements of Naomasa's military reform agenda already under way.

This chapter explores how Naomasa seized leadership of coastal defense reform between 1846 and 1855, first by gaining the support of fellow defender at Nagasaki, Fukuoka lord Kuroda Nagahiro, and then by cultivating a network of influential daimyo throughout Japan who lobbied Abe on his behalf to approve Saga military projects. After receiving Abe's assent for these initiatives, Naomasa then solicited the technological assistance of prominent military expert and shogunal intendant (*daikan*) Egawa Tarōzaemon, establishing a bridge of military collaboration between Kyūshū and the Kantō region. The chapter concludes by analyzing Saga's construction of Tokugawa Japan's first reverberatory furnace and how using domainal-cast cannon to fortify the Shinagawa batteries at Edo Bay revealed the application of military lessons learned in Nagasaki to central Japan.

Abe Masahiro and Kantō Security

Abe was gathering "best practice" ideas about coastal defense at this juncture precisely because in August of 1845 he reinstated the post of coastal defense officer (*kaibōgakari*)—an office only intermittently filled since its inception in 1792 as a response to Russian threats—to coordinate maritime security efforts. Not only did Abe resurrect the position; he also named himself as one of the post's appointees.[1] In spite of the position's ostensible realm-wide purview, Abe's primary concern was in securing the Kantō region and assessing the possibilities for its shoreline defenses from the expert perspective of Nagasaki's longtime defenders. This priority catalyzed his request of the Fukuoka and Saga lords. Borrowing from the Nagasaki system to overhaul Edo-area defenses, however, had begun even before the reinstitution of the post of coastal defense officer in mid-1845. After a survey of Kantō defenses following the 1837 *Morrison* incident, when an American ship entered Edo Bay ostensibly to return shipwrecked Japanese castaways but with the goal of establishing trading privileges, shogunal inspector Torii Tadateru recommended that the Edo gateway be fortified by castle-holding daimyo who would model their efforts on the defenders of Matsumae, in southern Ezo, and Nagasaki.[2] From 1843, the shogunate redeployed one Dutch interpreter from Nagasaki to Uraga to help interrogate foreign ships. By 1849 the Uraga magistrate (defensive administrator of the larger Edo region) gained responsibility for negotiating with foreign ships over their departure, a charge that explicitly invoked the precedent established in Nagasaki (Nagasaki *omote no furiai o motte*). Two years earlier, the shogunate had granted the holders of the position of Uraga magistrate a rank equivalent to that of their Nagasaki counterpart (junior fifth grade); by 1852 they achieved ritual status equivalent to that of the magistrate of finances, three grades above that of the Nagasaki magistrate.[3] These promotions not only awarded the Uraga magistrate status equal to that of other

1. Masato, "Bakumatsu gaikō ni okeru shomondai." The other appointees were Makino Tadamasa, *rojū*; Ōoka Tadakata, *wakadoshi yori*; and Honda Tadanori, *wakadoshi yori*.

2. Mitani, *Escape from Impasse*, p. 44, and Mitani, *Perii raikō*, p. 43, quote Torii as recommending that Uraga Bay should be "fortified according to the model of Nagasaki and Matsumae" (Nagasaki, Matsumae *okatame no ofureai ni ainari sōrō*).

3. Miyake, "Kōkaki ni okeru Edo kinaki keiei," p. 49; Tanji, "Kōkaki ni okeru Edo wan bōbi mondai," p. 250.

magistrate peers, but also granted him stature sufficient to issue military orders to daimyo providing shoreline troops. As Miyake Satoshi has observed, Abe was crafting Uraga as an indispensable defensive and diplomatic portal—adding a fifth "guchi" to Arano's four-site rubric (of Matsumae, Tsushima, Nagasaki, and the Ryūkyūs)—a new "gateway" on par with that of Nagasaki. Naomasa's Saga-cast cannons would be the centerpiece of its firepower. As these measures reveal, contrary to histories that emphasize the flurry of defensive improvements that began with the arrival of Perry, important organizational changes had already emerged in the 1840s. Yet these modest reforms in the Kantō region largely concerned personnel and military oversight; Naomasa would offer critical ideas for improving strategy and infrastructure.

Edo officials recalibrating Kantō defenses by broadening the powers of the Uraga magistrate did not realize, however, that its analog in Nagasaki was undergoing a process of decentralization. Military authority incrementally, yet continually, shifted farther from the Nagasaki magistrate to the domains across the early nineteenth century. Between 1821 and 1842, the average tenure of the Nagasaki magistrate was 5.4 years, but from 1842 to 1852, the average dropped 54 percent to 2.5 years, more than halving the time the appointee occupied his position. This decrease reveals that the latter group of magistrates had hardly sufficient exposure to the duty (especially when they resided in Nagasaki only in alternating years) to fully grasp the intricacies of their defensive responsibilities. This lack of on-site experience made all the more necessary increased domainal military agency in the post–Opium War East China Sea Basin. The lingering assumption in Edo that the Nagasaki magistrate effectively controlled Nagasaki's defenses, however, provided Naomasa and other Saga officials an institutional "cover" to strengthen security in that harbor according to their own vision.

Defensive reconfiguration in the Kantō region during this period included not only adjusting the Uraga magistrate's stature to more closely resemble that of his Nagasaki counterpart. It hinged on increasing the number of stationed troops. Following American commodore James Biddle's departure from Uraga Bay in the summer of 1846 after having shocked the shogunate with a request for trade, the Uraga magistrate noted that the firepower of Biddle's two ships had outgunned his shore fortifications by a factor of nine to one.[4] With the inefficacy of its defenses

4. Mitani, *Escape from Impasse*, p. 63; Mitani, *Perii raikō*, p. 59.

exposed, between 1846 and 1849, the shogunate increasingly concentrated Kantō shoreline military authority in the hands of the Uraga magistrate and added the troops of two additional domains, Hikone (*fudai*, 290,000 *koku*) and Aizu (*shimpan* 230,000 *koku*), to the two existing forces of Kawagoe (*shimpan* 170,000 *koku*) and Oshi (*fudai*, 100,000) domains, which had guarded the bay since the 1810s.[5] The new forces increased the total available manpower to defensive potential roughly equivalent to that of Fukuoka and Saga domains in Nagasaki (whose combined *kokudaka* at roughly 830,000 *koku* approximated that of 790,000 *koku* for the Kantō-assigned domains). Charged with defending a coastline more than twice the length of the Nagasaki shore, in which total artillery emplacements housed fewer firearms than those on board Commodore Biddle's two warships, Kantō troops needed greater quantities of cannon to have any chance at effective defenses.[6] Naomasa helped address this deficiency with the reverberatory furnace project in Saga, which ultimately produced cannon for the Shinagawa batteries of Edo Bay. This new technology transfer initiative gained momentum as Naomasa first brokered the support of his partner in Nagasaki security and critical ally for defensive overhaul, Kuroda Nagahiro, lord of Fukuoka domain.

Negotiating Kuroda Nagahiro's Support for Military Reform

Naomasa emerged as a central architect of this new era of coastal defense not merely because of knowledge gained through military experience in Nagasaki, but also because he was astute at cultivating networks of political support throughout the realm. These horizontal alliances of like-minded daimyo and other Tokugawa elite cemented a broad base of support that helped extract shogunal permission for military projects that otherwise might have been prohibited as potentially seditious or too

5. *Shimpan* refers to a category of daimyo which were blood relations of the Tokugawa family.

6. Tanji, "Kōkaki ni okeru Edo wan bōbi mondai," p. 229. While Edo Bay firearms included thirty-four pieces of nine-pound shot or greater, and thirty-six of six pounds or less, Biddle's vessel *Columbus* carried eighty-three pieces of eighty-seven-pound shot or greater, and the *Vincennes* twenty-three pieces using approximately fifty-two-pound shot.

costly. Naomasa's creation of this "defensive coalition" of advocates of maritime military reform underscores the ubiquity of networks among Tokugawa elites explored by numerous scholars such as Anna Beerens, Bettina Gramlich-Oka, and Eiko Ikegami. Unlike the work of these historians, however, which examines social networks focused on airing more general political discontent or exploring aesthetic concerns, the case of Naomasa reveals how pan-daimyo coalitions achieved specific policy goals through collective pressure.[7]

Naomasa began with a coalition of two. Seven months before Abe officially solicited opinions on defense from Saga and Fukuoka, Naomasa had corresponded with Fukuoka lord Nagahiro about how best to strengthen the Nagasaki fortifications using insights gained from the *Palembang*'s 1844 visit. The two domains' collaboration seemed all the more urgent following the arrival in Nagasaki in the summer of 1845 of the British surveying ship *Saramang*, whose presence presaged broader British interest in visiting the port. Two months later, Nagahiro stopped in the Saga castle town on his way home from Nagasaki to consult with Naomasa about harbor improvements. The shogunate normally prohibited daimyo from meeting each other privately in their domains to limit opportunities for plotting rebellion. But in the wake of successive visits by the *Palembang* and the *Saramang*, the threat of external attack overshadowed concern about internal insurrection. The shogunate permitted the two lords to consult without censure.

When these two daimyo first met in the fall of 1845 to discuss their response to Abe's request for suggestions about Nagasaki maritime security, both men were in their midthirties, with each having presided over domain affairs and Nagasaki defense for more than a decade.[8] They were contemporaries, and also fourth cousins, but this meeting first revealed Naomasa's singular assertiveness toward the shogunate regarding defense and divergence from Nagahiro's embrace of the status quo in Nagasaki. Nagahiro seemed reluctant to propose far-reaching change in

7. Beerens, *Friends, Acquaintances, Pupils and Patrons*; Gramlich-Oka, *Thinking Like a Man*; Ikegami, *Bonds of Civility*.

8. Nakano, *Nabeshima Naomasa kōden*, 3:214; Nakano, *Nabeshima Naomasa nenpyō, sakuin, sōmokuroku*, p. 82. Kuroda Nagahiro was the son of Shimazu Shigehide, and Shigehide's second daughter (Nagahiro's older sister) was the wife of Shogun Ienari. Nabeshima Naomasa married the daughter of Ienari, so these two men were closely linked in a web of marital connections. See Hidemura Senzō, *Fukuoka kenshi, tsūshi hen, bunka*, 1:164.

Nagasaki because his domain was located more than 100 miles from the harbor, meaning his troops and provisions traveled more than twice the distance of those from Saga to reach the port. Fukuoka's most eminent Dutch scholars at midcentury also had concentrated on translating books related to medicine or natural history instead of military science (as had Saga). This lack of internal expertise in Western weapons technology prevented Nagahiro from embracing artillery improvements that his domain could not help implement. As well, his domain faced continuing financial difficulties. Attempts to improve Fukuoka's fiscal health during the Tempō reforms in the 1830s with the forced repayment of loans and with public spectacles, such as sumo tournaments, largely failed. Thus, the Kuroda administration entered the 1840s without the fiscal surplus that Saga had and that was necessary to entertain large-scale defensive improvements.[9]

In their discussions about Nagasaki defense that began in late 1845, Fukuoka and Saga domains both acknowledged that improvements to harbor security were critical. But whereas Fukuoka proposed strengthening the existing batteries in the inner harbor, Saga favored building new fortifications on the sea islands, farther out at the harbor entrance, to shell foreign vessels well before they approached the city proper. The core difference in these propositions was that between a strategy focused on the inner batteries, which would require minimal upgrades to existing infrastructure at proximate sites, and one focused on the outer batteries, which would require construction of new garrisons well beyond the mainland, particularly on the island of Iōjima. As the Fukuoka liaison in Nagasaki, Kiriyama Ichirō Daiyu, repeatedly argued, his domain objected to Saga's insistence on fortifying the outer harbor because this was precisely the area most difficult (and expensive) to reach. Further, since these islands were part of Saga domain territory, Fukuoka officials argued that Naomasa alone should shoulder the responsibility for strengthening and manning these sites.[10]

It took a full calendar year, until the fall of 1846, for Fukuoka and Saga to craft a consensus report and recommend strengthening the batteries only at the harbor entrance, the "*minato guchi*." Both daimyo agreed that given the recent advances in Western firearms technology, which gave deck-mounted guns longer trajectories, ships should no longer be

9. Shibata, "Fukuoka han no Tempō kaikaku."
10. Nakano, *Nabeshima Naomasa kōden*, 3:306–7.

pulled into the inner harbor, as had been the custom.[11] This compromise position, a minimalist strengthening of the status quo, was undergirded by Saga retainers' detailed mapmaking and situated their domain as leader of the initiative even as they presented it to Abe as a consensus opinion.[12] To encourage the shogunate to fund these improvements to defend both Dutch guests and Japanese residents, both domains emphasized that the original batteries constructed in the 1650s had been built by a third-party domain, Hirado, and that previously Edo had provided a majority of weapons and ammunition to arm the soldiers stationed there.[13] Armed with Kuroda lord Nagahiro's tacit support for whatever projects Naomasa might finance and implement without significant contributions from Fukuoka, Naomasa next turned to garner allies among a diverse group of daimyo for ever more ambitious military reform.

Mobilizing Marital and Political Ties for Reform

An exploration of the tangible goals of Naomasa's network of supporters reveals that in the 1840s and 1850s, these individuals were not explicitly focused on undermining Tokugawa authority, but their appropriation of national leadership in military affairs effectively subverted the shogunate's claim to control the execution of the monopoly on violence. Naomasa (fig. 4.1) soon spread his network building to daimyo beyond Kyūshū, and beyond the *tozama* class (of which both he and Kuroda Nagahiro were members), to bolster the diversity of a growing coalition of lords interested in concrete improvements in artillery capabilities. Unlike the defense policy propositions of bureaucrats and Confucian scholars in the Kantō, such as Koga Tōan or Fujita Tōko, who had no experience on the front lines of maritime security, Naomasa's ideas gained attention as legitimate and practical because of his long-standing exposure to on-the-ground service in Nagasaki. Naomasa had been planning multipronged military improvements in Nagasaki long before Abe solicited his opinions. These initiatives included not only the construction of a reverberatory furnace to produce Western-style cast-iron cannon, but also the joining of the Nagasaki sea islands of Shirōjima

11. Ibid., 3:281.
12. Kajiwara, "Kōkaki no Nagasaki keibi no tsuite."
13. Nakano, *Nabeshima Naomasa kōden*, 3:282–83.

FIGURE 4.1 Portrait of Nabeshima Naomasa, Saga domain daimyo, 1830–61, photograph, 1859. Courtesy of the Nabeshima Hōkōkai Foundation, Saga City.

and Kannoshima with landfill to close one of the most frequently used harbor entrances from the open sea, and the building of a naval yard and port for warships in the nearby Amakusa Islands.[14] The centerpiece of this agenda was building a new foundry near the Saga Castle to allow the domain to become self-sufficient in mass-producing cannon. After

14. Ibid., 3:285

convincing Abe and Kuroda Nagahiro of his vision, Naomasa continued to build support for these projects among broader networks of key political actors using his marital ties. Historian Yoshida Masahiko's analysis of mid-nineteenth-century Tokugawa political organization identifies the emergence of a new category of "activist daimyo," who joined forces across traditional daimyo classifications (linking *tozama*, *shimpan* and *fudai* categories alike) to lobby for greater consultation between Edo officials and daimyo.[15] Yet few scholars have examined in detail how these networks of political alliance mobilized to achieve a particular concrete objective, such as that of Naomasa's foundry.

Naomasa's assertive cultivation of his domain's military capacity was both ambitious and brave, since eminent advocates of Western-style defense, such as Nagasaki city elder Takashima Shūhan, had been imprisoned for organizing infantry drills, even when conducted at the request of the Tokugawa shogunate. Nabeshima marital connections to the shogunal house, however, contributed to the unusual latitude Edo officials granted him in his technological experiments, as well as his ability to craft consensus among daimyo networks for defense-related projects. In 1824, while still eleven years old, Naomasa had wed Morihime, the seventeenth daughter of Shogun Ienari.[16] The pairing may have been a political strategy of Ienari to burden the powerful Nabeshima house with the additional ritual expenditures necessary to accommodate the daughter of a reigning shogun.[17] Despite the fiscal hardship to the domain, the marriage significantly benefited Naomasa's political stature and his ability to execute his maritime defense duties.

His wife's familial ties first brought Naomasa concrete advantage following his accession to daimyo in 1831. During Naomasa's initial residence in Edo on alternate attendance, Morihime personally petitioned the shogun, her father, to grant Naomasa ritual privileges to increase the stature of his alternate attendance cortege. As a result of her successful appeal, Naomasa received two honors. Naomasa gained the distinction, first, of having a *kinmon hasamibako*, or gold storage box carried on poles, with the Nabeshima crest leading his entourage and, second, of using the hollyhock crest of the Tokugawa house on ritual implements carried

15. Yoshida, *Bakumatsu ni okeru Ō to hasha*.
16. Nakano, *Nabeshima Naomasa kōden*, 2:68.
17. Nagano, *Sagahan to hansharo*, p. 39; Sugitani, *Nabeshima kansō*, p. 4.

by his retinue during the return trip to the Saga castle town.[18] In another instance of marital advantage, following the destruction of the Saga Castle's *ni no maru* tower by fire in the spring of 1835, Morihime again interceded with her father to help secure a loan of 20,000 *ryō* to subsidize the rebuilding of the castle.[19] As an additional sign of favor, later that same year, the shogunate elevated Naomasa's stature by granting him the honorific title of *ukonoue no shōshō*, an advancement in court rank that was a particularly important measure of status for *tozama* lords who could not improve their social standing through appointment to positions in the shogunate, as could *fudai* daimyo.[20] Although Naomasa had succeeded his father, Narinao, as daimyo in 1830 at the age of seventeen, Naomasa did not actually control domainal affairs until he managed the response to the catastrophic burning of Saga Castle in 1835. The shogunate's granting of the reconstruction loan, and subsequent title, officially recognized Naomasa as new de facto master of Saga domain, including oversight of defense.

Special shogunal loans continued to benefit Naomasa's treasury, to the extent that Edo officials seemed to be searching for ways to justify them. During a fire that broke out near the Nabeshima Sakurada residence in Edo that same year, the staff delayed in evacuating Morihime because the retainers attending the residence were a skeleton crew, a deficiency attributed to the dispatch of so many Saga samurai to defend Nagasaki. Although this shortcoming may instead have been part of more general measures to economize during the domain's Tempō retrenchments, Naomasa secured a subsidy from the shogunate to finance extra attendants who could ensure Morihime's safety in future emergencies.[21] Even these token gifts were certainly appreciated given that only five years earlier, in 1830, when Naomasa first departed Edo to return to Saga as daimyo, his retinue had set out at night to avoid Edo merchants who were demanding repayment of Nabeshima loans.[22] As lord, Naomasa

18. Nakano, *Nabeshima Naomasa kōden*, 2:70–75. Constantine Vaporis notes that having these accoutrements "embossed in gold" was an important marker of social status in daimyo processions. Vaporis, *Tour of Duty*, p. 97.

19. Nakano, *Nabeshima Naomasa kōden*, 2:215–24.

20. Sugitani, *Nabeshima kansō*, p. 4; Hori, "A Study of the Early Modern Samurai Ranking System."

21. Nakano, *Nabeshima Naomasa kōden*, 2:249.

22. Morris-Suzuki, *Technological Transformation of Japan*, p. 5; Sugitani, *Nabeshima kansō*, pp. 5–6.

reduced the Saga domain debt some 60 percent (from 20,570 *kan* to 8,209 *kan*), so that by 1838 he was able to set aside a fixed sum each year for military affairs.[23] This fiscal conservatism allowed Naomasa to double Saga expenditure on Nagasaki defenses in the decade between 1830 and 1840.[24]

Beyond these monetary perquisites, which helped the young lord finance Nagasaki military improvements, Morihime's links to successive shoguns also ensured recognition of Naomasa's Nagasaki defense service. After her father, Ienari, stepped down in 1837, her brother, Ieyoshi, became shogun. While Naomasa was in Edo on alternate attendance in early 1842, Morihime had an audience with her brother, the shogun Ieyoshi, in which Ieyoshi congratulated Naomasa for his superlative performance in Nagasaki.[25] Twice within a five-month period, between late 1845 and early 1846, Morihime again received congratulatory greetings from Ieyoshi to recognize her husband's contributions in Nagasaki. She quickly relayed those commendations to Naomasa by letter.[26] Ieyoshi praised Naomasa for his overall "exceedingly satisfactory" performance in port, and particularly for his efforts during the visit of the 1844 Dutch embassy aboard the *Palembang*. Even though Abe Masahiro prioritized the security of the Kantō region when he assumed the position of chief senior councillor of the shogunate in 1845, Shogun Ieyoshi continued to acknowledge the efforts of his brother-in-law, Naomasa, in protecting Nagasaki. These commendations ended the following year, 1847, however, with Morihime's death, suggesting that without these familial connections to the shogun, Naomasa's military efforts would receive less public recognition in Edo, but also less scrutiny.

A web of marriage alliances continued to connect Naomasa to many of the most influential political figures in mid-nineteenth-century Japan, creating indispensable daimyo support for his defense projects. After his first wife, Morihime, died, the political connections gained through Naomasa's new wife, as well as through the marriage of Naomasa's daughter, Mitsuhime, preserved his ties to the Tokugawa while creating links to other powerful lords who shared his commitment to developing Western firearms technology. Only months after Morihime's death,

23. Nagano, *Sagahan to hansharo*, pp. 98, 100–101.
24. Sugitani, *Nabeshima kansō*, p. 14.
25. Nakano, *Nabeshima Naomasa kōden*, 2:97.
26. Ibid., p. 269.

Naomasa married Hitsuhime of the Tayasu house, one of the three powerful *sankyō* branches of the Tokugawa family, which had been established to provide heirs for shogunal succession. Hitsuhime's older brother was the influential lord of Fukui domain, Matsudaira Shungaku, who, like Naomasa, had embraced Dutch military science.[27] Shungaku became a particularly important advocate for Naomasa in persuading Abe to endorse his Nagasaki plans, along with the daimyo of Uwajima, Date Munenari, who was married to Naomasa's older sister, Naohime. The powerful Satsuma lord, Shimazu Naraikira, was Naomasa's elder cousin by five years and would prove an important ally in cultivating defense.[28] In 1854, Naomasa arranged, with the assistance of Munenari and Shungaku, to marry his daughter, Mitsuhime, to Kawagoe Matsudaira Naoyoshi, the ninth son of the powerful Mito Nariaki.[29] Naoyoshi's older brother, Nariaki's seventh son, would be adopted into the Hitotsubashi house (another *sankyō* branch) and become the final Tokugawa shogun, Yoshinobu, in 1866. Correspondence with Nariakira, Shungaku, and Munenari about Saga military initiatives cemented Abe Masahiro's support for Naomasa's petitions for the further strengthening of Nagasaki harbor batteries in 1850. Without their critical advocacy of his vision of upgrading Nagasaki defenses, Naomasa might otherwise have been censured by shogunal officials jealous, and suspicious, of his successes.

Coalition Support Secures Abe's Assent

In 1847, Naomasa informed this core network of influential lords with interest in strengthening coastal defenses of his plans to produce additional cast-iron cannon for the Nagasaki outer harbor, a cleverly nuanced revision of the more conservative proposal, focused on the inner harbor, that he had submitted with Fukuoka in late 1846. They pressured Abe on numerous occasions to support Naomasa's request for permission to execute these more ambitious plans.[30] Naomasa first enlisted the backing of his cousin, Shimazu Nariakira, Satsuma domain scion preoccupied with the defense of the Ryūkyū archipelago, who in the spring of 1847

27. Nakano, *Nabeshima Naomasa kōden*, 2:235.

28. Ibid., 3:3, 151.

29. Ibid., 4:232–33.

30. Yoshida Masahiko discusses the singular political influence of these "power domains" (*yūhan*) in *Bakumatsu ni okeru Ō to hasha*.

wrote Tokugawa Nariaki, former Mito lord and influential Abe adviser, asking him to secure shogunal financial support for the Nagasaki upgrades.[31] Cognizant of how shogunal permission for Naomasa's projects might serve as a precedent for obtaining approval for similar plans in Satsuma, Nariakira noted that the defense of Nagasaki would also help secure the Ryūkyūs. Later that same year, Uwajima daimyo Date Munenari, another well-connected lord and Naomasa's brother-in-law, wrote Nariaki lamenting the poor state of maritime defenses and acknowledging Naomasa's concern about Nagasaki.[32] That Naomasa cultivated a vocal group of advocates signaled his awareness of the difficulty in securing Abe's assent for his outer-harbor and foundry plans. In spite of these attempts to sway Abe's opinion through Nariaki, one of the young councillor's closest advisers, at the end of 1848, Abe rejected Naomasa's proposals. But both Naomasa and his fellow daimyo advocates refused to accept this response as a final answer. And the group seemed confident that they could persuade Abe to reverse his ruling.

Abe's conservative response revealed the continuing dominance in Edo of defense policy based on conflict avoidance. His rejection of Naomasa's plans was a dismissal less of new weapons technology than of the larger strategy of prioritizing outer-harbor fortifications. Abe argued that plans for strengthening the outer harbor, in particular the island of Iōjima, would "exhaust" the two domains of Saga and Fukuoka because of transportation and lodging costs. Thus, Abe agreed only to the strengthening of existing batteries on the islands of Naginata Iwa and Takaboko at the immediate harbor entrance (objects of reform in the 1846 joint Fukuoka/Saga proposal) in a way that would not be noticeable (*medatanai*). Presumably, this caution was taken to avoid projecting to the Dutch increased Tokugawa belligerency.[33] During the 1804 Rezanov incident, the Nagasaki magistrate had issued edicts that admonished surrounding domains to mobilize troop reinforcements in a way that did not attract attention as well, but this stance had perhaps been necessary to avoid provoking a belligerent response from the Russian ships. Now, in a time of peace, it reflected fiscal conservatism.

Abe's dismissal of Naomasa's proposal also revealed a reluctance to divert shogunal attention from reinforcing Kantō security. But his greater

31. *Shimazu Nariakira monjo*, 1:71–74, quoted in Sakai, "Shimazu Nariakira and National Leadership in Satsuma," p. 220.

32. Kihara, *Bakumatsuki Sagahan no hanseishi kenkyū*, p. 174.

33. Nakano, *Nabeshima Naomasa kōden*, 3:339.

fear seems to have been the potential fiscal burden on the shogunal treasury of any improvement to Nagasaki fortifications, which Naomasa repeatedly hinted that Edo should help finance. In 1845, the total annual shogunal income had been only 4 million *ryō*. Estimates of the cost of strengthening the Nagasaki batteries according to Naomasa'a plan were 189,000 *ryō*, about 5 percent of shogunal revenue.[34] Following the *Phaeton* incident in 1808, Fukuoka and Saga domains had shouldered the construction costs of the most recent improvements, nine new and expanded Nagasaki batteries.[35] But the shogunate had funded the original inner-harbor battery construction in the 1630s, and the domains repeatedly appealed to this precedent in their petitions during the late 1840s. Discussions of the funding source for improvements were inconclusive. Yet, to Edo officials wary of the military power that Naomasa's experiments might provide him, Abe could dismiss these fears by emphasizing the extraordinary cost of these projects to the domain.

Saga production of cast-iron weapons ultimately allowed the shogunate to make use of domainal efforts without investing significant Tokugawa funds. Abe's approval of Naomasa's request to undertake defensive experiments, therefore, can be understood as the product of his vision for Saga as a defensive subcontractor for the shogunate.

In spite of recognizing these obstacles to obtaining Abe's assent, in early 1849, Uwajima lord Date met with Abe to advocate again for Naomasa's ambitious military plans.[36] Satsuma daimyo-in-waiting Nariakira also continued to write to Nariaki, emphasizing the need to improve Nagasaki harbor defenses with those of Uraga, the shoreline foremost in the minds of shogunal officials.[37] These lords' awareness that Naomasa would soon have a translation of Ulrich Huguenin's (1755–1834) seminal text on the construction of the Liege reverberatory furnace of the Dutch National Cannon Foundry, and their expectation that this information would be available to their own technicians, certainly bolstered their enthusiasm for Saga's plans.[38] In a mid-1849 letter to Tokugawa Nariaki, Nariakira wrote that through Saga physician Itō Genboku,

34. Yoshida, *Bakumatsu ni okeru Ō to hasha*, p. 211.

35. Ibid., pp. 211n72, 246–47.

36. Nakano, *Nabeshima Naomasa kōden*, 3:348.

37. *Shimazu Nariakira monjo*, 1:205 (Nariakira to Tokugawa Nariaki, 1849/4/3).

38. *Het gietwezen in's rijks ijzer-gesch gieterij te Luik*, 1834 (The casting process at the National Iron Cannon Foundary in Liege). This title is usually translated in Japanese as 大砲鋳造法 (Taihō chūzō hō).

the father of Sugitani Yōsuke (Saga retainer and translator of Huguenin's text), he had seen the first two volumes of an unfinished translation on cannon casting. He offered to share them with Nariaki as part of the common exchange of translations of Dutch texts.[39] A year later, in mid-1850, Nariakira again wrote to Nariaki, informing him that he had seen the completed translation and offering to send copies of the illustrations.[40] Both of these men were interested in improving coastal security and producing cast-iron cannon in their own domains. Abe's endorsement of Naomasa's plans for Nagasaki, in addition to addressing widely acknowledged critical weaknesses in Nagasaki security, might serve as a useful precedent for as yet unapproved defensive improvements in their own home territories.

A development that made the political environment favorable to Naomasa's increased military agency was Emperor Komei's issue of a rescript on coastal defense in the summer of 1846. Remonstrating the shogunate for its failure to "despise" the Western enemies, it instructed Tokugawa officials to be more vigilant about the protection of its maritime borders. This document was an explicit challenge to the efficacy of Tokugawa foreign policy and broader shogunal authority.[41] Tacitly allowing Naomasa's weapons experiments was a convenient tool for the shogunate to counter court claims that it was not adequately concerned about coastal defense.

In early 1850, Abe finally approved Naomasa plans for adding cannon to the outer harbor. This permission implicitly sanctioned construction of a reverberatory furnace, since no other facility existed to produce cast-iron cannon—superior to bronze guns because of their sustained strength during repeated firings—in the realm. Saga technicians immediately began planning for its construction. Although the continued pressure of eminent political figures seems to have worn down Abe, in the first month of 1850, he had encouraged all daimyo to consider constructing "permanent defenses." Increasing domestic production of cast-iron

39. *Shimazu Nariakira monjo*, 1:216 (Nariakira to Nariaki, 1849/5). Nagano Susumu identifies this volume as Huegenin's text in Nagano, *Sagahan to hansharo*, p. 167.

40. *Shimazu Nariakira monjo* 1:363 (Nariakira to Nariaki, 1850/5/21). By the eleventh month of 1849, Nariakira noted that he had met twice (recently) with Naomasa, although his letter did not specify the contents of their discussion (Nariakira to Nariaki, 1849/11/5), p. 250.

41. Nakano, *Nabeshima Naomasa kōden*, 3:274.

cannon was indispensable for this initiative.[42] Abe's assent, however, was not primarily an endorsement of Saga's agenda for expanding Nagasaki defenses. He knew that plans were already under way to transfer some existing Nagasaki firearms to Edo Bay fortifications.[43] Naomasa's successful casting project would enable upgrades to the defensive environment in Nagasaki, while subsidizing expanded firepower in the Kantō maritime region.

So how had Naomasa's daimyo network achieved its concrete goal of gaining Abe's permission so quickly? First was the shifting tenor of military policy discussions in Edo, which briefly considered the use of peasant militias (*nōhei*) and the construction of large naval ships, in addition to improving coastal batteries. But even given the enthusiastic support of Abe and the Uraga magistrates for the former two initiatives, only the latter method was ultimately endorsed. Between 1846, when Naomasa first began to pressure Abe, and 1850, when the senior councillor finally granted permission, bolstering static coastline defenses with greater quantities of weapons transformed from one of several options for strengthening maritime security to the primary method of choice. After Abe acknowledged his inability to broker support in Edo for the more ambitious measure of permitting construction of large naval vessels, in January of 1850 he issued what has come to be called a "Gratitude to the Nation" coastal defense order, which called for mutual support among neighboring domains, settlement of samurai in strategic areas, and the creation of peasant militia.[44] The linchpin of this vision, however, was the improvement of shore fortifications, and soon after the shogunate directed daimyo to cast artillery pieces. Naomasa's furnace project was a cornerstone of this initiative.

Abe might not have been as receptive to Naomasa's tenacity and coalition building had his own attempts to initiate a substantial overhaul of Kantō-area defenses succeeded. Yet, even given his most desperate efforts, between 1846 and 1851, the only significant material improvement to Edo Bay security was the strengthening of a single battery at Kannonzaki.[45] The string of surprise visits by foreign warships beginning with the June 1846 landing of French admiral Jean-Baptiste Cécille in the

42. Yanai, *Tsūkō ichiran zokushū*, 5:49.
43. Tanji, "Kōkaki ni okeru Edo wan bōbi," p. 163.
44. Mitani, *Escape from Impasse*, p. 68.
45. Ibid., p. 69.

Ryūkyūs and then in Nagasaki to establish diplomatic relations with the Tokugawa, the arrival of Commodore James Biddle of the U.S. East India Squadron at Edo the following month, and the May 1849 surveys by the British gunship *Mariner* off Edo Bay did not provide sufficient impetus for radical policy change in the Tokugawa capital. Although Naomasa could not yet independently build a navy, as would become possible in the 1860s when the shogunate's ability to control the distribution of the monopoly on violence essentially dissolved, he gained relative freedom to produce a new generation of weapons for use onshore.

Egawa Tarōzaemon: The Collaborative Bridge

Although the support of powerful lords throughout Japan was critical for securing shogunal councillor Abe's permission to construct Saga's new furnace, the collaboration of a network of shogunal coastal defense specialists was equally significant for executing this plan. Naomasa's relationship with Egawa Tarōzaemon, shogunal administrator (*daikan*) of much of the Kantō region, was especially pivotal in the success of Saga artillery projects and the later use of these cannons in Edo Bay. In the summer of 1847, Naomasa had first estimated to Abe that approximately 100 large-bore cannon (apparently eighty-pound "boncannon," or Paixhans guns with exploding shells, weapons he first viewed on board the *Palembang* in 1844) were necessary for the harbor reinforcements.[46] Naomasa emphasized that Western firearms research had produced ships like water fortresses (*kaijō*) and created hulls so strong that standard shot of one *kanme* (roughly 8.7 pounds) could not penetrate them, making necessary the domestic construction of larger cannon.[47] Yet Saga artisans had no experience with producing cast-iron guns, so Naomasa actively solicited the advice of defense expert Egawa, who provided key technical advice after he had failed to build his own reverberatory furnace at his Nirayama headquarters on the Izu Peninsula.

Egawa had long been one of the few shogunal officials committed to educating himself about the science of European developments in weapons technology. He was descended from a long line of hereditary holders of the office of Nirayama *daikan*, local administrator of shogunal lands spanning the Izu Peninsula to the northern Kantō region (including

46. Arima, "The Western Influence on Japanese Military Science," p. 364.
47. Nakano, *Nabeshima Naomasa kōden*, 3:315.

the provinces of Kai, Sagami, Suruga, and Musashi) whose traditional responsibility had been collecting taxes, resolving judicial disputes, and maintaining the public peace. Given that all of these provinces, except for Kai, bordered the sea, in 1837, when the American ship *Morrison* entered Edo Bay, Egawa petitioned the shogunate for permission to strengthen the defense of coastal areas under his purview. This request marked the broadening of the responsibilities of this post from those of traditional administrator to also include maritime security. To develop expertise in military matters, Egawa studied under the preeminent Western firearms expert in Japan at the time, Takashima Shūhan, and by 1842 the shogunate asked Egawa to cast Western-style cannon. Egawa was one of a growing number of weapons experts convinced that more durable cast-iron firearms, rather than traditional bronze pieces, were the key to effective defenses, and arranged for subordinates to translate a Dutch volume (apparently Huegenin's text) on constructing a reverberatory furnace so that he could manufacture cast-iron pieces at his Nirayama headquarters. By 1848, however, Egawa acknowledged that he did not have the technical expertise to build the furnace, or sufficient funds (even though he had been charged with the project by shogunal officials) because of the fiscal conservatism of the shogunate's finance bureau. He remained convinced that domestic production of cast-iron weapons was critical for securing the shoreline under his oversight, particularly since he anticipated that foreign vessels would increasingly appear in those very waters so close to the Tokugawa capital at Edo. Thus, Egawa began to support Naomasa's efforts.

Even before Naomasa received official permission from Abe to begin his furnace project in 1850, he met twice with Egawa to discuss firearms technology, reflecting the broadening of his network of allies beyond fellow daimyo. In early 1848, as Naomasa traveled through the Mishima station of the Tōkaidō on his trip home to Saga from alternate attendance in Edo, the two men met to discuss Naomasa's interest in continuing the reverberatory furnace project initiated by Egawa.[48] During this conversation, Naomasa ordered two guns from Egawa, requested to borrow diagrams of cannon, and discussed collaborating on the translation of Huegenin's text.[49] The two men talked at least twice more over the next three years, in addition to corresponding by letter, as Egawa

48. *Nirayama juku nikki*, p. 27 (1848/3/24).

49. Kashiwagi Sōzō to Egawa Tan'an, 1848/3/26, quoted in Nakada, *Nirayama daikan Egawa shi no kenkyū*, p. 559.

encouraged Naomasa's leadership of the furnace project.[50] In early 1850, just after receiving Abe's assent to begin construction of the furnace, Naomasa wrote to Egawa asking him to send one of his best metallurgical technicians, Hasegawa Keibu, and two assistants to aid Saga as it prepared to build its new foundry.[51] Naomasa's success would benefit from the lessons of a shogunal failure.

Egawa assisted Naomasa not only by sending technicians from his suspended furnace project, but also by training Saga retainers, such as Motojima Tōdayū, in firearms technology at his Nirayama headquarters. Some seven years earlier, Motojima had first studied with Egawa, and apparently this experience preselected him for a second apprenticeship. Motojima was a member of the low-ranking *teakiyari* category of Saga samurai, whose original charge had been to make bladed weapons as an artisan-samurai. The function of these retainers was in transition following news of Britain's victory over neighboring China in the First Opium War.[52] In the wake of China's defeat, in late 1842, the followers of various Saga domain schools of firearms technology who belonged to this category of retainer agreed to cooperate in executing Nagasaki duties to improve the efficacy of their responses to defensive emergencies.[53] By late 1844, following the departure of the *Palembang*, the men identified a practice facility for a newly created composite school of Saga weapons study, ambitiously titled the "projecting authority afar" (*ien-ryū*) group.[54] Motojima's training in Western-style firearms methods emerged during a period in which Saga retainers had begun to embrace a more syncretic, and collaborative, approach to artillery exercises that transcended strict adherence to the practices of one tradition. In this environment, he was appointed head of a newly formed group of low-level samurai trained to man the cannon on the soon-to-be-strengthened outer batteries.[55] By 1850, this background prompted Naomasa to assign Motojima responsibility for overseeing renovations of the Nagasaki fortifications after consulting with Egawa.

50. Serizawa, *Yōshiki seitetsu no hōga*, p. 92. The dates of their meetings as recorded in Egawa's journal were 1848/3, 1849/10, and 1851/10 (See *Nirayama juku nikki*).

51. Nakada, *Nirayama daikan Egawa shi no kenkyū*, p. 563.

52. Ōhashi, "Kindai tetsu kōgyō no akebono," p. 226.

53. Kajiwara, "Bakumatsu Saga han ni okeru kajutsugumi," p. 375.

54. Nakano, *Nabeshima Naomasa kōden*, 3:184.

55. Nagano, *Sagahan to hansharo*, p. 159.

Motojima arrived at Nirayama in early 1850 to learn from Egawa's experience constructing a reverberatory furnace, but also to explore what lessons he could apply to Nagasaki from the strengthening of Uraga Bay, which Egawa had executed.[56] Yet, this short tour did not evidence pioneering technological innovations that revealed that Edo Bay was the leader in a new generation of shoreline defense. After several days in Izu, Motojima spent four days touring the stretch of batteries from Uraga, at the entrance to Edo Bay, southward to the Sarujima battery and finally across the bay to Fujitsu on the Bōsō Peninsula, the precise coastal areas Egawa had helped reinforce. Both Saga officials and local subordinates of the Uraga magistrate, who was charged with the security of the Edo Bay area, requested that Motojima keep secret his survey of these fortifications. Egawa's assistant, Saitō Yakyurō, allowed Motojima to view the shogunate's secret cache of firearms housed in the local armory at Uraga, including cannon named "big tiger" (*otora*) and "little tiger" (*kotora*), but these weapons were old-style, bronze construction. Later firing demonstrations from midsize twenty-six- and forty-three-pound cannons recorded no "hits."[57] Although some shot traveled roughly a mile, this was not a sufficient distance to hit vessels in the middle of the bay, which at its narrowest point was at least three miles wide. This tour reflected that Kantō defenses were in dire need of more effective artillery to protect the capital region. The most important result of this sharing of supposedly "privileged" information was that it demonstrated the willingness of both Egawa and the broader shogunate to help Naomasa succeed in producing larger cannon so that they might be installed on this very coastline.

Building Saga's New Foundry

Permission for Saga domain retainers to inspect fortifications of the capital region shoreline, when the specifics of these military installations were highly guarded state secrets, revealed the shogunate's growing realization that the best answers to national maritime security might not come from its innermost circle of advisers. Material evidence that the shogunate was more than a closet supporter of Naomasa's furnace project surfaced in the first month of the following year, 1851, when the shogunate granted Saga a loan of 50,000 *ryō*. This sum was only half of

56. Hideshima, *Saga han jūhō enkakushi*, pp. 417–51.
57. *Bakumatsu gijutsu no kiseki*, p. 48.

what Saga officials had requested over the past two years, and officially the shogunate identified the loan as disaster relief, likely because Edo did not want other domains coming forward requesting assistance for maritime defense expenditures.[58] Some historians have interpreted this advance as a special courtesy extended primarily because of Naomasa's marriage to a daughter of the Tayasu branch house. Yet, the most convincing explanation is that Abe supported Naomasa's artillery plans for expanding Nagasaki fortifications as a "test" laboratory for the Kantō.[59]

In addition to financial support, however, Saga's success also hinged on the domain's cultivation of Dutch scholars specializing in the translation of texts related to military science, whereas linguists of other domains, such as Fukuoka, concentrated on translating books related to medicine or history. The primary source of information for the construction of Saga's new reverberatory furnace was a translation of Huguenin's *Het gietwezen in's rijks ijzer-gesch gieterij te Luik* (1834), a single volume that described the state-owned ironworks in modern-day Liège, Belgium. Saga retainer Sugitani Yōsuke (1820–66) had translated it into Japanese beginning in 1847.[60] The exact provenance of Sugitani's copy is unclear, but the original volume had arrived in Nagasaki on board the Dutch vessel *Mary en Hillegonda* in 1836, two years after publication, and multiple translation efforts proceeded simultaneously across the realm.[61] Like Motojima, Sugitani was a low-ranking Saga samurai who studied in the important Edo medical academy of Itō Genboku, also of Saga, after beginning Dutch studies in Nagasaki.[62] He had begun work on the translation just as Naomasa approached Abe with the idea of strengthening Nagasaki harbor using large-bore cannon, an initiative that required a new furnace for producing the cast-iron artillery Naomasa envisioned.[63]

In mid-nineteenth-century Japan, the traditional hand-bellows-blown furnace method of iron making continued to dominate and was fine for small objects such as pots and pans, but it could not produce the

58. Mitani, *Escape from Impasse*, p. 72; Nakano, *Nabeshima Naomasa kōden*, 3:525.

59. Kihara, *Bakumatsu Sagahan no hanseishi kenkyū*, p. 181; Mitani, "Tempō-Kaei ki no taigai mondai."

60. Goodman, *Japan and the Dutch*, p. 154.

61. MacLean, "The Introduction of Books and Scientific Instruments into Japan," p. 47.

62. Nagano, *Sagahan to hansharo*, p. 161.

63. Ibid., p. 166.

volumes of homogenous molten iron necessary for mass-producing cast-iron cannon.[64] In spite of the production of articles for daily life, metallurgical innovations in early modern Japan had focused on refining small-scale steel production for laborious, hand-crafted sword making. Thus, the challenges to successful adaptation of imported technology lay not merely in mastering new science, but also in embracing a proto-industrial mentality of economies of scale. The primary innovation of furnaces such as that at Liege, which had been used in Europe since the seventeenth century, was that the iron to be smelted was placed in a separate chamber rather than directly on top of the fuel in the furnace. An arched interior roof forced the flames of the fire back onto the surface of the iron "so that impurities of the fuel were less likely to contaminate the smelted metal." This process resulted in a purer product, less apt to crack when fired, that could be manufactured in mass quantities.[65]

The setbacks in adapting this reverberatory furnace technology were numerous and might have been expected given the contemporaneous thirty-year quest to develop an effective smallpox vaccination in Japan, a success celebrated by Naomasa's vaccination of his own son and heir in 1849. Yet, the urgency of protecting the nation catalyzed the shogunate's optimism that mass production would evolve within a few years rather than a few decades, and it soon placed orders for hundreds of cannon from the Saga foundries. Even as Saga completed its first furnace by late 1850, problems in casting persisted because of lack of knowledge about supporting technologies and differences in the types of earth materials available in Europe and Japan. One of the first failures identified was the inability to elevate the furnace temperatures to sufficient level, a process that required coke, a coal fuel that burned hotter and longer than charcoal. Although Huguenin's text identified coal, preferably coked, as the superior fuel source for the furnace, charcoal was the primary fuel at the Saga foundry until 1855 or 1856.[66] Bituminous veins running through the nearby Takashima fields contained the coal grades necessary for producing coke, but Saga technicians, initially preoccupied with the chemical composition of the iron sand used in the furnaces, took several years to learn how to produce it.[67] Moreover, instead of using pig iron

64. Ibid., p. 57.
65. Morris-Suzuki, *Technological Transformation of Japan*, pp. 58–59.
66. Serizawa, *Yōshiki seitetsu no hōga*, p. 74.
67. Monroe, "Mineral Wealth of Japan," p. 378.

(an intermediate product made by smelting iron ore with a high-carbon fuel such as coke) as the base material (as Huguenin's text recommended), early castings used remelted sword blades. Saga artisans did not have a local iron source and later used iron sand from Ishimi, present-day Shimane Prefecture. Yet, the chemical composition of this iron sand, not understood at the time, made it difficult to melt.[68] Saga domain encountered its most sustained success only after it began importing European iron in 1859.[69] Cognizant of these shortcomings, but uncertain of their resolution, Saga retainers overseeing production, such as Sugitani and Motojima, frequently visited the Dutch at the Dejima trading compound in Nagasaki with questions, at times carrying samples of the flawed cast iron with them.[70]

Early failures made the shortcomings of the furnace immediately apparent, but it would take years to identify their source, and often decades to rectify them. Within four months, after four failed attempts at casting, Saga artisans finally produced a cast-iron cannon in late 1851, but it cracked three days later, when test fired, revealing pits in the metal.[71] By the fifth month of the following year (1852), Saga technicians had produced what was identified as "close to the caliber of Western weapons," but difficulties continued.[72] Because of these repeated obstacles, through the 1850s, half of the initial foundry site at Tsukiji in the Saga castle town was still devoted to the older crucible furnaces, producing bronze weapons.[73]

In this transitional phase of experimenting with new, imported defensive technologies, which often failed, Saga domain also used traditional techniques for smaller-scale defense projects whose success was assured. In the spring of 1851, just as the Tsukiji furnace site had cast its first cannon, Saga domain hired two experienced stonemasons to tour the harbor islands of Kannoshima and Shirōjima and submit an estimate of the cost

68. Nagano, "Zairai gijutsu to inyū gijutsu no setten," p. 70.

69. Ibid., p. 68.

70. Hideshima, *Saga han jūhō enkakushi*, pp. 329–30. Consultations with the Dutch in Nagasaki recorded for 1854/6/6; 1854/i 7/10; 1854/i 7/26. This final consultation, which included discussion of the construction of the cannons' wheeled mounts, lasted more than a week.

71. Nagano, *Sagahan to hansharo*, p. 191.

72. Ibid., p. 196.

73. Hideshima, *Saga han jūhō enkakushi*, image 44; Nagano, "Zairai gijutsu to inyū gijutsu no setten," p. 64.

for filling the narrow strait separating them.[74] This focus underscored Naomasa's conviction, contrary to that of Abe, that outer-harbor improvements were still the key to Nagasaki's defense. These artisans, identified only as Seibei and Manbei of Bizen Province on the Inland Sea, an area known for its stonemasons, estimated a cost of 60,000 *ryō* to fill the strait, about 800 feet long and 60 feet deep. Clever rumors circulated in Nagasaki that the domain was "sinking" its money by dumping boatloads of rocks for naught when currents and sea winds made them drift off target. A popular ditty that chided, "Plop, plop the stones go, and where they stop nobody knows," was reportedly heard around the harbor.[75] But by the third month of the following year, 1852, the project was complete, providing evidence that Naomasa could execute his ambitious vision for the harbor. The cost of this project alone was more than half of Naomasa's original proposed budget for the entire overhaul of harbor defenses, so one wonders why he proposed it at all when the likelihood of sailing ships choosing to navigate this narrow strait was remote. Yet as casting cannon with Western standards of craftsmanship proved elusive, producing public symbols of Saga's military leadership, even using centuries-old, labor-intensive methods, was critical. As well, oversight of this project by artisans of another domain, selected for their village's tradition of overseeing large-scale stone building projects such as the 1,200-foot-long jetty at Awaji Island in the Inland Sea, further underscored the increasingly collaborative, supradomainal nature of maritime defense.

Soon after this landfill project was complete, a gargantuan task employing thousands of local laborers and their boats, Saga began to install newly cast cannon on the outer-harbor batteries. While the reverberatory furnace was being refined, the production of bronze firearms remained double that of cast-iron weapons, and so most of these cannon first installed were bronze construction.[76] In mid-1851, Saga domain received permission from the shogunate to place thirty-four cannon on Kannoshima, ranging from two 150-pound cannon to twelve 24- and 12-pound cannon. Iōjima would receive twenty-six cannon, ranging from six 80-pounders to four 4- and 12-pounders.[77] The average size of

74. Nakano, *Nabeshima Naomasa kōden nenpyō, sakuin, sōmokuroku*, p. 104.

75. Ibid., p. 562.

76. Nakano, *Nabeshima Naomasa kōden*, 4:6. In 1852, the domain cast forty bronze cannon ranging from 20-pound shot to 250-pound shot, and twenty-one iron cannon with shot between 2.5 pounds and 134 pounds.

77. Nakano, *Nabeshima Naomasa kōden*, 3:571.

the cannon positioned at the batteries increased only slightly with these additions: now there were fifty-four cannon of 12-pound shot or greater in Nagasaki harbor, whereas previously there had been only fifty cannon of 8.7 pounds or greater.[78]

The variance in categories for counting weapons across different types of documents, as well as the likelihood that many cannon emplaced did not function, makes it difficult to precisely compare the firepower strength of Nagasaki harbor across the decades. But the collective conclusion of multiple sources is that by 1854, following what many historians have previously identified as the most ambitious strengthening measures in the history of Nagasaki garrison security, the total number of cannon protecting the shoreline remained roughly equal to that of forty years earlier, before the Opium Wars and the arrival of the *Palembang* (fig. 4.2).[79] Had artisans focused instead on mass-producing bronze pieces instead of struggling to perfect a new technology, and had the energies of Saga's technicians not been diverted to produce cannon for Edo, this number might well have been higher. Even with the marginal increase in firepower at the Nagasaki batteries, the weapons Saga produced lacked the rifling (providing increased accuracy and distance) of the deck guns on board vessels now entering Nagasaki Bay, advances imperative for hitting steam-powered gunboats, which could maneuver much more quickly than their predecessors with sails. In the eighth month of 1854, while on board Russian admiral Evfimii Putiatin's flagship *Pallada*, the head of the Saga furnace project, Motojima, observed rifled guns for the first time—which the Dutch explained to him allowed ammunition to travel farther and with greater precision—as well as sights, which had recently been added to firearms in the West.[80]

What Naomasa's enthusiastic optimism for these weapons experiments could not predict was the long and uneven process of adapting imported technology to local conditions. Although cast iron better retained its strength and shape than bronze during repeated firings, cast-iron artillery had become the predominant naval weapon in Europe during the previous half century largely because mass production made it less expensive to make than bronze pieces. These economies of scale

78. Hara, *Bakumatsu kaibōshi no kenkyū*, p. 9; Hideshima, *Saga han jūhō enkakushi*, pp. 395–97, 404–405.

79. Hara, *Bakumatsu kaibōshi no kenkyū*, p. 201.

80. Nakano, *Nabeshima Naomasa kōden*, 4:64; Howard, *Sailing Ships of War*, p. 247.

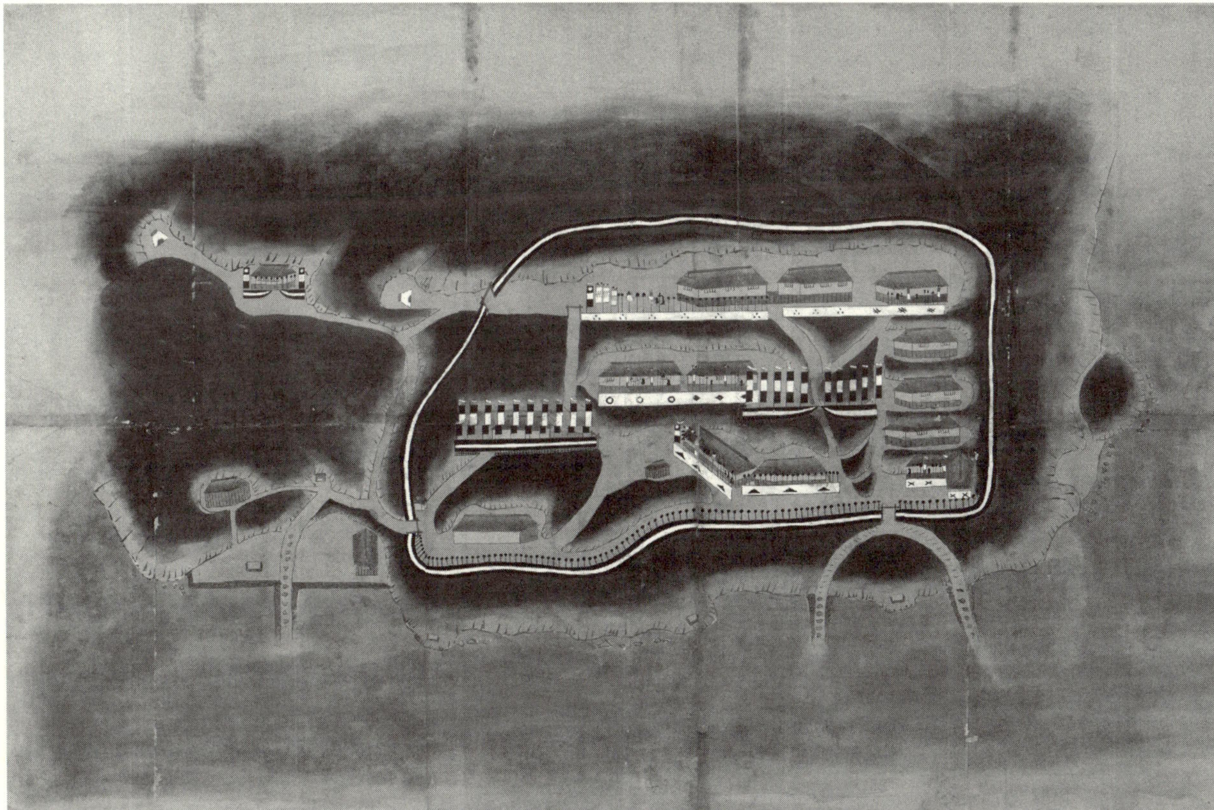

FIGURE 4.2 Tomachi battery in Nagasaki harbor flying the black-and-white heraldic regalia of the Fukuoka domain. *Tomachi gobansho kazarizu*, late Edo period. Itami collection no. 564. Courtesy of the Fukuoka City Library.

would take decades to achieve in Japan. Naomasa's embrace of this technology was rooted in the assumption that cast iron was categorically superior in terms of reliability (it was noncorrosive), range, and destructive power, when the adoption of cast-iron weapons on Western gunboats was not entirely the product of these metrics, but rather finances. Historians have long neglected examining the political process of building and operating the first reverberatory furnace in Japan because the quantity of its production was so small and the reliability of its weapons so uncertain. That the majority of firearms used in the Boshin War of 1868–69 were imported (from Germany, the Netherlands, Britain, and the United States) speaks to the inability of Japanese technicians to perfect this process over the next fifteen years so that domestic mass production of cast-iron artillery was feasible. During this very period, Western nations in fact developed rifled, breech-loading, and even repeating weapons while Japanese still struggled to fabricate a basic smooth-bore, muzzle-loading cannon. Yet the process of constructing a furnace, while only modestly successful in adapting new technology, yielded substantial political results in placing domains at the vanguard of military innovation and in providing a concrete goal to mobilize military cooperation among daimyo.

Saga Cannons at Edo Bay

Even as mass production at the Saga foundry proved elusive, following the arrival of Commodore Perry in 1853 to request fueling and provisioning privileges for American sailors, the shogunate placed orders for cast-iron artillery from those new furnaces to be installed in Edo Bay. Perry's aggressive response to the initial shogunal rejection of his demands, that he would return with additional warships to extract an affirmative reply the following year, prompted an atmosphere of panic in Edo and beyond. The centrality of nearby Kantō domains in mobilizing troops for a military response to Perry's return visit is frequently noted, but the critical role of Saga is less well-known. Almost immediately, the shogunate began to construct a string of six landfill fortresses in Shinagawa Bay to serve as a barrier against potential attack on the capital.[81]

81. Although eleven were originally planned, only five were completed due to financial constraints and the competing Goryōkaku fortress project in Hakodate.

Edo officials then ordered Naomasa to produce two hundred cast-iron cannon to fortify these batteries, although the shogunate decreased this number to fifty pieces when technical difficulties with the Saga furnaces made the initial quantity seem unreasonable.[82] To fulfill this order, between the fall of 1853 and spring of 1854 Saga technicians built a second reverberatory furnace at a site known as Tafuse in their castle town. Because the Saga foundry production was intermittently successful, shogunal artisans also began producing bronze cannon at a new Yushima furnace in Edo.[83] Apparently, the shogunate was content to allow domains to shoulder the unpredictability and financial liability of experimenting with cast-iron production, choosing to sponsor more reliable bronze casting in its own facility. At the peak of Saga's production for the Shinagawa batteries, associated costs comprised 40 percent of annual domain revenues, revealing the still elusive benefits of economies of scale that had made cast-iron weapons ubiquitous in Europe.[84]

By mid-1855, Saga artisans at last loaded the cannon they had cast for the Shinagawa forts on three barges of Nabeshima Naomasa and the Osaka magistrate for transport to Edo. Given production shortfalls, this shipment included only half of the fifty pieces requested, each marked by a different letter of the Japanese syllabary for tracking.[85] The first two barges completed their voyage, but the third vessel, the *Junsei-maru*, encountered high winds off of Hibizaki in Kishū domain and sank, although its crew escaped after replacing a ripped sail with one hastily made from their clothes to maneuver close to shore.[86] Records are unclear regarding exactly how many cannon had been loaded on this vessel, but evidence suggests that at least six cannon were lost in the

82. *Bakumatsu gijutsu no kiseki*, pp. 66–70, 103; Hideshima, *Saga han jūhō enkaku shi*, p. 329. This order included twenty-five 36-pound cannons and twenty-five 24-pound cannons. The request for movable mounts revealed the newly recognized necessity of swiveling shore cannon given the increased maneuverability of Western steam-powered vessels.

83. This facility was constructed in an area of firebreak bordering the Yushima Seidō, a Confucian temple that later housed the Hayashi Confucian academy. Asakawa, *Odaiba*, p. 110.

84. Nagano, *Sagahan to hansharo*, p. 162. Nagano does not precisely date this figure, calculated from data in the *Daikōjū seizōroku*, but it is for some year in the early 1850s.

85. Ibid., p. 333.

86. Hideshima, *Saga han jūhō enkakushi*, p. 224.

accident.[87] The shogunate had originally forecast that the Yushima foundry would provide 118 bronze cannons for the Shinagawa batteries, the Nirayama site would supply 109 cast-iron cannon (none of which were made), and Saga 50 cast-iron cannon, with 5 cannons transported from Osaka, for a total of 282 pieces.[88] A tally of cannon actually in place in the late 1850s, however, revealed only 124 weapons installed, slightly less than half of the original number, with only between 15 and 17 from Saga.[89] Although the Saga numbers were modest, the inclusion of domain-produced weapons as the only new cast-iron cannons in Edo Bay was a potent symbol of the leadership role of enterprising daimyo in helping Japan embrace a new generation of military technology.

More central to our understanding of larger maritime defense strategy during the mid-1850s, Saga domain's inclusion in the fortification of Shinagawa Bay reflected a new and evolving understanding of Western motives in Japan. The batteries on these landfill islands of Shinagawa replicated the Nagasaki model of offshore fortifications on proximate islands as a second line of defense for artillery situated on the mainland, of which Edo had many emplacements as well. The Shinagawa Bay battery project also revealed the growing embrace of national security based on defense of a handful of "core ports," which would soon include not only Nagasaki and Edo, but also Hakodate, and then Yokohama, as well. This "core port" initiative replaced the impossible idea of fortifying the entirety of the Japanese coastline. Yet, the placement of these cannon in the *naikai* or *naime* ("inner sea"), as contemporary documents identified the Shinagawa Bay, rather than the entrance of the larger Uraga Bay, some thirty miles to the south, demonstrated a rejection of the outer-harbor (*sotome*) strategy Naomasa had embraced in Nagasaki. Following Perry's initial visit to Edo in 1853, numerous shogunal officials, including Egawa, had briefly accepted the concept of an outer-harbor defense at the mouth of Uraga Bay (map 5).[90] The shift to an inner-harbor strategy

87. Asakawa, *Odaiba*, pp. 113–14. Some documents place the number of cannon contributed by Saga as high as thirty-six pieces, although the actual number in place and serviceable (after subtracting weapons out of service due to cracked bores) was less than half this number; Hideshima, *Saga han jūhō enkakushi*, pp. 330–31.

88. Asakawa, *Odaiba*, p. 107.

89. Ibid., pp. 107, 113. Satsuma, Nirayama, and Mito all contributed cannon to Edo Bay, although Satsuma's furnace was not operational until 1853, Nirayama's until 1855, and that of Mito until 1856. Nagano, *Sagahan to hansharo*, p. 37.

90. Asakawa, *Odaiba*, p. 56.

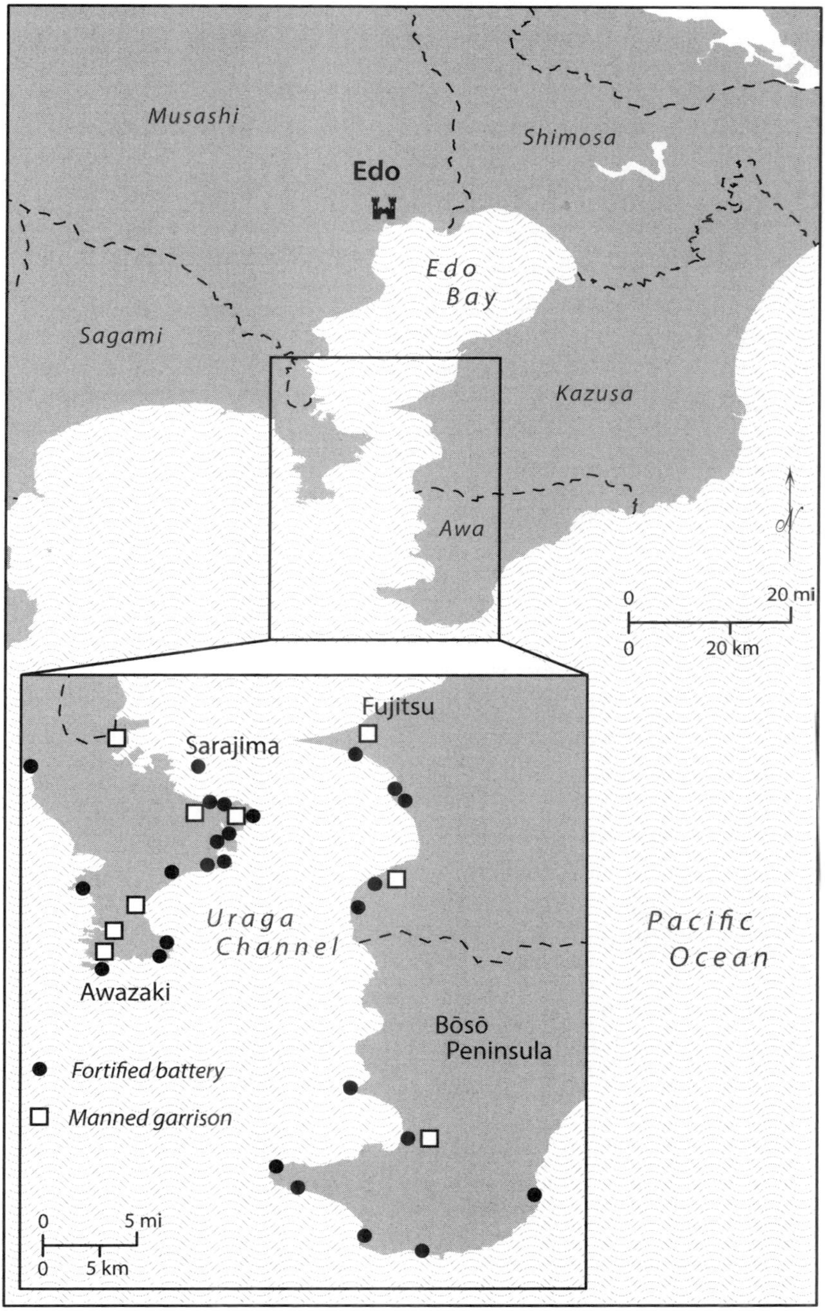

MAP 5 Uraga Bay defenses (adapted from Hara, *Bakumatsu kaibōshi no kenkyū*, 13).

at the capital was largely the product of growing realism about the limited number of shore cannon available in the Kantō and the need to concentrate them in a single location to provide effective defense of the Tokugawa capital city.[91] Initial interactions with Perry suggested that the Americans would not indiscriminately attack remote stretches of beach (such as those along the outer Uraga area, several days' journey from Edo proper). They were not planning a full-scale invasion of Japan, as had been feared.[92] Rather, they were most interested in commercial relations to broaden their expanding trade network across East Asia. This strategy would engage Tokugawa officials at core port cities where Western diplomats could most efficiently negotiate while also surveying potential trading harbors.

A related concern in building the landfill Shinagawa batteries, however, was protecting the Tokugawa castle from Western naval shelling with sea island "obstacles" that would physically prevent warships from approaching the Edo coast close enough for their ordnance to reach the castle walls. The draft of Perry's largest vessels was in the range of sixteen to twenty feet, the depth of the harbor about a mile out from the batteries, so at the closest, ships could only come within four miles of the castle (three miles inland from the batteries), too far away to shell.[93] Thus, the embrace of the inner-harbor plan at Shinagawa, while adopting the Nagasaki template of sea island fortifications, emerged not due to a simple transfer of strategy but due to the intermingling of other singular, geographical concerns of the Tokugawa political capital.

By early 1856, following the arrival of the Saga-cast cannons at Shinagawa, Naomasa surveyed the batteries in Edo Bay, where his cannon were now installed, to inspect the utility of his military reforms in Nagasaki for the larger Tokugawa realm.[94] His visit to the Shinagawa batteries was only the most recent by a string of coastal defense officials and dignitaries, which had even included an ailing Shogun Iesada in 1854 (fig. 4.3). In early 1857, however, two of the thirty-six-pound cannon cast

91. At the time of Perry's 1853 arrival, the total number of Tokugawa firearms on the 100-mile periphery of Uraga Bay was ninety-nine, and about 80 percent of those pieces discharged shot of twenty-four pounds or less. The smallest of Perry's sixty-three naval guns, which could be moved en masse, was a cannon of thirty-two-pound shot. Hara, *Bakumatsu kaibōshi no kenkyū*, p. 60.

92. Hara, "Bakumatsu ni okeru Edo wan no bōbi," p. 52n45; *Dai Nihon komonjo: Bakumatsu gaikoku kankei monjo*, 1:534, 538–39.

93. Asakawa, *Odaiba*, p. 87.

94. Hideshima, *Saga han jūhō enkakushi*, p. 236.

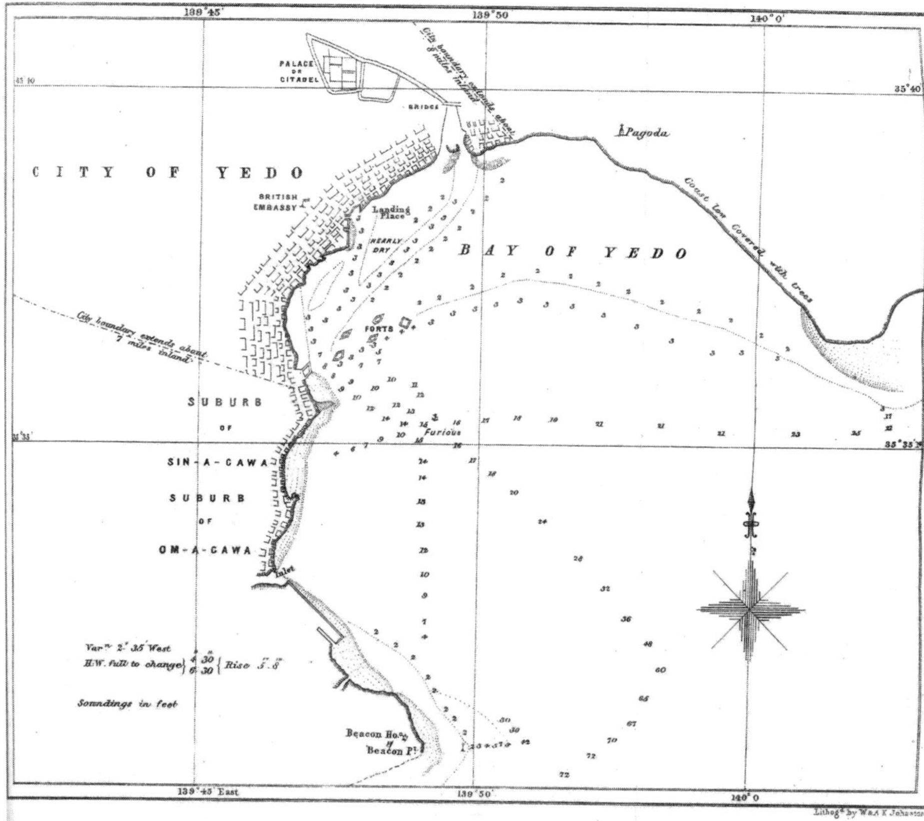

FIGURE 4.3 Shinagawa batteries, lithograph, 1860, reproduced from Laurence Oliphant's *Narrative of The Earl of Elgin's Mission to China and Japan, in the Years 1857, 1858, and 1859*, vol. 2.

in Saga cracked when fired at Shinagawa batteries numbers five and six. Because of this development, Saga retainers reduced the amount of powder used at the newly cast cannon on Iōjima and Kannoshima in Nagasaki batteries by a quarter.[95] After reports that the Shinagawa cannon barrels had multiple splits, discussions in Saga concluded that this damage resulted from the inability to heat the furnaces to sufficiently high temperatures and the continued presence of impurities in the ore, prompting the import of coal from Europe.[96] By year's end, however, shogunal councillor Iwase Tadanari's vision of a Kantō-area port where foreigners could be sequestered, as in Nagasaki, came to dominate diplomatic discussions with the United States during negotiations over the Treaty of Amity and Commerce. Following Kanagawa's selection as this site in early 1858, attention to the Shinagawa batteries waned as officials realized that most foreign ships would soon cease traveling to Edo proper, instead stopping several miles south at the Kanagawa inlet. This site transformed into the centerpiece of Kantō-area security as the neighboring village of Yokohama became the official port site. Although no defensive shots were ever fired from the Shinagawa batteries, their legacy of securing an inner harbor shaped defense of the treaty ports at both Hakodate and Yokohama as the template originally established in Nagasaki continued to spread.

Conclusion

In the decade between 1844 and 1854, Saga domain's metallurgy projects and its construction of new fortifications in Nagasaki were the most important laboratories for updating military technology in Japan. While the immediate material improvements in defensive capabilities were minimal, the specific goal of building a reverberatory furnace catalyzed a network of information sharing and political collaboration that endured beyond this particular project. Contrary to a trajectory of antagonistic military rivalry emphasized in previous studies of defensive developments in mid-nineteenth-century Japan, the intellectual exchange Naomasa brokered demonstrates how the cultivation of defensive technology was a cooperative project, often domain led. Given that initial attempts to build

95. Ibid., pp. 242–43.
96. Ibid., p. 243.

a shogunate-sponsored reverberatory furnace at Nirayama had failed in the early 1840s, senior councillor Abe recognized by the late 1840s that his direct subordinates would not be able to guarantee long-term, centrally orchestrated development of Western firearms technology. The absence of a champion for Western-style artillery in Edo, at the very moment it was most critical, created an opportune environment for Naomasa's leadership.

Drawing on Saga's success, furnaces were soon constructed at Kagoshima in Satsuma domain, at Hagi in Chōshū domain, and at Mito, with the shogunate rebuilding its own facilities in Nirayama by 1854. Saga, at the vanguard of this process, was not proprietary about its accomplishments with the reverberatory furnace or its shore batteries. In fact, Naomasa invited observers to study these improvements, in part because they were shogunate-sanctioned enterprises, but also because Japan was not yet engaged in the internal political struggle of the late 1850s that would transform domains into military opponents. By the 1860s, these metallurgical projects became politicized as Saga cast replicas of the latest Armstrong cannon that were used in the Battle of Ueno to defeat Tokugawa forces.[97]

Histories of nineteenth-century Japan often omit this episode of the technology of defense because the cannons Saga domain produced were already a generation behind the rifled bores of Western firearms even before leaving their site of production. Yet, the case of Nabeshima Naomasa reveals how domainal initiatives to strengthen coastal defenses benefited from the exchange of ideas with Dutch scholars and weapons experts in both Edo and Nagasaki in a fluid knowledge network similar to that of mid-nineteenth-century physicians who collaborated in developing a successful vaccination against smallpox.[98] The trajectory of deliberations over improvements to the infrastructure and technology of defense during the 1840s and early 1850s reveals a more allied, reciprocal process of intellectual sharing among key actors than that of the debates over larger defense policy, which were antagonistic and divisive.

As early as mid-1853, we see the reciprocity of knowledge sharing come full circle, in which Saga artisans, previously the students of Tokugawa administrator Egawa's experiments on the Izu Peninsula, had become instead the mentors for Egawa's technicians to consult following

97. Cobbing, *Kyushu: Gateway to Japan*, p. 217.
98. See Janetta, *The Vaccinators.*

Saga's construction of a successful furnace.[99] By the end of the year, three more of Egawa's retainers visited Nagasaki to see Russian envoy Putiatin's steamships, and inspected the reverberatory furnace compound at Saga on their return home.[100] They reached Izu with maps of the newly reinforced Nagasaki harbor batteries, diagrams that Egawa had requested as a reference for planning expanded defenses in the Kantō region.[101] Exploring this two-way process of information exchange not only demonstrates Nabeshima Naomasa's furnace as a success produced by collaboration with Egawa, even though previously many historians have framed it as solely the victory of domainal persistence. It also reveals the reverse flow of technical information from Kyūshū to the Kantō, from domain to shogunate, in the mid-1850s. During Commodore Perry's return in the spring of 1854, U.S. diplomats made clear that they would not accept Nagasaki as one of the first "open" ports because it symbolized restrictions on foreigners due to the sequestration of the Dutch on Dejima. When these initial negotiations settled on opening ports at Shimoda and Hakodate, the crux of Tokugawa maritime security, and the flow of defensive preparations, shifted northward from Nagasaki to the Kantō region, and then to Ezo. It is to the defense of these sites, and the political implications of the militarization of these newly created international ports, that we turn in chapter 5.

99. On 1853/6/17, the same day the news reached Saga that Perry's ships had arrived in Uraga Bay, Egawa's subordinate, Hatta Heisuke, arrived in Saga domain to consult with Motojima about constructing a reverberatory furnace in Nirayama. Nakano, *Nabeshima Naomasa kōden*, 4:30; Nagano, *Sagashan to hansharo*, p. 37.

100. Nakada, *Nirayama daikan Egawa shi no kenkyū*, p. 568.

101. Ibid., *Bakumatsu gijutsu no kiseki*, p. 150.

CHAPTER FIVE

Reconfiguring Coastal Defense at the Treaty Ports

In early 1856, artist Utagawa Hiroshige first produced woodblock prints of the Shinagawa Bay fortresses, located roughly a mile offshore of the Tokugawa capital at Edo. One of several images of the forts, *View of the Shiba Coast*, foregrounded channel markers and Japanese sailing ships, relegating silhouettes of the dark batteries to the background (fig. 5.1). Two other renditions, *Shinagawa Susaki* and *Takanawa Ushimachi*, depicted the fortifications in a similar vein, as uninhabited gray harbor islands, convenient horizontal foils for an image teeming with vertical masts of Japanese sailing vessels portrayed in greater detail.[1] Hiroshige's focus on maritime images, a characteristic historian Henry Smith has referred to as the "pervasiveness of water," reflected a growing public interest in the Japanese seascape. Yet as Hiroshige's inclusion of military forts revealed, water spaces were now not merely a commercial zone of fishing vessels and cargo ships, but also territory to be systematically defended. The goal of coastal defense was recalibrated to protect not only Tokugawa lands, but also proximate sea spaces, converting surrounding littoral zones into sovereign territory as the concept of "Japanese space" was redefined. This chapter is the story of how domainal troops helped defend that vital Tokugawa space during the treaty-port era, gaining new perquisites and augmented military agency for manning coastal garrisons as shogunal officials increasingly focused, instead, on diplomacy as the key to national security.

1. *View of Shiba Coast* (plate 108), *Shinagawa Susaki* (plate 83), and *Takanawa Ushimachi* (plate 81) in Smith and Poster, *Hiroshige: One Hundred Famous Views of Edo*. Christine Guth explores how nineteenth-century visual culture reflects this growing interest in water spaces in her incisive essay, "Hokusai's Great Waves."

FIGURE 5.1 Utagawa (Andō) Hiroshige (Japanese, 1797–1858). *View of the Shiba Coast,* no. 108 from the series *One Hundred Famous Views of Edo*, woodblock print, second lunar month of 1856, sheet: 14 3/16×9¼ in. (36×23.5 cm). Courtesy of the Brooklyn Museum, Gift of Anna Ferris, 30.1478.108.

Hiroshige's images, and the construction of the Shinagawa batteries (explored in chapter 4), demonstrated the broadening recognition of proximate ocean spaces as territory to be defended well beyond Nagasaki's harbor. They did not reveal, however, the reconfiguration of the military contract between the shogunate and domains, designed to establish Japanese control over these waters. Between 1854 and 1868, the Western treaties brought a permanent, bustling foreign commercial and military presence to Tokugawa maritime space, raising unprecedented security concerns. Such new threats to Japan's sovereignty required practical adjustments to the country's defense structure, including further devolution of the monopoly on violence to domains. Most notably, the shogunate had to provide defense for the newly opened treaty ports of Yokohama, Hakodate, and other international harbors. Doing so meant heightened levels of domainal troop mobilization for extended periods of time at new sites, prompting revisions to the way military authority had been delegated in the long-operating Nagasaki system. These changes included the appointment of increasing numbers of domains to guard Tokugawa lands (domains now often located hundreds of miles from the shorelines they were assigned to defend), the granting of numerous "entrusted lands" (*azukari dokoro*) to domains charged with defense, and cash payments (instead of the usual ritual granting of prestige gifts) as compensation for military service.

The assignment of growing numbers of domains to coastal defense duties at the major ports (from a handful of domains in the 1840s to more than fifty within a decade), combined with the constant shuffling of assignments among them, made continuity of execution on the ground difficult. To address the inconsistencies of this turnover in manpower, the shogunate implemented two important practices. First, it transformed the previously disjointed and port-specific treatment of foreign ships to a standardized system of rules and regulations, regardless of the port of call or provenance of the vessel. The creation of universal, trans-site norms helped shoreline troops avoid confusion over varied privileges of navigation among Western powers. Codifying these regulations in writing ensured their replicability and consistent transmission across the growing number of harbors identified as treaty ports. Clear articulation of the regulations was equally important for ports like Kobe and Niigata, which lacked experience dealing with foreign vessels, and those such as Nagasaki, which already had some proficiency in doing so. Second, the shogunate assigned many port-city magistrates—including those at

Nagasaki, Yokohama, and Hakodate—to serve concurrently in the central government post of magistrate of foreigners. While these simultaneous appointments facilitated coordination among the various local magistrates, the individuals serving in these dual capacities regularly privileged the shogunate's growing interest in nurturing stable economic and diplomatic relations with treaty powers over improving defenses at the ports. The former practice, the creation of trans-site norms, made relinquishing execution of defense to new domains all the more possible because now written rules, rather than merely custom, existed to guide, and standardize, their responses to foreign ships. The latter shift in port magistrates' priorities, to now privilege diplomacy over military affairs, left the majority of decisions about port defenses to the domains manning local fortifications and providing troops.

With these developments in the background, this chapter examines how defense at the three largest treaty ports of Nagasaki, Yokohama, and Hakodate reveals continued changes in the partitioning of the monopoly on violence, augmenting domainal agency in new ways (map 6). In Nagasaki, the failure of the shogunate to punish domains for defensive shortcomings, particularly in the Seymour Incident of 1856, and resident Westerners' resistance to continued domainal construction of batteries in an era of escalating attacks on foreigners, reflected the shogunate's inescapable military reliance on domains and diminishing enforcement capability. As port fortification moved northward to Kantō harbors, the vast numbers, and often distant location, of domains required to protect an imperiled capital region prompted the shogunate to offer new perquisites for military service in the form of entrusted lands and cash payments. As Yokohama emerged as the primary harbor of this region and the largest port in Japan, shogunal officials there paid growing attention to its diplomatic and commercial affairs, leaving its military concerns almost exclusively in the hands of domains. Finally, in Hakodate, defense of Japan's northernmost treaty port revealed new military challenges as the shogunate charged domains with protecting not only the harbor proper, but also the larger island of Ezo from anticipated Russian incursion. In each of these sites, domains gained increasingly generous privileges from the shogunate in exchange for their coastal military service, signaling the definitive dissolution of the daimyo obligation to freely aid the Tokugawa with troops, as their seventeenth-century power-sharing arrangement had required.

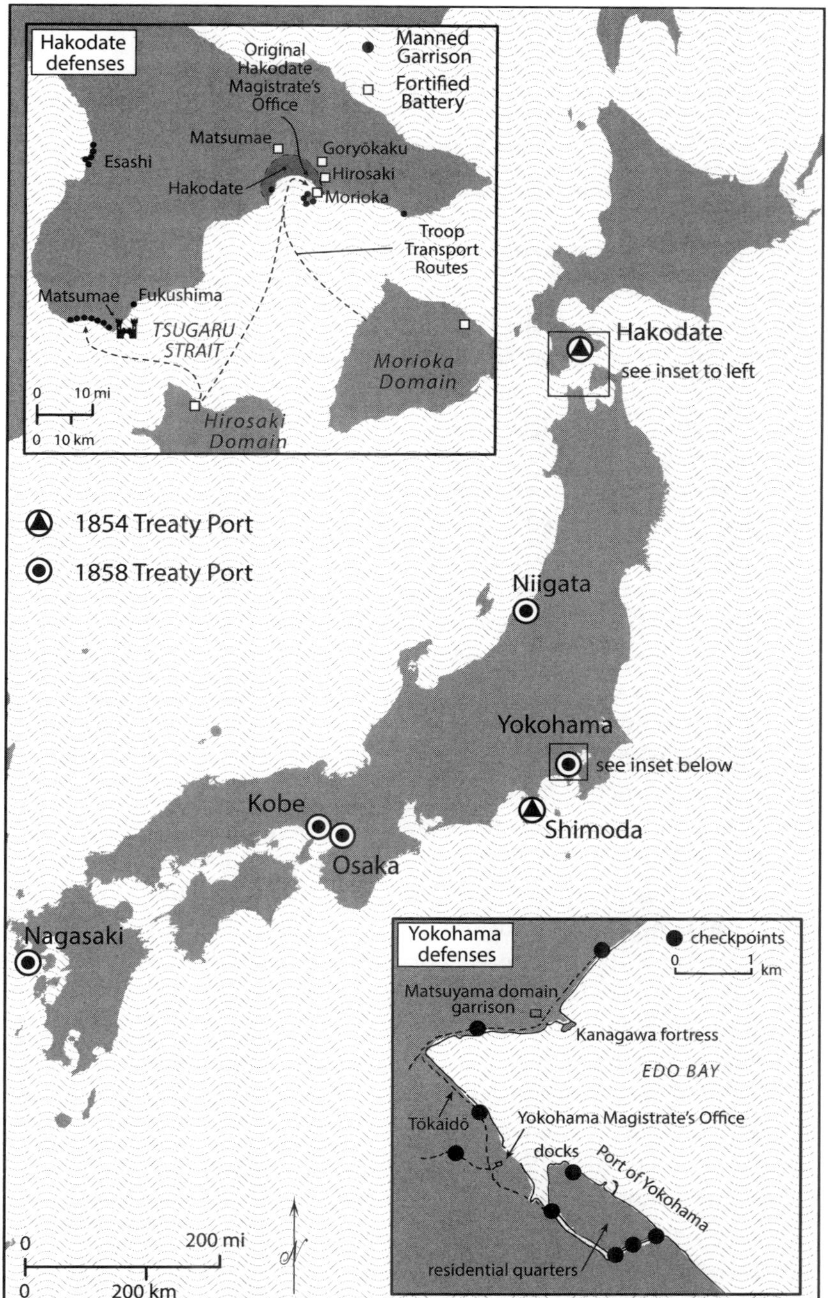

MAP 6 Treaty ports with insets of Hakodate and Yokohama (adapted from Hara, *Bakumatsu kaibōshi no kenkyū*, 107, 141).

Domains and the Military Response to Westerners in Nagasaki

Even though Nagasaki had a centuries-long and routinized harbor defense system in place by the 1850s, it continued to serve as an important military laboratory where the domainal role in maritime security evolved in two important ways. First, the 1856 Seymour Incident, in which Saga vessels failed to prevent the British steamship *Barracouta* from entering the Nagasaki inner harbor, revealed that domains would not be punished for defensive failures. Second, the continued domainal construction of shore batteries, in the face of Western consular opposition, reflected growing foreign fear about the ability of the Tokugawa to control the actions of shoreline domainal troops during a period of escalating and violent xenophobia directed at resident foreigners. In both cases, domains were critical agents in establishing Tokugawa norms of engagement for ports opened to a new Western presence.

To understand the significant political and defensive implications of the 1856 Seymour Incident for domains—in which an aggressive charge by the British steamship *Barracouta* sank two Saga domain vessels in Nagasaki harbor—we must first briefly survey debates over what constituted an "open" port in the mid-1850s. British rear admiral Sir Michael Seymour's destructive charge was sparked by the refusal of the Nagasaki magistrate to honor the more generous interpretation of what "open" meant in Hakodate port regulations. After the shogunate signed the 1854 treaties granting an array of Western nations provisioning rights at select Japanese ports, the future shape of maritime defense rested on the interpretation of the term "open port" (*kaikō*), which held a central place in the language of the treaties. Much scholarship has focused on how the meaning of the term "open" was negotiated to delimit the boundaries of foreigners' travel on land outside the port cities proper. Yet historians have generally overlooked how this same notion was interpreted to demarcate the precise water spaces within each harbor in which foreign vessels were allowed to freely circulate. The political complexities of creating a mutually agreeable definition of exactly what sections of harbor water spaces were open to the free movement of foreign vessels emerged almost immediately after the initial treaties were signed.

Tensions over this concept first arose two years before Seymour's arrival, when the British and Japanese in Nagasaki negotiated the scope of British privileges in that port allowed by the 1854 Anglo-Japanese Convention. Interpretations of what "open" should mean for the harbor of Nagasaki clashed when Rear Admiral Sir James Stirling, commander of the British Navy of the Far East, made a dramatic entrance in October of 1854 aboard the fifty-two-gun sailing frigate HMS *Winchester* to establish formal diplomatic relations with the Tokugawa. Tokugawa unwillingness to embrace Stirling's request for his ships' virtually unrestricted movement in port resulted in the Seymour Incident two years later.

The timing of Stirling's 1854 arrival and of British interest in a treaty with the Tokugawa shogunate coincided with the Crimean War, then raging in Europe over control of the territories of the declining Ottoman Empire (fig. 5.2). Whereas the Americans and Russians first came to Japan to acquire refueling and provisioning privileges, Britain's primary interest was in locating and destroying enemy ships of the Russian navy, their rivals in the Crimean conflict. This military goal meant that British captains needed immediate access to the entirety of Japanese harbors so that they could identify any Russian vessels attempting to hide there. Such an aim was not explicitly covered by the 1854 Anglo-Japanese Convention that Stirling acquired, which allowed British ships to enter Nagasaki and Hakodate only for supplies. As these official terms applied at Nagasaki, ships had to first anchor at Iōjima—the furthermost island of the outer harbor, beyond sight of the city center—and await permission to proceed.[2] Stirling, whose primary military mission of locating elusive Russian vessels required alacrity, demanded the complete opening of all the water spaces of Nagasaki and the right to freely enter the harbor without first requesting permission from the magistrate. To prove his point, when he returned the following year to ratify the convention, he forced his way into the inner harbor. This provocation demonstrated the domainal harbor guards' inability to enforce port restrictions on British steamships and then prompted the discussion of amending Nagasaki harbor regulations for foreign ships to mirror the more generous arrangements of the newly opened port of Hakodate.

On reentering Nagasaki in May of 1855, Rear Admiral Stirling soon moved his entire squadron to the inner Nagasaki harbor, without a domainal response, on the grounds that weather conditions made the

2. Nagasaki port regulations as recorded in "Minutes of a Communication between the Governor of Nagasaki and Rear Admiral Sir James Stirling," *British and Foreign State Papers*, pp. 716–17.

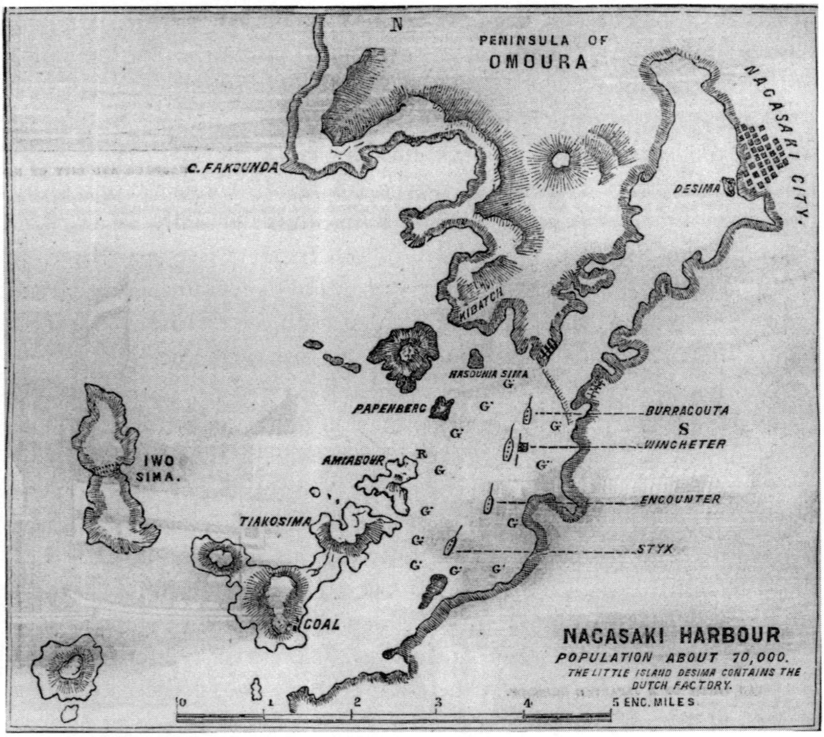

FIGURE 5.2 Stirling's 1854 visit to Nagasaki, lithograph, reproduced from the *Illustrated London News*, Jan. 13, 1855, p. 43.

mooring at Iōjima, in the outer harbor, unsafe. He attempted to make this practice of automatically proceeding to the inner harbor standard protocol. Stirling sent a revised draft of port regulations to the magistrate proposing that when weather conditions required, British ships be allowed to enter the inner harbor without having to undergo questioning.[3] After the magistrate rejected this amendment, Stirling traveled to Hakodate to investigate port regulations there in the hopes that they were more favorable and might be used for negotiating leverage in Nagasaki.[4] Hakodate port regulations did not distinguish between an inner and an

3. Beasley, *Great Britain and the Opening of Japan*, p. 133; *Dai Nihon komonjo: Bakumatsu gaikoku kankei monjo*, 10:192, 308.

4. Beasley, *Great Britain and the Opening of Japan*, p. 136.

outer harbor since its natural geography created a single concave basin, surrounded on three sides by land; it had no sea islands similar to those of Nagasaki dotting Hakodate's harbor entrance.[5] Stirling employed this finding to argue for the creation of universal, trans-port regulations, specifically ones that would follow Hakodate's favorable use of the term "whole port," for "open port," interpreted to mean foreign vessels' free movement in all water spaces of the harbor.[6] In response, the Nagasaki magistrates insisted that Nagasaki's rules of engagement historically distinguished between rules for the inner and outer harbors and therefore should "naturally" continue.[7] The magistrates also underscored that each open port at that time (Shimoda, Uraga, Hakodate, and Nagasaki) had its own local regulations, suggesting that even if the Nagasaki custom would not supply the template for other ports on this issue, they would not necessarily use Hakodate as a model either.[8] The magistrates may have clung tenaciously to precedent in part because they were career bureaucrats, steeped in a political culture of rule by custom. From a more practical angle, they likely wanted to tightly control the movement of foreign vessels to prevent British and Russian ships from attacking each other in Japanese waters and sparking collateral Japanese damage.

Once the Japanese rejected Stirling's proposal to adopt more favorable Hakodate regulations, the British admiral then drafted what he termed a "liberal explanation" of the Nagasaki restrictions. This version was informed by his knowledge of the absence of the distinction between an inner harbor and an outer harbor at Hakodate, and by resistance. He proposed a compromise in saying that the "[treaty] *opens the whole and every part of those Ports*, but Ships must be guided in anchoring by the Directions of the Local Government" [emphasis added].[9] Despite the conciliatory tone of this language, at a later meeting, Stirling threatened to bring his entire force past the rowboat chain, which sat in the harbor at the ready to block aggressive British movements, if the magistrate did

5. British commodore Charles Elliot observed that Hakodate had relatively few regulations, the most onerous of which was the requirement to buy supplies through local authorities. Grainger, *The First Pacific War*, p. 94.

6. *Dai Nihon komonjo: Bakumatsu gaikoku kankei monjo*, 12:451, 480.

7. Ibid., 12:480.

8. Ibid., 12:304.

9. Beasley, *Great Britain and the Opening of Japan*, p. 137.

not amend the port regulations according to his scheme. Under duress, the magistrate agreed to "the whole and every part" clause, but only upon confirmation by officials in Edo. Stirling left, apparently satisfied that he had won.

Stirling's successor, Rear Admiral Sir Michael Seymour, arrived in Nagasaki in the fall of 1856 to retrieve the shogunate's reply to the request for more generous port regulations. Seymour immediately announced his intention to proceed toward the city center from the outer harbor in order to show that he expected the shogunate to grant British requests for freedom of movement. He then gave the magistrate one hour to remove the rowboats, which were strung across the water at the main batteries of Tomachi and Nishidomari, blocking his path. Despite Nabeshima Naomasa's midcentury improvements to artillery on the Nagasaki outer-harbor islands, domainal troops continued to employ a rowboat blockade of oared vessels as a second line of defense. These boats, in effect, created a floating barrier at the entrance to the inner Nagasaki Bay. Seymour, even more forcefully than Stirling had, exposed the folly of this measure in an age of steam power.

Commanding the British six-gun paddle steamer HMS *Barracouta*, Seymour overran the rowboat chain, capsizing two vessels of Saga domain, which was the on-duty defense force in Nagasaki that year.[10] According to John Tronson, an officer accompanying the British mission, the episode occurred as follows:

> Steaming at a fair rate, onward we went; the connecting chain between two of the junks snapped asunder when we touched it; then the lower yard caught the masts of the junks on each side. The junk on the port side tottered, struggled, heeled over, and went down, soldiers, armament and all. We dragged the other, attached by its mast, to the yard abreast of the Dutch Factory, then cast off the *Pique* and returned for the flagship [*HMS Winchester*].[11]

The Saga ship *Wakatake-maru* emerged undamaged, but its *Sumida-maru*, which had been rammed on the starboard side, was sunk. Neither side

10. The audacity of the British was all the more shocking because it was the first encounter of Nagasaki residents with a steamship. In his memoirs, a British consul at Hakodate called this a "very plucky thing" to do. Hodgson, *A Residence at Nagasaki and Hakodate*, p. 187.

11. Tronson, *Personal Narrative of a Voyage to Japan*, p. 398.

disputed these results. The primary disagreements that did arise were between the magistrate and officials from Saga domain, whose rowboats had been destroyed, over how they should resolve the incident.

In an apparent attempt to exonerate its defensive forces, which had failed to stop the *Barracouta*'s advance, Saga domain underscored the belligerent and illegal nature of British actions. Saga officials, for example, repeatedly claimed that the British had stolen a pennant of Ogi, an affiliated Saga domain, from the vessel *Wakatake-maru*.[12] The magistrate did not directly address this claim, although he did send the British a letter requesting that they desist from such aggressive behavior in the future. In an attempt to keep the peace with a treaty nation, he immediately invited the twenty-eight-member crew of the *Barracouta* to his residence to discuss the matter. Saga officials lamented the preparation of a "grand banquet" for foreigners who had committed "illegal acts." At the same time, they recognized that the domain's role as a special guard for the magistrate during this reception provided an opportunity to recover their martial pride.[13]

In choosing to de-emphasize Saga's complaints, the magistrate prioritized his role as chief Tokugawa diplomatic officer in Nagasaki over his responsibilities as de jure commander of local defenses. The magistrate minimized the material damage of this episode in the interests of promoting goodwill in treaty negotiations. His diplomatic efforts seemingly worked. Within two weeks, the British delivered a letter of apology to the magistrate for their "mistake." But Saga did not feel it had received the backing it deserved. The magistrate's failure to address the purported theft of the Ogi pennant, or to offer repairs for the sunk and damaged boats, prompted Saga officials to continue vilifying the British in domainal documents for years to come.[14]

This 1856 *Barracouta* episode, although seldom mentioned in history texts, was the most aggressive and destructive behavior by foreigners in Nagasaki since the kidnapping of Dutch secretaries by the British in the 1808 *Phaeton* incident. Comparing the two incidents reveals important changes in the logic of coastal defense across the first half of the nineteenth century, the most significant being domains' exemption from punishment for defensive shortcomings. In the 1808 episode, seven Saga retainers committed suicide to claim responsibility for failing to defend

12. Hideshima, *Saga han kaigunshi*, pp. 104–113.
13. Ibid., pp. 104, 106.
14. "Letter of apology," *Ishin shiryō kōyō*, AN056-0834 (1856/8/5).

the harbor. Beyond these acts of contrition and duty, the shogunate placed the daimyo, Nabeshima Narinao (Naomasa's father), under house arrest for 100 days since he held ultimate responsibility for military oversight. Further, to punish the entire domainal population for its collective negligence in securing Nagasaki, the shogunate levied commercial restrictions on Saga as a whole. As the penalties in 1808 made clear, the punitive burden of failure fell on Saga domain.[15]

During the 1856 incident, almost half a century later, Saga was again the on-duty domain. This time, however, the shogunate assigned responsibility for negligence to only a handful of individuals instead of the collective domain. The magistrate did remonstrate Saga domain generally for negligence in preparing for emergency incidents.[16] But the Saga lord, Naomasa, and vassals escaped censure with the exception of the commander of the Saga harbor guard, Nabeshima Samasuke, who was sentenced to thirty days of house arrest.[17] Samasuke proved a convenient scapegoat to allow Saga domain, and the shogunate, to quietly deflect responsibility from themselves for the incident. While the magistrate of 1808 committed suicide in expectation of criminal proceedings against him, in 1856 the magistrate avoided taking responsibility. In the magistrate's 1856 letter of reproach to Saga, he exonerated himself, and the domain, by noting that the high speed of a steam vessel presented unprecedented difficulties. This resolution preserved unsullied the reputation of the magistrate, as well as that of the Saga lord, Naomasa.

So why was the assignment of responsibility and punishment so different in 1856 than it had been in 1808? The precarious balance of international and domestic relations was key. First, in 1856, the magistrate needed to avoid shogunal reproach to maintain his prestige as he oversaw diplomatic negotiations with the British and other treaty powers in Nagasaki. Second, given Saga's demonstrated leadership in weapons technology, the shogunate could not risk antagonizing its lord, Naomasa, with official rebuke at a moment when it desperately needed his support to arm the broader Tokugawa coastline. At the time of the incident, with treaty negotiations ongoing, most Western powers had not yet officially committed to amicable relations with Japan. Tokugawa fear of attack persisted. Moreover, punishing Saga domain more harshly might have also

15. Wilson, "Tokugawa Defense Redux."
16. Nakano, *Nabeshima Naomasa kōden*, 4:394–95.
17. Ibid., 4:395.

discouraged those domains assigned coastal defense from diligently executing their responsibilities, especially if any failure might be considered a criminal offense. Indeed, the frequency with which domains declined or requested reassignment of defensive duties in the Kansai and Kantō areas during this period suggests that they attempted to avoid responsibilities in locations where they were most likely to confront steam vessels.

Despite Seymour's efforts, the wording of the port restrictions had not changed by the time the Ansei Treaties were signed two years later, in 1858. When Britain's high commissioner for China, Sir James Bruce, eighth Earl of Elgin, traveled to Nagasaki on his way to sign the Treaty of Amity and Commerce, the captain ignored all Japanese boats and officials on the way into the harbor, just as Seymour had done, but without capsizing domainal vessels.[18] The British adopted a cavalier and aggressive attitude, selectively interpreting port regulations to their advantage. Tokugawa officials there did not challenge them this time. The captain followed a similar course of action when approaching Edo weeks later. The HMS *Furious*, Elgin's vessel, passed Uraga and defied precedent at that harbor by moving up the channel toward Edo without stopping for inspection as protocol required. The paddle frigate, a "steamer of 400 horse power," traveled so fast that none of the Japanese officials' vessels could intercept it. Elgin's secretary, Laurence Oliphant, recorded the moment: "Two boat-loads of two-sworded officials pushed off in haste as we steamed up, and by gesticulations and gestures of entreaty, invited us to stop; but we passed on, utterly indifferent to their signals; and as we left them far behind, we could still discern them tugging hopelessly after us."[19] In an era when the shogunate was still wary of trusting Western nations to follow the contractual terms of trade and foreign relations outlined in treaties, these instances of British disregard for Tokugawa rules of conduct validated Japanese concerns over defending themselves against potentially hostile acts by the treaty powers. Fortifying harbors to be able to mount reasonable artillery resistance against the fast and agile steamships emerged as an important defensive strategy, even as the shogunate delegated these projects to the domains.

18. Osborn, *A Cruise in Japanese Waters*, p. 29. He served Seymour aboard the HMS *Furious*.

19. Beasley, *Great Britain and the Opening of Japan*, p. 186; Oliphant, *Narrative of the Earl of Elgin's Mission*, p. 91.

Western Concerns over Nagasaki Batteries

As the meaning of the term "open" was standardized across ports, and ships of all treaty nations gained the privilege of proceeding directly to Nagasaki's inner harbor without first confirming their provenance, domainal fortifications close to the city proper became increasingly important. Saga domain's 1862 construction of firing platforms at its residence compound in the heart of Nagasaki first reflected this change. Two years later, in 1864, the principal inner-harbor batteries previously located at Tomachi and Nishidomari (whose structures had been demolished the year before) were moved to Inasa, across a narrow finger of water from the city center. By 1866, the batteries at Kōzaki, Naginata Iwa, Kage no O, and Koyagishima, all fortifications in the outer harbor, were dismantled to privilege defense of the city core. Yet it was precisely during this period in the early 1860s, as Western fear of attack by xenophobic Japanese escalated and increasing numbers of foreigners resided in the port cities, that consular representatives began to protest the construction of additional coastal fortifications by domains.

The shogunate was aware of these defense initiatives and supported them, even if this backing was not apparent to Westerners. Cognizant of the mounting costs of Nagasaki defenses to Fukuoka and Saga domains in this era of increasing foreign water traffic, the shogunate extended the domains successive favors to compensate their continued assistance with coastal defense. In the late 1850s and early 1860s, the shogunate granted repeated favors to these domains. It forgave both domains a 50,000-*ryō* loan that had been extended to refortify the gun batteries at Iōjima and Kaminoshima. Saga domain received an indefinite release from Tokugawa corvée labor obligations. The shogunate excused both domains from providing boats to transport the Nagasaki magistrate from Shimonoseki and Kokura to Osaka, as had been custom. Domainal troops posted in Nagasaki received standing permission to leave in the ninth month, even if the Dutch merchant ships had not departed, as was usual. The shogunate also released these two domains from dispatching reinforcements to Nagasaki when ships of treaty nations arrived. These increasingly generous exemptions from military service, and monetary compensations, signaled the desperation of Tokugawa officials to maintain domainal cooperation in coastal defenses given the growing water traffic in treaty port Nagasaki.[20]

20. *Ishin shiryō kōyō*, AN122-0629 (1858/9/25) and MA006-0706 (1860/3/29).

The increasing fortification of Nagasaki proper, however, was not all driven by a sense of external threat. The Japanese also armed the port city to ensure the public safety of a population of roughly 30,000 during a period of escalating anti-Western violence in urban areas. In a geopolitical environment where treaty nations constantly scrutinized one another's motives, the Tokugawa decision to prioritize security of the inner Nagasaki harbor concerned Western diplomats who feared Japanese might use the fortifications in and around the city to attack foreign residents. Fears of attack existed on both sides and were not unfounded.

By early 1863, tensions with Britain over the September 1862 Namamugi Incident, in which Satsuma domain samurai attacked and killed the British merchant Charles Richardson, were rising. The increasing mobilization of troops on the Nagasaki hillsides reflected the persistent fear that Nagasaki, and not the Satsuma domain seaside castle town of Kagoshima, would be the British navy's target for retribution.[21] As a result, the Nagasaki magistrate ordered Saga domain to transfer cannon from Iōjima (in the outer harbor) to both the domain's Nagasaki residence at Daikoku-machi and to Inasa area (both located on the inner-harbor perimeter). Presumably this transfer of firepower would assuage the fears of local residents and protect the city from potential shelling by Western gunboats. Although Nagasaki remained at peace, a retaliatory attack by the British did materialize in Kagoshima later that year, heightening mutual distrust throughout the realm. Anticipating an assault on Nagasaki, many Western residents, such as Dutch adviser and missionary Guido Verbeck, fled to Shanghai, leaving the foreign settlement a "ghost town."[22] The secretary of the British legation in Japan, Edward St. John Neale, contested Saga's transfer of arms to the magistrate of foreign affairs in Edo and requested that the new inner-harbor weapons be removed.[23] In response, the Nagasaki magistrate argued that Neale's suspicions undermined the professed "amity" of the treaties. Moreover, he insisted, these preparations were for the security of all nations.[24]

Not only the transfer of weapons, but also the construction of new domainal shore batteries, perpetuated this conflict. The following year, just as the Western powers were planning to shell Shimonoseki in retaliation for unexpected attacks on their vessels by Chōshū batteries, Saga

21. Cobbing, *Kyushu: Gateway to Japan*, p. 223.
22. Ibid.
23. Hara, *Bakumatsu kaibōshi no kenkyū*, pp. 56–57.
24. For Neale's title, see *The Foreign Office List*, pp. 126–27.

domain began constructing a new battery at Inasa, against the foreign counsels' continued protest. Apparently fearing a Western coalition naval attack on Nagasaki similar to that mounted against Chōshū, shogunal officials ordered the magistrate to postpone construction. To the Western counsels' protestations that the new batteries threatened foreign residents, Saga—as on-duty domain—countered that since Western warships entering Nagasaki harbor carried lethal armaments, an absence of new shore batteries would require the Japanese to prevent foreign ships from anchoring in the inner harbor. Furthermore, altering the nation's defensive installations because of the objections of foreigners would be a "blow to the country's prestige."[25]

Despite these justifications for proceeding with construction, Rutherford Alcock, first British minister in Japan, sent a letter to the shogunate with two demands. First, he requested removal of the fence around the Nagasaki foreign compound, which had originally been proposed by the Japanese to better protect the residents from hostile attacks by violent anti-Western factions, but which he considered to violate treaty conditions. Second, he demanded that battery construction cease. Alcock intimated that foreign residents might perceive the goal of the battery project as hostile, rather than protective. In support of Alcock, the French consul, Léon Roches, and the Dutch consul, Dirk de Graeff van Polsbroek, sent similar letters. In the end, Alcock used a convenient reversal of the Japanese logic, suggesting that the Saga lord, Nabeshima, might launch cannonballs at foreigners just as the samurai in Chōshū had done in shelling Western vessels at Shimonoseki.[26] His persistence paid off, and by the end of the month, construction at Inasa halted. Alcock's rationale revealed the growing Western understanding that domainal control of shoreline batteries, while allowing the shogunate to focus on diplomacy as the first line of defense, would continue to undercut the cooperative tenor of state-to-state negotiations if renegade domains, acting contrary to shogunal policy, threatened foreign vessels. The shogunate's control of the monopoly on violence seemed momentarily resurgent after its ability to rally coalition domainal troops to rout Chōshū loyalist forces earlier that year. Yet as daimyo were increasingly called to deploy forces to quell escalating peasant protests, subdue masterless samurai

25. Nakano, *Nabeshima Naomasa kōden*, 5:444–49.

26. Letter written in Yokohama by Alcock, *Ishin shiryo kōyō*, GE050-0154 (1864/11/8).

(*rōnin*), and guard barrier points, they became, as Conrad Totman has observed of the mid-1860s, "less obedient than ever before and less capable or less willing" to support the Tokugawa.[27] The shogunate had long anticipated the need to provide special compensation to domains to ensure their assistance with coastal defense as the Western presence increased, particularly in central Japan. To understand the significance of these changes in the Kantō region during the treaty-port era, we must first examine territorial perquisites that emerged there in the late 1840s and early 1850s to reward domains newly assigned to defense duties.

New Territorial Arrangements in the Kantō

Whereas developments in treaty port Nagasaki reflected the influence of domainal coastal defense projects on diplomatic relations, troop deployments to the Kantō shoreline revealed important revisions to the military contract between domains and the shogunate. From the 1840s, as detailed in the previous chapter, the shogunate anticipated a heightened Western naval presence in the Edo region and began to grant domains charged with coastal defense there new forms of compensation, including cash payments and new territorial possessions known as "entrusted lands" (*azukari dokoro*). These perquisites far outstripped those previously offered to Saga and Fukuoka domains for Nagasaki defense service, revealing a shift in the structure of military relationships. Previously based on customary, reciprocal obligation, they were now undergirded by financial compensation. Shogunal political legitimacy explicitly rested on the ability to extract military service from its daimyo, freely rendered with the possibility—although not the guarantee—of some modest benefit (such as release from a single corvée labor project). The broadening expectation from the late 1840s of permanent, increasingly generous financial compensation in exchange for military service revealed the collapse of a 200-year-plus martial premise of the political order. Obligatory domainal military service to the shogunate, a fundamental component of the original Tokugawa political settlement in the early seventeenth century, was no longer discharged primarily out of a sense of duty. In effect, samurai posted to the shores of the Kantō region had now become soldiers for hire.

27. Totman, *The Collapse of the Tokugawa Bakufu*, p. 203.

This process of the shogunate providing the domains discharging maritime duty with augmented incentives to execute their military responsibilities evolved incrementally from the 1840s as Kantō defenses first expanded to respond to an accelerating sense of threat. Within a decade, the practice penetrated wide swaths of the main island of Honshū. Domains had intermittently defended the Kantō coast in the early nineteenth century following the 1824 landing of a British whaler at Mito, but the environment of alarm soon abated, leading to the withdrawal of all troops except a skeleton crew. Only in 1842, to increase security in the region following the withdrawal of the "shoot to repel with no second thought" order, did the shogunate replace the lapsed defense system that had been managed by the Uraga magistrate—who possessed no troops of his own—with one led by two local domains: Oshi domain on the Bōsō Peninsula, forming the northern border of Uraga Bay, and Kawagoe domain on the southern, Sagami side.[28] The region's security gained heightened importance following the 1846 visit of the French Indo-China squadron to the Ryūkyūs and the arrival of U.S. commodore James Biddle at Uraga the same year. The shogunate promptly reinforced both the Bōsō Peninsula, by adding Aizu troops to those of Oshi domain, and the Miura shores bordering Uraga Bay on the south, by adding forces from Hikone domain to those of Kawagoe. The Tokugawa monopoly on violence, while still the purview of the warrior class, was gradually extended to an increasing number of domains, their retainers, and even in many cases the peasant classes, reconfiguring what once had been a monopoly of the few as a monopoly of the many.

These expansions of coastal defense in the late 1840s began to transform the military relationship between the shogunate and domains through the granting of "trust lands" (*azukari dokoro*) to daimyo as compensation for their defensive duty.[29] This move reflected a reversal of the defensive logic driving the aborted 1843 *agechi rei*, in which the Tokugawa had attempted to centralize control of defense in the capital region by forcing lords to exchange their land holdings within ten *ri* (roughly twenty-five miles) of Edo for low-yielding shogunal lands in other parts of the archipelago. As Harold Bolitho argues in his analysis of the Tempō Reforms, this strategy made good sense for the maritime

28. *Kanagawa kenshi, tsūshi hen 3, kinsei 2*, p. 1012.

29. "Trust lands" is John Hall's term. See Hall, "The *Bakuhan* System," pp. 169–70.

security of the Tokugawa political center, yet the involved lords, although formally subordinate to the shogun, balked at this incursion into territorial rights that they thought "were inviolable, theirs to be held in perpetuity."[30] Thus, the turn to assign *azukari dokoro* in the Kantō region reflected a change in military tactics: the shogunate would now protect its capital region not by formally converting all of the immediate territory into *tenryō* (Tokugawa lands), as had been the idea with the 1843 edict. Instead, it would provide incentives, through the granting of land rights, to lords—who were wealthier, and controlled larger retainer bands, than the generally small lords of the Kantō—to defend lands of the capital region as if they were the lords' own.

Originally, trust lands had been shogunal territories that sat at a distance from Edo. Lords near the lands were assigned to administer them instead of a more conventional shogunal proxy, such as a local intendant (*daikan*), as a cost savings to the shogunate. By 1839, roughly 18 percent of shogunal lands were managed in this way by twenty-seven domains, primarily in the areas north of Echigo and south of Mimasaka at the extreme reaches of the main island of Honshū.[31] In these areas, proximate daimyo shouldered "caretaker services" such as gathering taxes, settling disputes, and prosecuting criminals, although the degree to which they followed shogunal instructions for their duties varied.[32] From mid-century, however, these lands were granted increasingly close to the capital, not primarily to outsource their administrative oversight, but to compensate distant domains for coastal defense service in the Kantō region.

With its 1847 appointment to coastal defense duty along Uraga Bay, Hikone precipitated a new category of trusteeship for domains assigned coastal defense responsibilities, a class of ownership close to outright sovereign control that provided them with increased benefits for their military service. Hikone was the first domain granted the right to manage shogunal trust lands "as if they were domainal lands" (*shiryō dōyō* or *shiryō*

30. Bolitho, "The Tempō Crisis," p. 154.

31. Totman, *Politics in the Tokugawa Bakufu*, p. 67. Totman suggests that nearly half of the 2 million *koku* of shogunal lands in these areas were *azukari dokoro*. Given that the shogun's own landholdings comprised roughly 4 million *koku*, these areas in the northern and southern extremes of the island of Honshū constituted the majority of *azukari dokoro* territory. Totman emphasizes the variation in shogunal ability to enforce the daimyo's execution of its instructions. Harafuji lists twenty-seven domains in 1839. See Harafuji, *Daimyō azukari dokoro no kenkyū*, pp. 169–70.

32. Bolitho, "The *Han*," p. 205.

dōzen) for defense-related purposes. This new classification emerged as the rationale for granting domains the management of trust lands shifted, from that of a tool to aid the shogunate in managing territory to that of a mechanism to assist (and reward) domains in executing maritime defense. Following Hikone's appointment to coastal defense duties, the shogunate granted the domain 14,600 *koku* of lands in Kamakura, Sagami *kuni*, just south of the capital. In turn, the domain was to return an equivalent amount of land to shogunal control from its home territory of Ōmi *kuni*, near Lake Biwa, so that it would not appear to have gained inordinately in new tax revenues or stature (in an increased "assessed domainal income" [*kokudaka*]) with the arrangement. To multiply the benefit of this exchange to the domain, however, these lands in Ōmi, which were first converted into shogunate-administered lands, then reverted to domainal oversight as trust lands throughout which Hikone received rights of "treatment equal to that of domainal lands" (*shiryō dōyō*).[33] Previously this right of de facto domainal control of trust lands had been granted to only four domains—Aizu, Kanazawa, Ōzu, and Shonai—and never to facilitate a military arrangement.[34] Hikone established a precedent for other domains to receive trust lands as compensation for coastal defense duties. Significantly, this precedent began with a *fudai*-class domain, traditionally considered a loyal Tokugawa ally and located relatively close to Edo, before extending to outside (*tozama*) domains as well.

Despite their overall territorial gain, Hikone officials were discontented with the arrangements and sought further compensation for their Kantō military service. Unhappy with surrendering lands that previously belonged to them, they petitioned for the newly designated trust lands in Ōmi *kuni* to revert to full domainal possession. The shogunate granted this request. Hikone then petitioned to gain *shiryō doyō* rights in its Sagami trust lands in the Kantō, which had not originally been permitted. The shogunate granted this as well, in 1851. Furthermore, when the shogunate assigned Hikone additional defense responsibilities in West Uraga the following year, it gave Hikone another 6,000 *koku* of trust lands. This time, the territory carried the *shiryō doyō* prerogative from the beginning.[35]

33. Harafuji, *Daimyō azukari dokoro no kenkyū*, p. 188.
34. Takemoto, "Chōshū han no Sōshū keibi," p. 101.
35. Harafuji, *Daimyō azukari dokoro no kenkyū*, p. 188.

Granting increasingly distant domains significant territory bordering the Kantō shorelines assigned to them to defend reflected the shogun's urgent concern about the capital region's security. This system emerged because of the need to supply troops far from home with lodging, boats, men and horses for labor, and food supplies. In the case of Hikone, which ended up stationing more than 2,000 of its samurai along the Suruga coast, the privileges of administrating this region "as if it were domainal lands" meant it could circulate and use domainal currency (*hansatsu*) on-site.[36] This practice benefited Hikone officials, who could purchase goods without negotiating a separate local currency. Thus, the acquisition of *shiryō dōyō* privilege provided material and financial benefits since the assigned domain could more easily requisition rice, rowers, sentries, or even timber for fortifications from the surrounding population.

While the granting of *shiryō dōyō* privileges for defense purposes was new, the broader practice of entrusting domains with shogunal lands to facilitate the execution of coastal defense was not. In 1672, the shogunate granted the *fudai* lord of Shimabara, Matsudaira Tadafusa, trust lands of 1,300 *koku* in nearby Amakusa (just south of Nagasaki, in neighboring Kumamoto domain) to offset predicted costs of military service in Nagasaki. Even though Shimabara's military contributions were minimal, by the late eighteenth century, the domain's trust territories had increased to 33,000 *koku* of lands in Kyūshū. Legal scholar Harafuji Hiroshi attributes this surprisingly large total to the shogunate's gratitude for Shimabara's decades of service as Tokugawa inspector[37] But rewards were not always commensurate with actual service. Fukuoka and Saga domains certainly offered more significant contributions than Shimabara in Nagasaki, and for generations. At times both domains made exorbitant financial sacrifices. Costs associated with the 1647 mobilization in response to the unexpected arrival of Portuguese vessels, for example, compelled the fiscally strapped Fukuoka daimyo to withhold 10 percent of his retainers' stipends. Given such a record of loyal service, one might expect the shogunate to have given these domains greater compensation, such as Shimabara received for its lesser contributions. After all, Fukuoka

36. Asakawa, "Hikone han no Sōshū keibi," p. 65. Hikone had the largest contribution at 2,000 men. Next was Aizu with 1,397 (1848), followed by Kawagoe at 667 (1852) and Oshi at 97 (1850).

37. This amount was roughly half of Shimabara's assessed income.

and Saga were the defenders of the country's only international port. Yet the shogunate did not.[38] Such a disparity did not appear to be an issue at the time. But once the shogunate began awarding trust lands more freely in the mid-nineteenth century, Saga domain fought for its fair share.

Aware of mid-nineteenth-century defense-related developments in the Kantō, Saga lord Nabeshima Naomasa petitioned the shogunate twice, in 1853 and again in 1860, to convert Amakusa lands and Kyūragi village (Tokugawa land within Saga, administered by the Hida intendant) into Saga's trust territories. The main thrust of his argument concerned the need to control lands where he planned to build a naval base (permission for which was later denied). He also contended that *shiryō dōyō* privileges would facilitate Saga's recruiting of oarsmen for defense vessels and harnessing of the local saltpeter production necessary for gunpowder.[39] The shogunate denied these seemingly reasonable requests.

Maintaining careful control of its lands had always been key to Tokugawa rule. The shogunate had the power to disburse lands in new configurations but did so only after considerable calculation. Edo was apparently reluctant to grant these Kyūshū lands to a domain with a permanent defense responsibility in Nagasaki, meaning that its trusteeship would be in perpetuity. As well, the Amakusa grant (25,000 *koku*) would be well beyond the size of any trust lands in the Kantō. Entrusting lands in the capital region was in many ways a simpler matter than doing so in Kyūshū. The defense responsibilities in central Japan rotated frequently, presumably to prevent domains from forming a substantial military power base close to the capital city. Consequently, no single domain would become entrenched as a trustee of shogunal territory the way Saga, with its constant duty in Nagasaki, might. Without doubt, the shogunate felt gratitude for the response of Saga and Fukuoka domains in various defensive emergencies in Nagasaki. Yet, it reserved the status and financial benefits of trust-land management primarily for long-standing, allied domains, and not *tozama*-class domains, as were Saga and Fukuoka. This preferential treatment persisted until the 1850s.[40]

38. Harafuji, *Daimyō azukari dokoro no kenkyū*, pp. 36–38.

39. Kihara, "Bakumatsuki Sagahan no bakuryō azukari."

40. Of the ten largest *azukari dokoro* holdings in the mid-nineteenth century, only one was entrusted to a *tozama* domain, Yonezawa, whose holdings ranked just behind those of Aizu and Ogaki domains. The remainder were managed by *kamon* and *fudai* domains, although primarily by *fudai*. Harafuji, *Daimyō azukari dokoro no*

These developments reveal how the military contract between shogunate and domain had been evolving years before the arrival of Perry in 1853, including increasing compensation in land and cash for military service in the Kantō area. For example, in 1851, the shogunate forgave Oshi and Kawagoe domains, charged with defending Edo Bay, loans of 15,000 *ryō* and granted newly appointed coastal defenders Hikone and Aizu domains 10,000 *ryō* each. Domainal commitment to maritime duty, however, varied. Kawagoe and Aizu were diligent, Hikone and Oshi less so. Hikone balked at its assignment to guard Edo Bay, in part because it also held the weighty post of defender of the imperial capital of Kyoto. In 1851, the domain proposed that defense of the Kantō be assigned to large castle-holding (*kunimochi*) lords, which its daimyo was not, implying that the shogunate instead marshal the greater human and material capital at their disposal. Soon after making this proposal, however, as Hiroshi Mitani has observed, the domain distributed the extravagant sum of "150,000 *ryō* among its retainers, towns, and temples to celebrate Ii Naosuke's investiture as daimyo." This largesse suggests the domain's proposal was less about advocating a superior model of military organization and more about protecting its own coffers.[41]

Perry's arrival in 1853 catalyzed a full-blown security crisis, and the need to mobilize the resources and manpower of larger, wealthier domains became clear. The shogunate soon decided to grant trust lands to outside (*tozama*) domains, marking a seismic shift in late Tokugawa political culture. It began organizing Kantō-area defenses in accord with Hikone's idea. When Chōshū domain replaced Hikone on Edo Bay in 1853, it received trust lands equivalent to those held by Hikone (20,686 *koku*), with the same right of *shiryō dōyō*. Chōshū then distributed the burden of service among its branch domains (Chōfu, Kiyomatsu, Tokuyama, and Iwakuni), as had Saga in Nagasaki and as would Kumamoto in the Kantō.[42] The existence of branch domains, among which the primary

kenkyū, pp. 170, 599–602. Of course, not all domains embraced the management of shogunal trust lands as a privilege, but rather as a burden, such as Kanazawa, which asked to have its trust territory jurisdiction reclassified as *shiryō dōyō* because of its inability to resolve infighting among peasants across domainal/*azukari dokoro* lines.

41. Mitani, *Escape from Impasse*, pp. 67, 71. The domain had already requested a transfer of troops from Sagami to an area closer to Edo to lessen the military burden on the domain.

42. Asakawa, "Hikone han no Sōshū keibi," p. 65.

domain could distribute its responsibility, was likely part of the shogunate's calculus in selecting domains for maritime duty.[43] Outside domains were now not only assigned defense duty in the capital region. Instead of being delegated these responsibilities as an onerous and uncompensated burden, they were rewarded for their service. This development signaled the dire defensive concerns of the Tokugawa, who felt forced to accept *tozama* troop mobilizations within an easy march of Edo.

Not only did the shogunate assign Chōshū domain; it assigned three other outside domains the same year—Kumamoto, Okayama, and Yanagawa—to replace the military service of Kawagoe, Aizu, and Oshi in the capital region. Given that only two of these domains, Chōshū and Okayama, were located on the main island of Honshū, this restructuring required massive outlay by the domains for transporting men and supplies. With these assignments, six of the ten largest *tozama* domains in Japan were supplying coastal defense forces far from their home domains.[44] By the end of 1854, as further compensation for their service, the shogunate also granted the Kumamoto and Chōshū lords the ritual privilege of carrying *sanbon-yari* (three ceremonial spears) in alternate attendance processions and accelerated the process for increasing the court rank of the Yanagawa lord.[45] Together, these appointments demonstrate the enduring ability of the shogunate to elicit military service from powerful daimyo. At the same time, entrusting several of the largest domainal militaries in Japan with the security of the capital region suggests the government's desperation. The shogunate now felt imperiled. The protection of the Tokugawa by allied, but numerically inferior, forces of hereditary and collateral domains that had been leveraged to that point was no longer sufficient.

As these outside (*tozama*) domains began to discharge their Kantō service, fiscal hardship, and not merely avarice, prompted them to repeatedly petition the shogunate for permission to more directly manage,

43. Takemoto, "Chōshū han no Sōshū keibi," p. 104. Kumamoto, assigned in the same year, would also benefit from distributing its defensive burden among its two branch domains.

44. These were Sendai (with duty in Ezo), Kumamoto, Fukuoka, Chōshū, Saga, and Okayama.

45. Harafuji, *Daimyō azukari dokoro no kenkyū*, pp. 188–89. Ornamental spears were an important marker of social status in daimyo processions, with the shogun's retinue carrying five, the *gosanke* houses four, and the following elite lords, generally with a *kokudaka* of 300,000 or greater, three (*sanbonyari*).

or to increase the size of, trust lands. During the first year of their service, in 1853, Kumamoto sent 1,691 troops to the Kantō shores. Chōshū sent 1,638, Okayama 850, and Yanagawa 593, for a total of 4,772 soldiers (not counting some porters and oarsmen).[46] That Kumamoto domain dispatched the greatest number of troops is not surprising since it was the largest of the four domains and had been a candidate for defender of Nagasaki in the mid-seventeenth century. Yet it was also the farthest away, almost 600 miles south in Kyūshū. This hardship of distance prompted it to continually ask for increases in its trust lands during its maritime defense tenure. Within a year, the domain complained that it could not obtain enough materials and labor in the original trust lands to effectively execute duty and so requested additional lands. The shogunate approved an increase of 2,500 *koku* additional lands. But when Kumamoto asked for an extra portion of the local rice harvest, ostensibly to feed its resident troops, the request was denied.[47] Two years later, in 1856, Kumamoto used another tactic in requesting an increase, arguing that its trust territory was smaller than that of Chōshū, Okayama, or Yanagawa. This time the shogunate acquiesced and then granted an additional 10,000 *koku*. Kumamoto's concern about offsetting its mounting defense expenditures was legitimate. Its first assignment alone had led to 300,000 *ryō* in loans, and by the end of the first year of duty, the domain had promulgated a retrenchment edict (*kenyaku rei*), to be in effect for five years.[48]

For the short term, these domains did not mount a collective petition for the abolition of, or diminution in, alternate attendance duties—a parallel manifestation of military obligation to the shogun—as Fukuoka and Saga had received for Nagasaki service. Yet for the domains of far western Japan now charged with Kantō defenses, the associated costs of these annual daimyo processions to the Tokugawa capital could monopolize "as much as fifty to seventy-five percent" or more of their cash revenue. Lessening this symbolic martial burden of fealty would have been an easy way to help the domains economize and devote resources instead to active-duty military service on the shorelines.[49] In this initial

46. Ibid., p. 189. When appointed in 1847, Hikone sent 2,000 men.

47. Ibid., p. 191. Details of this petition are in the *Ishin shiryō koyō*, AN143-0925 (1859/5/21).

48. Harafuji, *Daimyō azukari dokoro no kenkyū*, p. 190.

49. Vaporis, *Tour of Duty*, p. 2.

period of escalating unease about the Western presence, however, the shogunate likely wanted to ensure the yearly presence of the great lords in Edo so that they could participate in discussion of Tokugawa foreign policy. As well, the institution of alternate attendance was one of the last vestiges of the early Tokugawa ability to control the behavior of its lords. Its continuation until 1862 revealed that only a decade after Perry's arrival did the shogunate finally view the resentments created by this mechanism as greater than its benefits to stability.

In keeping with the long-standing arrangement of pairing Fukuoka and Saga domains for alternating in Nagasaki, defense of the Kantō also mandated two sets of partner domains. In the five years from 1847 to 1853, the military capacity in the Kantō region increased significantly. The combined official assessed productive capacity (*kokudaka*) of the newly appointed domains in 1853 marked a 69 percent increase over that of 1847 (rising from 790,000 *koku* to 1,333,000 *koku*). The collective military potential now surpassed (at least when extrapolated from wealth in productive capacity) that of the Fukuoka-Saga pairing, which had approximated the combined *kokudaka* of the domains assigned Kantō duty in 1847. These figures quantify how the shogunate now prioritized the security of the Edo region over that of Nagasaki.

The shogunate's heightened sense of peril from the late 1840s is palpable in the granting of these new forms of compensation to the domains for military service. The perceived need to secure the immense stretches of the Kantō shoreline that these arrangements facilitated, however, gradually diminished with the opening of the treaty ports in 1858. Maritime security shifted from defending the Tokugawa capital shoreline at large to instead now focus almost exclusively on the treaty ports to ensure a safe environment for Western trade. In the Kantō, this core site was the port of Yokohama.

Guarding Yokohama

Once the shogunate agreed to open Yokohama to Western trade, previous efforts to fortify the Edo region at large redirected to instead defend this single port. After signing the Treaty of Amity and Commerce with the United States in 1858, senior councillor Ii Naosuke dispatched his newly assigned magistrates of foreigners (*gaikoku bugyō*) to survey ground for a new port at Yokohama. Yokohama and the surrounding villages at that time were part of Kanazawa domain, which was held by a *fudai* lord.[50] The foreign magistrate's orders to survey this area meant the lord would have to return this territory to the shogunate. The original goal of converting Yokohama into shogunal lands was to facilitate centralized control of foreign affairs, including defense and the mobilization of coalition forces without violating the military sovereignty of a local domain. Yet the reality of implementation over the course of the following decade revealed that commercial and diplomatic interests soon took precedence over security concerns, which were left to the domains.

This deliberate partitioning, and continued devolution of, defensive responsibilities to the domains was a conscious choice by the shogunate so that its officials could instead devote the majority of their attention to the intricacies of treaty negotiation. The amicable relationships initiated with the 1858 treaties resulted in a general decrease in fear of foreign attack. So even though the Kanagawa magistrate, a position created in mid-1859, officially oversaw trade, diplomacy, and security in the new port, in practice he devoted most of his efforts to the first two issues and only minimal attention to coordinating defenses. Port magistrates, whose principal role in external relations before 1855 had been defense, now increasingly focused their energies on regulating commerce and assisting with diplomatic negotiations instead. This change had already occurred in Nagasaki, as seen in the resolution of the Seymour Incident, where the magistrate privileged new Tokugawa state relations with the British over his long-standing political relations with Saga domain.

Diminishing shogunal focus on maritime security echoed in other positions as well. The abolition of the post of coastal defense officer (*kaibō gakari*), which had overseen maritime defense since 1845, exemplified this transition. Ii Naosuke refashioned this position into one called the office of magistrate of foreigners (*gaikoku bugyō*) in 1858. The new title—and revised administrative purview—minimized military affairs in the interest of nurturing commercial relations.[51] All of these magistrates of foreigners concurrently held the post of Kanagawa magistrate.[52] Since the charge of this newly created shogunal position was to "break the

50. Auslin, *Negotiating with Imperialism*, p. 48. As Auslin clarifies, this was the Kanazawa of Musashi Province and not the castle town of Kaga domain.

51. Nagao, "Ansei ki kaibōgakari no seidoshi teki kōsatsu," p. 53.

52. See chart of *kaibō gakari* in Masato, "Bakumatsu gaikō ni okeru shomondai to kaibōgakari," p. 55.

influence of the maritime defense officials over the formulation of foreign policy," as Michael Auslin has observed, in Yokohama, diplomatic issues soon took precedence over military matters in the magistrates' administration of the harbor.[53]

Despite the switch in administrative priorities of shogunal officials, Yokohama could not remain completely undefended and still project the military foundations of Tokugawa power, even if Western diplomats increasingly understood the limitations of this claim to martial supremacy. In preparing for the opening of the port, the shogunate initially assigned defense to two hereditary (*shimpan*) domains.[54] Fukui took responsibility for the area south of the harbor while Iyo Matsuyama domain, from Shikoku, took the area to the north. The year prior to this assignment, Matsuyama had constructed a modest battery at Namiki, in Kanagawa, to improve its capacity in guarding the nearby Kanagawa post station of the Tōkaidō. Once it held the assignment to guard the Yokohama coastline as well, the domain soon planned an additional shoreline garrison.[55] As the plans for the Kanagawa fortress came together, Fukui also proposed fortifying the Benten peninsula of Yokohama, a strategic strip of land jutting northward into the inner harbor.[56] Fukui never completed this project, however, suggesting the shift to a policy of a single, larger fort per harbor, as was also the case in Hakodate. The shogunate was unwilling to support outlays of capital for multiple garrisons at Yokohama when it had to fortify a string of new treaty ports around the larger Japanese coastline. Between them, Kanagawa and Fukui had a *kokudaka* of roughly 500,000 *koku*, only about 60 percent of the total held by Fukuoka and Saga. This discrepancy in wealth—along with the failure of the shogunate to grant Fukui and Matsuyama trust lands—provided fur-

53. Auslin, *Negotiating with Imperialism*, p. 47.

54. *Kanagawa kenshi, tsūshi hen 3, kinsei 2*, p. 1026; *Dai Nihon komonjo: Bakumatsu gaikoku kankei monjo*, 21:771–72. Iyo Matsuyama had also held important supervisory posts for Nagasaki defenses in the mid-seventeenth century. Supposedly, the previous daimyo of Matsuyama, Matsudaira Katsuyoshi, had requested this appointment as a vehicle for establishing his legitimacy in the domain because he was adopted from Satsuma domain. He died before construction of the fort began. "Kanagawa daiba no shimatsu" in *Ishin shiryō kōyō*, MA010—0493 (1860/6/19), p. 39.

55. *Yokohama shishi*, 2:248; *Dai Nihon komonjo: Bakumatsu gaikoku kankei monjo*, 21:871–72.

56. *Yokohama shishi*, 2:248; *Dai Nihon komonjo: Bakumatsu gaikoku kankei monjo*, 23:18–19, 154–55.

ther evidence of diminishing concern about an attack on Yokohama the longer the port remained open.

That construction of the Kanagawa fort did not begin until mid-1859, almost precisely when the port opened to trade, reflected the attenuating preoccupation about assault by foreign vessels in Yokohama (fig. 5.3).[57] Yet the fact that the primary fort for guarding Yokohama was not in fact built at Yokohama proper, but instead sat roughly a mile across the bay at Kanagawa, the original site for the treaty port, meant its management fell all the more decisively in the hands of the domain managing it, Matsuyama, which had long-standing ties to Kanagawa. Two factors justified the fort's location at what from a military standpoint would have been a less than optimal site. First, the choice to build the primary fort where Matusyama already stationed troops to guard the Tōkaidō post station facilitated the domain's oversight of constructing and operating the garrison. Second, a new Kanagawa fort could theoretically shell recalcitrant ships while also housing additional troops to provide extra security as Tōkaidō traffic increased daily due to the port's opening. Finally, the construction of the fort, across the water from Yokohama harbor, was also a conciliatory nod to Western diplomats miffed about the sudden change in their trading wharf's location (which had been originally planned for Kanagawa). A fortress across the bay at Kanagawa could neither threaten nor monitor the resident population of Western diplomats and businessmen in Yokohama the way one positioned in Yokohama might.

Despite the placement of Yokohama harbor's fort on the opposite side of the bay in Kanagawa, foreign opposition soon emerged. As construction advanced, the British consul, Francis Vyse, protested even this distant placement of the battery as a threat to resident Westerners in Yokohama.[58] Regardless, the shogunate completed the project as planned. Three years later, in 1862, the Yokohama magistrate began construction of an additional battery nearer to Yokohama, on the coast at Zogahana. He then instructed Western consulates to order foreign ships to refrain from entering the marked construction zone. The British consul in Yokohama by this time was Charles Winchester, who requested that construction be halted. Rather than have the Japanese increase their military presence, he wanted the security of the foreign residence quarters

57. *Dai Nihon komonjo: Bakumatsu gaikoku kankei monjo*, 22:689–90, 729–30.
58. *Yokohama shishi*, 2:249.

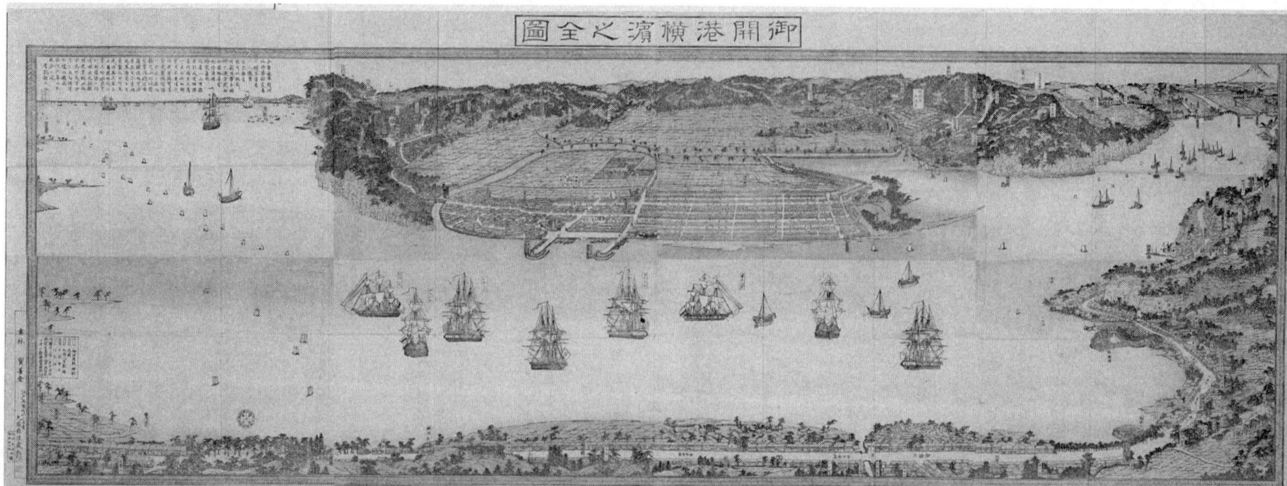

FIGURE 5.3 Hashimoto Sadahide (1807–73), *Complete Picture of the Newly Opened Port of Yokohama*, woodblock print, 1859. Courtesy of the Arthur Sackler Gallery, Smithsonian Institution, Washington, D.C., Gift of Ambassador and Mrs. William Leonhart, S1998.58a–h.

to instead be entrusted to British and French warships. British admiral Augustus Kuper supported this position with the strength of his fleet behind him.[59] Winchester's logic mirrored earlier arguments of the French ambassador Gustave de Bellecourt and French admiral Constant Jaurès who had also insisted—to no avail—that any battery construction in Yokohama constituted a hostile act toward the treaty powers. Their sentiments paralled similar complaints by Western diplomats in Nagasaki. Because of the widespread nature of Western discontent over such projects, the Yokohama magistrate agreed to temporarily shelve the project.

Part of the Yokohama magistrate's original motivation for an additional battery—to assuage the fears of the Japanese population about attack by foreigners in an atmosphere of escalating xenophobia—still held. The escalation worked from both directions, as the resident foreign officials had already been taking extra measures to secure their citizens. Even before construction of this new fortification, the HMS *Renard* had provided a British marine guard in 1861. By 1863, the British navy had stationed a fleet of twelve ships in Yokohama harbor and the following year expanded its presence with the addition of multiple regiments of ground forces. At the same time, the French also stationed a guard in Yokohama.[60] During this period, British, American, French, and Dutch forces on shore and aboard anchored ships numbered as many as 8,000 soldiers at one time in Yokohama.[61] These increases were largely a safeguard against growing fears stemming from rumors of impending attacks on foreigners that began circulating following the Tozenji attacks on the British legation in June of 1862 and the murder of Charles Richardson by Shimazu retainers the following September.[62]

Both Western and Tokugawa concern about defense focused on controlling the escalating violence because of the need to secure the most profitable port in Japan. From 1860, the total value of trade through the port of Yokohama exceeded that of Nagasaki.[63] In 1859, Nagasaki imports and exports had comprised 56.53 percent of the total value of national trade, while those of Yokohama trade were 36.8 percent. Within a single calendar year, the value of Yokohama trade was almost four times that

59. Ibid., 2:249n10, 252.
60. Cortazzi, "Yokohama Frontier Town," p. 199.
61. *Yokohama shishi*, 2:806.
62. Ibid., 2:793.
63. Ibid., 2:548.

of Nagasaki, 76.89 percent to 20.4 percent, and by 1865 the gap had widened to thirteen times. The defense of Yokohama was a new economic priority for the shogunate.[64] Among the Western treaty nations, Britain in particular was interested in the stability of Yokohama because from 1860, British commerce in Yokohama comprised 55 percent of the total value of trade there. Its control of both Yokohama imports and exports increased such that by 1865, its share increased to 85 percent.[65] The importance of securing the Yokohama commercial environment to the British, French, and Dutch governments was evident in their critiques of the efficacy and motives of local Tokugawa fortifications.

Given this reciprocal interest in trade relations, throughout the 1860s, domainal defensive responsibilities increasingly focused on maintaining the public peace in Yokohama and preventing attacks by Japanese on foreigners, rather than standing guard against an attack by Western vessels. Between 1861 and 1865, Yokohama defenses entered a turbulent period during which assigned domains changed from year to year, often serving only a few months at a time. In 1863 alone ten domains contributed troops to guard the city.[66] The flurry of new domainal maritime defense appointments and reassignments would have impeded effective response to a military emergency, but fortunately none occurred.

In fact, the Kanagawa fort did not fire a single defensive shot. The repeated appointment of handfuls of troops from very small domains reveals that military efficacy was not a central concern of the shogunate. In fact, during these very years when Yokohama anticipated the greatest unrest—the decade of the 1860s—the primary function of the Kanagawa fort transformed from defensive infrastructure to site of naval salutes. Even as Western diplomats had interpreted shoreline batteries as a threat to their expatriate populations, they expected, and accepted, some degree of functioning cannon emplacements to fire naval salutes. This diplomatic protocol was particularly important in Yokohama because

64. Ibid., 2:558.

65. Ibid., 2:565. The value of French trade followed at 8 percent, Dutch trade at 4 percent, and American trade at 1.5 percent.

66. Hara, *Bakumatsu kaibōshi no kenkyū*, p. 139. These domains included Hikone (*fudai*, 245,000 *koku*), Iiyama (*fudai*, 20,000 *koku*), Komoro (*fudai*, 15,000 *koku*), Tokushima (*tozama*, 257,000 *koku*), Sabae (*fudai*, 40,000 *koku*), Yunagawa (*fudai*, 14,000 *koku*), Mariyama (*fudai*, 10,000 *koku*), Kishiwada (*fudai*, 53,000 *koku*), Nobeoka (*fudai*, 70,000 *koku*), Koga (*fudai*, 80,000 *koku*), Sakura (*fudai*, 110,000 *koku*), Kakegawa (*fudai*, 60,000 *koku*).

of the succession of foreign dignitaries arriving in this treaty port closest to the Tokugawa political capital at Edo. Japan had long resisted the return of Dutch naval salutes in Nagasaki as a practice at odds with its own traditions, yet by the early 1860s this had become Tokugawa custom as well.[67]

By the mid-1860s, with the movement for treaty revision already under way, the priority for Japanese external relations was not defense but rather achieving status as a diplomatic peer in the eyes of Western states. The retooling of the Kanagawa fort as a site of naval ritual helped achieve this parity. The firing of generic ritual greetings when ships entered harbor soon ended because of the frequency with which treaty boats arrived. The use of salutes became more specific as the shogunate determined set numbers of shots to greet foreign diplomats of various ranks. In early 1862, for example, U.S. consul general Townsend Harris approached shogunal senior councillor Kuze Hirochika to negotiate the firing of salutes from Kanagawa to greet new American diplomats. His request was prompted by the imminent arrival of Robert H. Pruyn as new U.S. minister to Japan. Their discussions resulted in the designation of a specific number of shots for diplomats of various grades, including seventeen for Pruyn because he was classified as an official of the second rank.[68] In mid-1865, the Dutch consul also proposed exchanging naval salutes on the birthdays of heads of state, including that of the Dutch king and shogun. By the following year, discussions began over how to acknowledge the birthday of British queen Victoria with naval salutes as well.[69] Japanese salutes continued to be fired from the land-based battery at Kanagawa, rather than naval vessels (as were those of the Western nations). This reinvention of the use of the Kanagawa fort, as a site of state ritual rather than domainal military agency, revealed a growing shogunal awareness of the significance of adopting Western-style naval protocol in obtaining powers' recognition of Tokugawa sovereignty. By this point in 1865, however, with alternate attendance dissolved and domains only begrudgingly attentive to treaty-port defenses, the repurposing of forts as sites of ritual was a convenient way for the Tokugawa to save face as domains neglected coastal defense obligations

67. The Nagasaki magistrate first received shogunal permission to fire cannon salutes to entering foreign ships in 1857. *Ishin shiryō kōyō*, AN081-0062 (1857/8/6).

68. Ibid., BU034-0149, (1862/3/27).

69. Ibid., KE017-0193 (1865/5/22).

to the shogunate to instead focus on military reforms within their own domains.

The Defense of Hakodate and Ezo

The defense of the northernmost treaty port of Hakodate reflected the shogunate's attempt to reassert central control over the security of a harbor long managed by a single domain, Matsumae. The reclaiming of the port's territory there as shogunal lands, and its fortification, marked the culmination of a coastal defense network truly national in geographical scope, since defended Tokugawa harbors, situated on three of the four main islands, now stretched the length of the Japanese archipelago. Although the shogunate resurrected the post of Hakodate magistrate (suspended since 1822) to provide military coordination, this magistrate's priority quickly became diplomatic relations. The distance of Hakodate from the political center in Edo, and the dispatch of troops there from multiple domains without a clear command structure, meant these forces could largely operate at their discretion. Maritime defense installations were now national in spatial scale but continued to be local in the organization of military command at the very juncture when centralized military policy was most critical for retaining Japanese sovereignty.

The Tokugawa might have reclaimed tighter military control of domainal forces through the Hakodate magistrate because the military component of his assignment weighed heavier than that at other late-Tokugawa treaty ports. His defensive duties extended beyond securing the harbor proper to protecting the broader island of Ezo from anticipated Russian incursion. As with Yokohama and Nagasaki, at Hakodate, domains, this time from northern Japan, such as Hirosaki, Morioka, and Akita, provided the manpower for these defenses. But the magistrate regularly privileged diplomatic matters over managing these troops. As well, the sheer size of Ezo, some 33,000 square miles in land area, meant oversight of domainal troops posted on distant coastlines, such as hard to reach Mashike on the north coast or Shari in the east, was near impossible.

The defense of Hakodate, and Ezo, in the treaty-port era required a different strategic calculus than that of international harbors at Yokohama and Nagasaki. In contrast to these two ports, which had numerous surrounding domains at the ready to dispatch troops at a moment's notice, the wide and turbulent Tsugaru Strait separated Hakodate from the domainal forces of northern Honshū. Only the troops of nearby Matsumae to the west—the sole domain on the massive island of Ezo, occupying only the tiny southwest corner—could be mobilized with ease and alacrity. As well, the need to man remote coastal outposts, ravaged by extreme winter temperatures (often fatal to posted troops), meant the defensive burden to domains in both travel costs and manpower was greater than in other treaty ports. This meant that domains ultimately earned greater incentives than peers at other treaty ports, and also greater freedoms.

Commodore Perry's arrival at Hakodate in the spring of 1854, after first calling at Edo, prompted the shogunate to repossess the harbor's territory from Matsumae domain, as a first step in securing the port.[70] Reclassifying treaty-port lands as a shogunal territories (*tenryō*), as had occurred in Yokohama, is often explained as necessary to establish shogunal control of international trade regulations and broader economic activities in newly opened commercial entrepôts. Yet, we see in Hakodate, as also happened in Yokohama, that the shogunate's conversion of these lands was equally critical for allowing coalition forces of multiple domains to mobilize there without usurping the local domain's (in this case Matsumae's) territorial sovereignty. These military appointments reinstated the Ezo system of domain-led defenses begun in the late eighteenth century.

Following Adam Laxman's request for trade relations on behalf of Russian empress Catherine the Great in 1792, the shogunate created a domain-managed defense system in southern Ezo that explicitly drew on the Nagasaki model. A few military campaigns in Ezo before the late eighteenth century had hinged on coalition forces of multiple domains. These mobilizations, however, were ad hoc and the product of the daimyos' general military obligation to the shogunate (*gun'yaku*, originally conceived to suppress domestic rebellion), rather than the product of standing coastal defenses to guard against external incursion. For example, during the well-known 1669 Shakushain conflict, hundreds of Hirosaki domain forces were dispatched to Ezo, and troops from Akita and Morioka prepared to depart as reinforcements against an Ainu revolt. But these armies mustered only temporarily.[71] In the famous 1789 Ainu

70. Hara, *Bakumatsu kaibōshi no kenkyū*, p. 108. With this claim, it also reinstituted the office of Hakodate magistrate, which had been suspended since 1822. *Hakodate shishi, tsūsetsu hen*, 2:71.

71. Walker, *The Conquest of Ainu Lands*, pp. 63–65.

uprising, the shogunate initially ordered Hirosaki and Morioka troops to prepare to dispatch across the strait, but Matsumae domain forces ultimately suppressed the rebellion without reinforcements. Only in 1799, with lingering concern about Russian interest in Ezo following Laxman's visit, did the shogunate reclaim the majority of the island as Tokugawa territory to facilitate defense.[72] In correspondence with the northern Honshū domains of Hirosaki and Morioka, Edo officials ordered that "in all matters of service to the shogunate [in Ezo defenses], the practice of the Kuroda and Nabeshima in Nagasaki should be considered."[73] Troops from these two outside (*tozama*) domains, as had been the case in Nagasaki, were now charged with dispatching 500 men each to a central garrison at Hakodate, and then reassigning a portion of those troops to outposts along the distant, eastern Ezo coastline, including Nemuro, Kunashiri, and Etorofu.[74] The reference to the Nagasaki model in these instructions implied that northern Honshū domains should replicate not only the two-domain organizational structure there, but also its spotless record of defensive performance. In 1799, the year this edict was promulgated and nine years before the infamous *Phaeton* debacle, external attackers had never defeated Nagasaki domainal guards in an attack. The two-domain system of the permanent stationing of troops in Ezo would persist until 1807, when oversight of the island reverted to Matsumae domain. The reinstitution of a similar domain-manned structure of Ezo defense five decades later, in 1854, modified the 1799 system's configuration by offering domains new incentives in the form of "trust lands," similar to the arrangements in the Kantō.[75]

Perry's arrival at Hakodate in early 1854 catalyzed the shogunate's repossession of the harbor as Tokugawa territory, but only following the appearance of Russian vice admiral Evfimii Putiatin later that year did the two newly appointed Hakodate magistrates petition the shogunate to strengthen harbor fortifications.[76] These initial material improvements included reinforcements at seven preexisting garrisons around the harbor, remaining from the early nineteenth century. Hirosaki and Morioka domains in northern Honshū were also once again ordered to supplement

72. Hara, *Bakumatsu kaibōshi no kenkyū*, p. 96.
73. Quoted in Asakura, *Hoppōshi to kinsei shakai*, p. 124.
74. Hara, *Bakumatsu kaibōshi no kenkyū*, p. 97.
75. See ibid., p. 113n59.
76. These individuals were Takeuchi Yasunori and Hori Toshiaki.

Matsumae domain's harbor duty in Hakodate.[77] By year's end, however, the magistrates, with paltry police forces of their own, concluded that additional domains beyond these three were necessary to man an expansion of harbor garrisons as planned. The magistrates explained this strategy with reference to the success of Nagasaki defenses, where additional domains beyond Fukuoka and Saga had contributed troops in defensive emergencies. They proposed that all international ports in Japan (including Uraga, Shimoda, and Hakodate) adopt a system of expanded domainal military forces.[78] To execute this vision, in early 1855, the shogunate added Sendai and Akita domains to Ezo garrison duty, bringing the total number of domains assigned permanent duty there to five.[79]

Although Hakodate hosted the widest variety of domainal troops of any open Tokugawa port in the mid-1850s, the early issue of harbor regulations there allowed these forces greater independence overseeing foreign vessels' movements in the harbor than in contemporary Nagasaki. By the end of 1854, earlier than in Nagasaki, the shogunate had promulgated collective rules governing the activities of American, British, and Dutch vessels in Hakodate harbor (*Hakodate minato okite*). This document was one of the first texts to standardize harbor instructions for multiple nations, including restrictions on foreign vessels' movement in the water. This edict ordered that vessels enter only at the "Oki no guchi" garrison or Kameda River wharf, thus specifying the parameters of accepted ship movement.[80] Yet even with this small restriction on navigation rights, from the beginning all three nations enjoyed parity in this regard, unlike in Nagasaki.

Treaty port Hakodate did not face the problematic distinctions of inner and outer harbor present in Nagasaki, but the local topography of Hakodate played a critical role in shaping the security response, in particular the placement of the Goryōkaku Fortress. The location and design of this bastion reflected the indeterminacy of the shogunate's vision of what the military role of an international port's magistrate should be in this new commercial age. On the one hand, as administrative headquarters of the magistrate, the fort was an impressively grand negotiating venue that might awe visiting Western diplomats with the

77. *Dai Nihon komonjo: Bakumatsu gaikoku kankei monjo*, 7:9–10, 12.
78. Ibid., 8:311–12.
79. Ibid., 10:200–203.
80. Ibid., 8:58.

architectural sophistication of the Japanese; on the other hand, it was a military compound, constructed to serve as a battle command center in case of attack. In contrast to this behemoth, only a modest garrison was built at the harbor's edge for domainal troops posted to Hakodate.

Goryōkaku constituted an unusual port military project because it was located inland roughly a mile and a half from shore, instead of on the coast, as were fortifications in Yokohama, Nagasaki, and Niigata. The Hakodate magistrates constructed it to protect themselves and their immediate administrative subordinates, and not to shell foreign vessels or to shield frontline domainal troops on the shore. Dutch scholar Takeda Ayasaburō (1827–80) had designed the pentagonal encirclement to mirror the layout of earlier bastioned cities in Europe, apparently in the hope of impressing Western visitors with Japanese cosmopolitanism. What he did not realize was that these structures had become obsolete as European cities, in the age of urbanism, had expanded beyond their old walls.[81] At twenty-three acres, or about twenty football fields in size, the vast area of Goryōkaku might have easily provided refuge to the Hakodate population, some 12,000 people in 1864, during a naval attack by foreign powers.[82] Yet, the fort's only defensive use would be to protect Tokugawa loyalists entrenched against the Imperial Army in the final battles of the Boshin War during 1868 and 1869 (map 6).

Empowering the Hakodate magistrates with a European-style fortified residence projected to Western visitors the military prowess and modernizing mind-set of the Japanese government.[83] Yet, during its

81. Plutschow, *Historical Hakodate*, p. 194. Plans for the expansion of European port cities in the 1600s—such as those for Copenhagen and Gothenburg—often incorporated seaside citadels into their schema as an indispensable element of protection. But the most desirable ports for maritime defense were soon to be identified by their deep naval harbors—such as the Atlantic ports of Brest and Rochefort in France—and not land-based defenses. See Konvitz, *Cities and the Sea*, esp. chaps. 2 and 3.

82. *Hakodate shishi, tsūsetsu hen*, 1:703.

83. Interest in constructing an impressive site for diplomatic discussions was likely important to the first two Hakodate magistrates since they served simultaneously as coastal defense officers (*kaibō gakari*) during the first months of their tenure as magistrate. See chart of *kaibō gakari* in Masato, "Bakumatsu gaikō ni okeru shomondai," p. 55. Among the posts of Kanagawa, Nagasaki, and Hakodate magistrates, magistrates of Hakodate also concurrently held the post of magistrate of foreigners (*gaikoku bugyō*) more often than did their two peers, further underscoring their interest in diplomacy. *Hakodate shishi, tsūsetsu hen*, 2:89. Indeed, as the magistrates increasingly realized

construction, foreign diplomats did not oppose the project as they had new Japanese garrisons in Nagasaki and Yokohama. The comparatively small resident foreigner population in Hakodate and low volume of trade certainly contributed to this absence of protest. When Hakodate first opened to provisioning and trade in 1860, it hosted some nineteen foreign residents (seven British, six Americans, one Frenchman, and five Russians), and by 1869 that number had barely doubled to roughly forty.[84] This small Western population mirrored the modest number of foreign ships entering Hakodate: sixty-four vessels in 1860, a number that increased only 16 percent to seventy-four by 1867.[85] By contrast, in Nagasaki in 1865, there were 151 Western residents, and by 1868, 199.[86] Between 1859 and 1866, an average of forty-four foreign gunboats and 191 trading vessels arrived annually in Nagasaki, roughly twice the Hakodate total. In spite of a Japanese population in Hakodate of more than 10,000 in the early 1860s, the violent anti-Western sentiment that manifested itself in assassinations in central and southern Japan, and made consular representatives concerned that Tokugawa batteries in urban centers might be turned on the foreign population, did not reach Hakodate.[87]

The shogunate invested unprecedented sums, even greater than those invested in the Shinagawa batteries, to build the Goryōkaku Fortress, yet the destination of domainal troops dispatched to Ezo in the treaty-port era revealed that shogunal concern was less about Hakodate's security and more about the defense of the larger island. The case of the northern Honshū domain of Akita provides an important illustration. In 1856, Akita sent 462 men to Ezo for defense duty, but the majority (268 soldiers) continued to Mashike in Northern Ezo as a safeguard against Russian encroachment.[88] As further evidence of the growing primacy of Ezo security beyond Hakodate, in 1859, the shogunate divided Ezo into six defensive zones, assigning one domain each responsibility

---

that a foreign assault was unlikely, military installations were less significant for providing defense than for projecting national prestige.

84. *Hakodate shishi, tsūsetsu hen*, 1:146–47.

85. Ibid., 1:162.

86. Burke-Gaffney, *Nagasaki: The British Experience*, p. 47.

87. *Hakodate shishi, tsūsetsu hen*, 1:703.

88. Kanamori, *Akita han no seiji shakai*, p. 215.

for securing these sectors.[89] As part of its partitioned responsibilities, in 1864 Hirosaki domain deployed 300 troops to Ezo: 200 men at Hakodate and 100 at Tsube to the north.[90] Although Hirosaki sent two-thirds of its troops to Hakodate, it was one of only two domains (along with Morioka) charged with fortifying the city proper.[91] We do not have precise figures for Morioka's contributions in this period, but if it sent numbers similar to those of its partner domain, Tsugaru, the treaty-port harbor would have had at most 400 soldiers guarding its immediate perimeter.

Because no armed altercations occurred in the treaty-port period, by the 1860s, the domains posted to Ezo for military service became less fixated on defense matters and could leverage the economic benefits of their simultaneous assignments to populate the island and exploit its resources. Although Akita domain protested its original 1855 appointment to Ezo guard duty, arguing that these responsibilities would prevent it from effectively securing its own shorelines, within five years officials were reaping profits of 12,000 *ryō* from trading in dried abalone and herring through its defense outpost on the northwest Ezo shores in Mashike, near current-day Rumoi.[92] Reflecting Akita's growing commitment to economic development there, by 1862, the domain transferred oversight of that garrison from the military affairs section of the domain administration to that of economic affairs. This intertwined relationship between mobilizing domains for economic development (as a preemptive move against Russian seizure of local sea-product trade) and ensuring military security in Ezo characterized other northern Honshū domains as well. Three years earlier, the shogunate had inextricably linked natural resource development and defense in a directive to Sendai domain regarding "The Defensive Development of Ezo" (*Ezo kaihatsu shūei no gi*).[93] Thus, defense duties in Ezo, while a financial and manpower burden to the domains assigned them, could also emerge as opportunity to cultivate local trade connections for economic benefits not available in Yokohama or Nagasaki on the same scale.

89. These domains were Sendai, Shonai, Aizu, Akita, Morioka, and Hirosaki.
90. Asakawa, "Ezochi keibi to han zaisei," p. 21.
91. *Hakodate shishi, tsūsetsu hen*, 2:80–81.
92. Kanamori, *Akita han no seiji shakai*, p. 221.
93. Kikuchi, "Sendai han no Ezochi keibi ni tsuite," p. 43.

Conclusion

This chapter surveyed the defense of Tokugawa Japan's three largest international harbors in the treaty-port period to analyze how the constant Western presence and the heightened diplomatic function of port magistrates augmented further the role of domains in executing coastal defense. While the distinct political geography and topography of Nagasaki, Yokohama, and Hakodate made their foremost security concerns quite different, a comparison of the most important coastal defense developments at each site yields larger patterns of the accelerating attenuation of the Tokugawa shogunate's monopoly on violence in its final two decades of rule.

In the petitions by Western consular representatives in both Nagasaki and Yokohama to protest domain-manned fortifications there, we see foreigners' growing concern with the shogunate's inability to control domains' independent and aggressive use of military force, often contrary to shogunal opinion. The shogunate's failure to restrain the bombardment of Western vessels by both Chōshū, in its July 1863 shelling of foreign ships at Shimonoseki, and by Satsuma domain in its attack on British ships a month later, was a violent symbol of Edo's crumbling hold on domainal military forces. The continued construction of artillery batteries in the city centers of treaty ports, as we saw in all three harbors, exacerbated foreigners' fears about the possibility of xenophobic domainal soldiers turning these weapons on resident Westerners. Yet the Tokugawa also knew that they could not achieve their aspirations of treaty equality without these physical symbols of Western military power that were prominent in ports throughout Europe.

At the late Tokugawa ports, we see the codification of trans-site, trans-nation rules for foreign ship movement, which streamlined defensive readiness by allowing domainal forces across the harbors to respond to all treaty nations with the same stance. The institution of these universal norms and invocation of the Nagasaki system as a defensive model for new ports reveal the shogunate's conscious creation of a more comprehensive and standardized system of defense that stretched the length of the archipelago. Yet while these intimations of a nationalist vision of maritime security had emerged in Edo in the 1850s with the creation of the treaty-port system and new bureaucratic posts to manage the harbors' defense, by 1862 centrifugal forces predominated as domains became more self-absorbed with their own local defenses following the relaxation of the alternate attendance regulations. We turn to these developments in the 1860s, and the larger influence of the coastal defense system on the Tokugawa regime's collapse, in the conclusion.

Conclusion

Over the course of the Tokugawa period, the politics of coastal defense underwent significant change. In 1641, the shogunate created a quasi-centralized system of maritime security over which its closest deputies maintained careful oversight even as local lords provided the majority of the troops. Yet across the seventeenth century, in the absence of sustained external threat, the Tokugawa daimyo gained increasing independence in executing this coastal guard duty. By 1700, daimyo military autonomy over their retainer bands, an explicit element of the early Tokugawa partitioning of power, now extended to areas outside of daimyo sovereign territory (such as Nagasaki) and to foreign nationals (such as the Chinese and Dutch) through coastal defense service. The shogunal monopoly on violence, the primary premise of Tokugawa hegemony, was increasingly diffused. That domainal soldiers on coastal defense duty, instead of direct Tokugawa vassals, executed the most constant and active show of military force in the realm embodied a grave contradiction. How could the Tokugawa shoguns continue to claim legitimacy to govern as supreme military power in Japan if their subordinate lords repeatedly surpassed them in exercising martial power?

During the first century of coastal defense, as this book has shown, this incongruity did not yield epochal political change. Since for the most part only two domains, Saga and Fukuoka, permanently discharged this service in the seventeenth century, and solely in Nagasaki, the political implications of their implicit challenge to shogunal control of military force were limited to their jostling with the magistrate over who controlled military matters in port. Yet with the broadening of their duty to include the repulsion of Chinese smugglers (chapter 2) and protection of the Dutch (chapter 3), these domains gained incrementally greater political influence across the eighteenth century. Even as their defense responsibilities were discharged in the name of the shogun and constituted an often onerous fiscal burden to the domains, they provided unprecedented local military agency as domains usurped greater privileges than they had been delegated. Sometimes this agency manifested itself not in the unauthorized use of mortal force, but in passive resistance, such as domainal reluctance to join coalition forces in the early eighteenth-century Genkai area or Fukuoka domain's focus on socializing with the Dutch, to the exclusion of rigorous battery inspections, in the 1830s. The shogunate recognized this assertion of independence as an inescapable manifestation of what David Howell has labeled the "dissonance" between the interests of the Edo bureaucrats and those of domains that was intrinsic to the Tokugawa order.[1] While these frictions of authority and autonomy were not continual, they were cumulative in that early modern political culture relied on precedent. Once the shogunate ignored domainal resistance or extension of its customary agency, this broadened latitude of local independence became entrenched as tradition. These examples reveal how, contrary to the arguments of James White and others, the Tokugawa state lost its monopoly over the legitimate use of violence well before the *bakumatsu* crisis of the mid-nineteenth century.

The shogunate had periodically attempted to reclaim control of the monopoly on violence in the early nineteenth century, but as the sheer number of domains involved in coastal defense, and the geographical spread of fortified shorelines, grew from the 1840s and 1850s with heightened Western pressure, coastal defense obdurately remained a local project. The accretion of domainal autonomy in executing coastal defense in fact accelerated as the shogunate attempted to centrally organize its administration with the creation of new posts in Edo, such as the magistrate of foreigners and parallel regional positions, such as the Yokohama and Hakodate magistrates, to oversee port security. Even as the two other elements of foreign relations—trade and diplomacy—became incrementally centralized during this period, coastal defense remained more domain-centric than the other two areas of external affairs for three reasons. First, a growing percentage of domains across the archipelago were now asked to contribute troops to maritime security not only in

1. Howell, *Geographies of Identity in Nineteenth-Century Japan*, p. 22.

their home provinces but also at the treaty ports. Second, daimyo, and the domainal samurai who served them, were more reluctant to relinquish control of military affairs to central actors than diplomacy and trade because military duty was inextricably tied to their identity as members of the warrior class. Samurai with hereditary coastal defense responsibilities hesitated to forgo the very front-line martial duty that had allowed them to exercise their military function across the Tokugawa period. Third, although the shogunate created new bureaucratic posts to coordinate an increasingly complex coastal defense, as the threat of colonization, or even attack, by Western powers waned, these shogunal positions focused primarily on diplomacy and trade, rather than military protection, as the keys to retaining Japanese sovereignty. As Michael Auslin has shown of the 1850s and 1860s, "the key to strategy" in this new geopolitical environment was "negotiation, which the Japanese saw as the best weapon to defend themselves from the West."[2] Among shogunal officials, coastal defense took a backseat to diplomacy as the most likely guarantor of continued Japanese sovereignty, devolving further military authority to the domains.

By the 1860s, the shogunate definitively relinquished any prospect of reining in escalating domainal military independence as it had attempted in the early 1700s, with the assignment of inspectors to coordinate Genkai-area smuggling campaigns, or in 1808 with the punishment of Nabeshima Naohiro for the *Phaeton* incident. By 1862, the shogunate abandoned control of the monopoly on violence with the relaxation of the alternate attendance system. The reduction in requirements, so that most lords would now spend three months (specifically, 100 days) of every three years in the capital, instead of six months in alternating years, soon segued into suspension of the system, and then its abolition. The Tokugawa terminated the practice primarily to allow daimyo to redirect the exorbitant expenses of these annual processions to coastal defense projects in their home domains, ideally ones with future benefits to the realm as a whole. Yet, excusing daimyo from the most visible, constant, and widespread form of military obeisance to the shogun, to permit them to focus on maritime security initiatives in their own territories instead of being at the ready to contribute troops to an emergency in the capital, was the most conclusive evidence yet that the shogunate was unable and unwilling to centralize coastal defense efforts.

2. Auslin, *Negotiating Imperialism,* p. 4.

It is no surprise that two of the most vocal proponents of these alternate attendance "reforms," which constituted a first step toward the practice's abolition, were lords whose domains had shouldered an unusually large burden in defending the treaty ports, Matsudaira Shungaku (lord of Fukui domain and defender of Yokohama) and Nabeshima Naomasa (lord of Saga and defender of Nagasaki). Shungaku had been arguing since Perry's 1853 arrival that domains should cease wasting resources on alternate attendance displays and instead devote those monies to strengthening defenses. He was one of the primary figures to push through the 1862 alternate attendance reforms.[3] Revealing the early inklings of later, broader disenchantment with Tokugawa rule, Saga lord Naomasa also argued for the need for daimyo to reprioritize the "protection of their own home provinces" (*jikoku o mochikatame sōrō koto*) after a decade of heavily contributing to Kantō-area defenses.[4] This position was a far cry from his commitment in the 1850s to building a second foundry, largely at his own expense, to cast cannon for the protection of Edo Bay. The revision of the centuries-old custom of alternate attendance signaled the dissolution of shogunal authority because it visibly marked, throughout all the highways of Japan, the cessation of the Tokugawa ability to demand the most regular and long-standing symbol of feudal allegiance. This book contends that, more significantly, this concession also reflected the irreversible disintegration of the Tokugawa monopoly on violence, which made collapse of the regime inescapable.

By 1862, the practice of sporadically granting trust lands, or monetary rewards (as discussed in chapter 5), was no longer sufficient to compensate domains for coastal defense services. The shogunate recognized that in an environment of sustained political crisis, new, epochal measures had to be taken not just on a case-by-case basis, because the sheer number of involved domains had become so unwieldly, but through systemic change—diminution of most domains' largest annual expenditure, alternate attendance—to compensate lords for the burden of coastal defense service. Granted, the shogunate's ability to coerce domains into complying with alternate attendance had diminished over time, so the 1862 reform was in part a measure to save face. Yet, the relaxation of these requirements in fact vacated hundreds of thousands of domainal troops

3. Yamamoto, *Sankin kōtai*, p. 204.
4. Maruyama, *Sankin kōtai*, p. 251.

from Edo. From the early 1850s, as the shogunate had assigned larger *tozama*-class domains coastal duty in the Kantō area, Edo officials realized that these troops, within an easy march of the capital, could conceivably mount an overthrow. Yet before the signing of Western treaties beginning in 1858, concern about attack from without overshadowed fear of rebellion from within, making the appointment of these forces a rational, calculated choice. The shogunate tolerated the presence of these troops as a ready source of soldiers to protect the Tokugawa capital against foreign attack. By the time of the alternate attendance reforms in 1862, however, given waning support for Tokugawa rule, the shogunate interpreted these same troops as a greater source of potential sedition than protection.

The pace of growing domainal military autonomy accelerated with the dismantling of the alternate attendance system because Edo lost its primary method of monitoring daimyo activities, regular and compulsory residence in the capital. The shogunate was unwilling and unable to reverse this development because Edo was inextricably reliant on a domain-led defense system even as it debilitated Tokugawa legitimacy. As we saw with Nabeshima Naomasa's metallurgy experiments in the 1840s and 1850s, the shogunate had myopically assumed that domains, concerned about survival of the realm, would be willing long-term subcontractors for national defense. This was not so. By the 1860s, with more domains—such as Mito, Satsuma, and Chōshū—involved in artillery projects, we find that political differences over foreign policy and ideological schisms over the role of the emperor produced less technological sharing with the center and more local, proprietary use than the shogunate might have hoped. The Tokugawa could not count on all daimyo being national patriots.

As domestic warfare escalated from the mid-1860s, reflecting spreading opposition to shogunal rule, elite Tokugawa officials privileged military reforms that strengthened the limited troops directly loyal to the Tokugawa as its own daimyo house, rather than building proto-national forces of its trans-domainal federation.[5] The desperate shogunal military reforms of 1867 produced a Tokugawa army of roughly 24,000 men, an infantry 40 percent larger than three years earlier, to confront the great southwestern domains, which seemed certain to attack the Tokugawa

5. Totman, *Collapse of the Tokugawa Bakufu*, pp. 286, 345.

government.[6] Yet the very need to cultivate proprietary troops of this magnitude revealed the shogunate's fear that it could not extract sufficient numbers of forces from allied domains, as their foundational military obligations required. Creation of a completely centralized military was indispensable for the Tokugawa to reclaim their monopoly on violence, but this radical reorganization of military power was impossible under the system of delegated authority the daimyo class refused to relinquish.

Yet the inability of the shogunate to centralize military forces was also a product of the broader dispersal of the legitimate use of violence claimed by widening sectors of the population beyond the warrior class. Indeed, by the mid-1860s, commoners in the Kantō region were self-policing the countryside (with the permission of Edo) because of the shogunate's failure to preserve the public peace.[7] In a period of growing social unrest and widening xenophobia, the shogunate desperately needed additional actors to help maintain internal stability. Viewed from the perspective of coastal defense, the devolution of military authority to these new agents was not merely a product of the chaotic social environment of the 1860s. Rather, it was the latest stage in the dilution of the shogunate's control of violence that had begun in the 1640s in newly garrisoned Nagasaki.

The overthrow of the Tokugawa in 1868 demonstrated that the shogunate no longer controlled the use of force sufficiently to protect its hegemony. Early Meiji-era attempts to reconstitute the monopoly on violence so that the new government's authority and Japan's maritime borders were secure remained mired in the late Tokugawa approach, which privileged diplomacy over military centralization. When the new Meiji leaders, largely from domains that had routed the Tokugawa in land battles, did consider military affairs, they prioritized improving existing military competencies—that of the army—rather than rectifying weaknesses—the absence of a naval tradition. In their comprehensive study of the Japanese navy, David Evans and Mark Peattie argue that given Meiji Japan's relative military weakness compared to the West, and the costs of creating a modern navy (which would take decades), the only possible defense for Japan in the 1870s was continuing dependence on "static defenses" (*shuei kokubō*), consisting of shoreline artillery and

6. Ibid., pp. 346–48.
7. Howell, *Geographies of Identity in Nineteenth-Century Japan*, pp. 102–3.

ground forces, supported by naval units. This approach meant that in early Meiji defenses, "the army came first and the navy second" (*rikushu kaijū*).[8]

A Meiji maritime defense strategy based on static forts persisted only through the late 1870s, however, and then evolved in two stages into a defense, and soon after an offense, based on naval power. This trajectory mirrored trends worldwide in late nineteenth century, where a range of conflicts reflected the emergence of offense as the priority over defense in military strategy. Historian Jeremy Black has observed that during this period, strategic consensus emerged that "the best way to achieve political objectives [and security] was generally that of taking war to the enemy."[9] This emphasis on preemptive strike was evident in U.S. Army attacks on Native American groups in the 1860s and 1870s and Prussian field marshall Helmuth von Moltke's strategy in defeating Austria and France in 1866 and 1870.[10] Similar developments appeared in East Asia. In Qing China in 1874, government officials debated whether to expand the armies near the northern border provinces to suppress Muslim rebellions and to create a larger territorial buffer against Russia, or to fortify the southeast coastline against Japanese aggression following the invasion of Taiwan.[11] The Qing court opted for the former, an offensive campaign, which expanded the northern boundaries of the empire. As these examples illustrate, for continental states, a focus on offense meant primarily expansion of armies. For archipelagic Japan, any offensive strategy necessarily rested on naval power. Thus, although debates similar to those in China arose at approximately the same time in Japan, they had a different outcome. In mid-Meiji Japan, unlike contemporary continental nations characterized by a strategic focus on an army-led military, the turn to offense, which relied on naval power, meant a distinctive organizational obstacle for the Meiji state: namely, the struggle to coordinate and integrate the separate and vehemently independent supreme commands of the army, Japan's traditional military core, and the navy, a newly emergent geopolitical necessity. The Meiji state needed to demonstrate successful integration of a modern navy within its monopoly on violence to fully gain equal status in the eyes of the

8. Evans and Peattie, *Kaigun,* pp. 7–8.
9. Black, *Western Warfare, 1775–1882*, p. 184.
10. Black, *War in the Nineteenth Century*, p. 142.
11. Hsu, "The Great Policy Debate in China, 1874."

Western powers. Mastery of sea power would provide Japan with the threat of force as a diplomatic tool when negotiating revision of the unequal treaties.

The history of Tokugawa coastal defense is the story of the incremental clash between local military identity and the collective security concerns of an incompletely centralized political federation. These tensions culminated in the collapse of control of the monopoly on violence by the early modern Japanese state. While the strategy and hardware of this coastal defense system proved to be anachronisms beyond rehabilitation in the modern age, the centrality of politics in shaping its organization remained evident in Japanese state formation through the twentieth century, and to the present day. The rise of a world-class navy that would defeat China and then Russia, colonial expansion, the emergence of a military state in World War II, and postwar debates about the incursions on Japanese sovereignty by the U.S. military umbrella are each modern manifestations of the continual renegotiation of the state's control over the legitimate use of force. Thus, the story of Tokugawa coastal defenders, and their place within the evolution of the Japanese monopoly on violence, is ripe to be reclaimed.

Bibliography

The place of publication for Japanese-language sources is Tokyo, unless otherwise specified.

Adas, Michael. *Machines as the Measure of Man: Science, Technology, and Ideologies of Western Dominance*. Ithaca, NY: Cornell University Press, 1989.

Andrade, Tonio. *How Taiwan Became Chinese: Dutch, Spanish, and Han Colonization in the Seventeenth Century*. New York: Columbia University Press, 2008.

Arai Hakuseki. *As Told Round a Brushwood Fire: The Autobiography of Arai Hakuseki*. Translated by Joyce Ackroyd. University of Tokyo Press, 1979.

———. *Oritaku Shiba no ki*. Iwanami shoten, 2005.

Arano Yasunori. *Kinsei Nihon to higashi Ajia*. Tōkyō daigaku shuppankai, 1988.

Arima Seiho. "The Western Influence on Japanese Military Science, Shipbuilding and Navigation." *Monumenta Nipponica* 19, nos. 3–4 (1964): 352–79.

Asakawa Ariko. "Ezochi keibi to han zaisei." *Hirosaki daigaku kokushi kenkyū* 90 (Mar. 1990): 15–30.

Asakawa Michio. "Hikone han no Sōshū keibi to seiyōryū hōjutsu." *Kaikokushi kenkyū* 5 (May 2005): 64–80.

———. *Odaiba: Shinagawa daiba no sekkei, kōzō, kinō*. Kinseisha, 2009.

Asakura Yūko. *Hoppōshi to kinsei shakai*. Osaka: Seibundō, 1999.

Asao Naohiro. "Sakokusei no seiritsu." In *Kōza Nihonshi*, vol. 4, edited by Rekishigaku kenkyūkai and nihonshi kenkyūkai, 59–94. Tōkyō daigaku shuppankai, 1970.

Aston, W. G. "HMS Phaeton at Nagasaki in 1808." *Transactions of the Asiatic Society of Japan* 7 (1879): 323–36.

Auslin, Michael. *Negotiating with Imperialism: The Unequal Treaties and the Culture of Japanese Diplomacy*. Cambridge, MA: Harvard University Press, 2004.

Bakumatsu gijutsu no kiseki: Saga han shiryō "Matsu no ochiba." Edited by Sugimoto Akira, Sakai Taiji, and Mukai Akira. Kyoto: Shubunkaku shuppan, 1987.

Beasley, W. G. *Great Britain and the Opening of Japan: 1834–58*. New York: Routledge, 1995.

Beerens, Anna. *Friends, Acquaintances, Pupils and Patrons: Japanese Intellectual Life in the Late Eighteenth Century, a Prosopographical Approach*. Leiden: Leiden University Press, 2006.

Berry, Mary Elizabeth. *Japan in Print: Information and Nation in the Early Modern Period*. Berkeley: University of California Press, 2006.

Black, Jeremy. *Naval Power: A History of Warfare and the Sea from 1500*. New York: Palgrave Macmillan, 2010.

———. *Rethinking Military History*. New York: Routledge, 2004.

———. *War in the Nineteenth Century, 1800–1914*. Cambridge: Polity, 2009.

———. *Western Warfare, 1775–1882*. Bloomington: Indiana University Press, 2001.

Blussé, Leonard. "A Glimpse Behind the Screens: Some Remarks on the Significance of the Deshima Dagregisters for the Study of Tokugawa Japan." In *The Deshima Diaries, Marginalia, 1700–1740*, translated and edited by Paul van der Velde and Rudolf Bachofner, xv–xxiii. The Japan-Netherlands Institute, 1992.

———. "The Grand Inquisitor Inoue Chikugo no kami Masashige: Spin Doctor of the Tokugawa Bakufu." *Bulletin of Portuguese/Japanese Studies* 7 (2003): 23–43.

Blussé, Leonard, and W. G. Remmelink, trans. and eds. *The Deshima Diaries, Marginalia, 1740–1800*. The Japan-Netherlands Institute, 2004.

Bodart-Bailey, Beatrice. "The Economic Plight of the Fifth Tokugawa Shogun." *Kobe University Economic Review* 44 (1998): 37–54.

Bolitho, Harold. "The *Han*." In *The Cambridge History of Japan*, edited by John Whitney Hall, 4:183–234. New York: Cambridge University Press, 1991.

———. "The Tempō Crisis." In *The Cambridge History of Japan*, edited by Marius Jansen, 5:116–67. New York: Cambridge University Press, 1989.

———. *Treasures Among Men: The Fudai Daimyo in Tokugawa Japan*. New Haven, CT: Yale University Press, 1971.

Brown, Philip C. *Central Authority and Local Autonomy in the Formation of Early Modern Japan: The Case of Kaga Domain*. Stanford, CA: Stanford University Press, 1993.

Bunsei jūnen chōgai ku gatsu Oranda sen hokage mikakushi no ki. Akitsuki Kuroda ke monjo, Kyūshū bunka shi kenkyūjo, Kyūshū daigaku.

Burke-Gaffney, Brian. *Nagasaki: The British Experience, 1854–1945*. Kent, UK: Global Oriental, 2009.

Chaiklin, Martha. *Cultural Commerce and Dutch Commercial Culture: The Influence of European Material Culture on Japan, 1700–1850*. Leiden: Research School CNWS, 2003.

———. "Monopolists to Middlemen: Dutch Liberalism and American Imperialism in the Opening of Japan." *Journal of World History* 21, no. 2 (2010): 249–69.

Clulow, Adam. "From Global Entrepôt to Early Modern Domain: Hirado, 1609–1641." *Monumenta Nipponica* 65, no. 1 (Spring 2010): 1–35.

Cobbing, Andrew. *Kyushu: Gateway to Japan*. Folkestone, Kent, UK: Global Oriental, 2008.

Cortazzi, Hugh. "Yokohama Frontier Town." *Collected Writings of Sir Hugh Cortazzi*. Richmond, Surrey, UK: Japan Library, 2000.

Craig, Albert. *Chōshū in the Meiji Restoration*. Cambridge, MA: Harvard University Press, 1961.

Dai Nihon komonjo: Bakumatsu gaikoku kankei monjo. 51 vols. Tōkyō daigaku shiryō hensangakari, 1910–.

Earns, Lane. "The Nagasaki Bugyo and the Development of Bureaucratic Rule." *Asian Culture Quarterly* 22, no. 2 (Summer 1994): 63–73.

Elison, George. *Deus Destroyed: The Image of Christianity in Early Modern Japan*. Cambridge, MA: Council on East Asian Studies, Harvard University, 1988.

Evans, David C., and Mark Peattie. *Kaigun: Strategy, Tactics, and Technology in the Imperial Japanese Navy, 1887–1941*. Annapolis, MD: Naval Institute Press, 1997.

Fairbank, John King. *China: Tradition and Transformation*. Boston: Houghton Mifflin, 1978.

The Foreign Office List, Forming a Complete British Diplomatic and Consular Handbook. London: Harrison, 1865.

Fujii Jōji. *Edo kaibaku: Nihon no rekishi 12*. Shūeisha, 1992.

———. *Tokugawa Iemitsu*. Yoshikawa kōbunkan, 1997.

Fujita Satoru. *Bakuhansei kokka no seijishiteki kenkyū: Tempōki no chitsujo, gunji, gaikō*. Azekura shobō, 1987.

Fukuoka kenshi, Fukuoka han tsūshihen. vols. 1 and 2, Fukuoka: Nishi Nihon bunka kyōkai, 2000.

Gardiner, Robert. *Heavy Frigates: Eighteen pounder frigates*. London: Conway Maritime Press, 1994.

Garrett, Richard J. *The Defenses of Macau: Forts, Ships and Weapons over 450 Years*. Hong Kong: Hong Kong University Press, 2010.

Geerts, A. J. C. "The Arima Rebellion and the Conduct of Koeckebacker." *Transactions of the Asiatic Society of Japan* 11 (1883): 51–116.

Genkai nada no Edo jidai. Fukuoka: Fukuoka shi hakubutsukan, 1997.

Goodman, Grant. *Japan and the Dutch: 1600–1853*. Richmond, Surrey: Curzon Press, 2000.

Grainger, John D. *The First Pacific War: Britain and Russia, 1854–1856*. Woodbridge, UK: Boydell Press, 2008.

Gramlich-Oka, Bettina. "Nagasaki: A Thorn in the Eye of the Shogunate?" In *Mining, Monies and Culture in Early Modern Societies: East Asian and Global Perspectives*, edited by Nanny Kim and Keiko Nagase-Reimer, 43–86. Leiden: Brill, 2013.

———. *Thinking Like a Man: Tadano Makuzu: 1763–1825*. Boston, MA: Brill, 2006.

Guth, Christine. "Hokusai's Great Waves." *Art Bulletin* 4 (2011): 468–85.

Hakodate shishi, tsūsetsu hen. 3 vols. Hakodate shishi hensanshitsu, 1990.

Hall, John Whitney. "The *Bakuhan* System." In *The Cambridge History of Japan*, edited by John Whitney Hall, 4:128–82. Cambridge: Cambridge University Press, 1991.

———. "Notes on Early Ch'ing Copper Trade with Japan." *Harvard Journal of Asiatic Studies* 12, nos. 3–4 (Dec. 1949): 444–61.

Hara Takeshi. *Bakumatsu kaibōshi no kenkyū*. Meichō shuppansha, 1988.

———. "Bakumatsu ni okeru Edo wan no bōbi." *Gunji shigaku* 22, no. 4 (Mar. 1987): 47–66.

Harafuji Hiroshi. *Daimyō azukari dokoro no kenkyū*. Sōbunsha, 1981.

———. "Nukeni tsumi zakkō." *Hōseishi kenkyū* 6 (1955): 177–223.

Hayashi Fukusho, ed. *Tsūkō ichiran*. 8 vols. Kokusho kankōkai, 1912–13.

Hayashi Shunsai, ed. *Kai hentai*. 3 vols. Tōyō bunkō. 1958–59.

Hellyer, Robert. *Defining Engagement: Japan and Global Contexts, 1649–1868*. Cambridge, MA: Harvard University Asia Center, 2010.

———. "The Missing Pirate and the Pervasive Smuggler: Regional Agency in Coastal Defense, Trade and Foreign Relations in Nineteenth Century Japan." *International History Review* 27, no. 1 (Mar. 2005): 1–24.

Hesselink, Reinier. *Prisoners from Nambu: Reality and Make-Believe in 17th-Century Japanese Diplomacy*. Honolulu: University of Hawai`i Press, 2002.

———. "The Two Faces of Nagasaki: The World of the Suwa Festival Screen." *Monumenta Nipponica* 59, no. 2 (Summer 2004): 179–222.

Hidemura Senzō, ed. *Fukuoka kenshi*. 64 volumes. Fukuoka: Nishi Nihon bunka kyōkai, 1982–.

Hideshima Naritada, ed. *Saga han jūhō enkakushi*. 1934. Reprint, Hara shobō, 1972.

———. *Saga han kaigunshi*. Chishin-kai, 1917.

Higaki Motokichi, ed. *Yoshida kadenroku*. 3 vols. Dazaifu: Dazaifu Tenmangu, 1981.

Hirado Oranda shōkan no nikki. 4 vols. Translated by Nagazumi Yōko. Iwanami shoten, 1970.

Hodgson, C. Pemberton. *A Residence at Nagasaki and Hakodate, 1859–60*. London: Richard Bentley, 1861.

Hori Shin. "A Study of the Early Modern Samurai Honor Ranking System." Translated by Philip Brown. *Early Modern Japan* 6, no. 1 (1997): 10–16.

Howard, Frank. *Sailing Ships of War, 1400–1860*. New York: Mayflower Books, 1979.

Howell, David L. *Capitalism from Within: Economy, Society, and the State in a Japanese Fishery*. Berkeley: University of California Press, 1995.

———. *Geographies of Identity in Nineteenth-Century Japan*. Berkeley: University of California Press, 2005.

Hsu, Immanuel. "The Great Policy Debate in China, 1874: Maritime Defense vs. Frontier Defense." *Harvard Journal of Asiatic Studies* 25 (1964–65): 212–28.

Huibert, Paul. "De Coningh on Deshima: *Mijn Verblijf in Japan*, 1856." *Monumenta Nipponica* 32, no. 3 (Autumn 1977): 347–64.

Ikegami Eiko. *Bonds of Civility: Aesthetic Networks and the Political Origins of Japanese Culture*. New York: Cambridge University Press, 2005.

———. *The Taming of the Samurai: Honorific Individualism and the Making of Modern Japan*. Cambridge, MA: Harvard University Press, 1995.

Innes, Robert. "The Door Ajar: Japan's Foreign Trade in the Seventeenth Century." Ph.D. diss., University of Michigan, 1980.

Irimoto Masao. "Iemitsu seiken no ichi kōsatsu." *Nihon rekishi* 292 (Sept. 1979): 23–59.

Ishin shiryō kōyō. Online database from the Tōkyō daigaku shiryō hensanjo.

Iwao Seiichi. "Kinsei nisshi bōeki ni kansuru sūryōteki kōsatsu." *Shigaku zasshi* 62, no. 12 (1963): 1–40.

Jackson, Terrence. "Socialized Intellect: The Cultural Network of Rangaku in Late Tokugawa Japan." Ph.D. diss., Indiana University, 2004.

Janetta, Ann. *The Vaccinators: Smallpox, Medical Knowledge, and the "Opening" of Japan*. Stanford, CA: Stanford University Press, 2007.

Javellana, Rene B. *Fortress of Empire: Spanish Colonial Fortifications of the Philippines, 1565–1898*. Makati City, Philippines: Bookmark, 1997.

Jōjima Masayoshi and Sugitani Akira. *Saga ken no rekishi*. Yamakawa shuppansha, 1972.

Kaempfer, Engelbert. *Kaempfer's Japan: Tokugawa Culture Observed*. Translated and edited by Beatrice M. Bodart-Bailey. Honolulu: University of Hawai`i Press, 1999.

Kajiwara Yoshinori. "Bakumatsu Saga han ni okeru kajutsugumi sōsetsu no igi." In *Kinsei kindaishi ronshū*, edited by Kawazoe Shōji. Yoshikawa kōbunkan, 1990.

———. "Kansei bunka ki no Nagasaki keibi to Feyton go jiken." *Fukuoka daigaku jinbun ronsō* 37, no. 1 (2005): 339–77.

———. "Kōkaki no Nagasaki keibi no tsuite." *Fukuoka daigaku jinbun ronsō* 26, no. 4 (1995): 2043–76.

Kamishiraishi Minoru. *Bakumatsuki taigai kankei no kenkyū*. Yoshikawa kōbunkan, 2011.

Kanagawa kenshi, tsūshi hen 3, kinsei 2. Yokohama: Kanagawa ken kenminbu kenshi hensanshūshitsu, 1983.

Kanai Toshiyuki, ed. *Nagasaki sōsho, 4, Zōho Nagasaki ryakushi,* vol. 2. Nagasaki shiyakusho, 1926.

Kanamori Masaya. *Akita han no seiji shakai*. Momyōsha shuppan, 1992.

Karatsu shishi. Karatsu: Karatsu-shi shi hensan iinkai, 1962.

Karras, Alan. *Smuggling: Contraband and Corruption in World History*. Lanham, MD: Rowman and Littlefield, 2010.

Katsu Kaishū. *Kaigun rekishi*. Hara shobō, 1967.

Kawazoe Shōji and Fukuoka komonjo o yomu kai, eds. *Shintei Kuroda kafu*. 12 vols. Bunken shuppan, 1982–84.

Kihara Hiroyuki. "Bakumatsuki Sagahan no bakuryō azukari keikaku to Ii Naosuke." *Kagawa daigaku kyōikubu kenkyū hōkoku* 9, no. 1 (Sept. 1999): 85–108.

———. *Bakumatsuki Sagahan no hanseishi kenkyū*. Fukuoka: Kyūshū daigaku shuppankai, 1997.

Kikuchi Shin'ichi. "Sendai han no Ezochi keibi ni tsuite." *Keizai ronshū* 5 (Mar. 1966): 41–54.

Kimura Naoki. "17 seiki chūyō bakuhansei kokka no ikokusen taisaku." *Shigaku zasshi* 109, no. 2 (2000): 55–77.

Kiyō gundan. Edited by Tanaka Yasunao and Nakamura Tadashi. Kondō shuppan, 1974.

Kohan Nagasaki chizu chō. Kyōto koten dokō kai, 1977.

Konvitz, Josef. *Cities and the Sea: Port City Planning in Early Modern Europe*. Baltimore: Johns Hopkins University Press, 1978.

Kuroda Kazumi. "Shōhō yonen no nanban sen raikō jiken: Edo to genchi de no taiō." *Nihon rekishi* 694, nos. 2–3 (2004): 54–70.

Kuroita Katsumi, ed. *Shintei zōho kokushi taikei*. Vols. 38–47. *Tokugawa jikki*. Yoshikawa kōbunkan, 1929–35.

Lambert, Andrew. *War at Sea in the Age of Sail*. London: Cassell, 2000.
Leonard, Jane Kate. *Wei Yuan and China's Rediscovery of the Maritime World*. Cambridge, MA: Harvard University Press, 1984.

Mack, John. *The Sea: A Cultural History*. London: Reaktion Books, 2011.
MacLean, J. "The Introduction of Books and Scientific Instruments into Japan, 1712–1854." *Japanese Studies in the History of Science* 13 (1974): 9–68.
Maruyama Yasunari. "Bakuhanseika no Genkai nada kōtsū: kinsei zen/chū ki o chūshin ni." In *Genkai nada no Edo jidai*. Fukuoka shi hakubutsukan, ed. Fukuoka: Fukuoka shi hakubutsukan, 1997, 6–12.
———. "Kyūshū: kinsei no maku ake to tenkai." In *Kyūshū: sono kako, genzai, mirai*. Fukuoka: Kyūshū daigaku shuppan kai, 1988, 59–80.
———. "Nagasaki keibi to sankin kōtai no kankei." In *Saga han no sōgō kenkyū*, edited by Fujino Tamotsu, 977–97. Yoshikawa kōbunkan, 1981.
———. *Sankin kōtai*. Yoshikawa kōbunkan, 2007.
———. "Sankin kōtaisei no keisei, kakuritsu katei to Fukuoka han." In *Bakuhan taisei no shin kenkyū*, edited by Maruyama Yasunari, 1–72. Bunken shuppan, 1982.
———. "Tokugawa seikenka ni okeru sankin kōtai." In *Saga han no sōgō kenkyū*, edited by Fujino Tamotsu, pp. 939–81. Yoshikawa kōbunkan, 1981.
Masato Kazuhiro. "Bakumatsu gaikō ni okeru shomondai to kaibōgakari." *Komazawa shigaku* 35 (1986): 51–75.
Massarella, Derek. "Review of *The Deshima Dagregisters: Their Original Tables of Contents, Vol. III, 1700–1710*. Ed. Paul van der Velde and Ton Vermeulen. And *The Deshima Dagregisters: Their Original Tables of Contents, Vol. IV, 1710–1720* and *Vol. V, 1720–1730*. Ed. Paul van der Velde." *Monumenta Nipponica* 46, no. 4 (Winter 1991): 552–54.
Matsukata Fuyuko. "King Willem II's 1844 Letter to the Shogun." Translated by Adam Clulow. *Monumenta Nipponica* 66, no. 1 (2011): 99–122.
Matsuo Shin'ichi. "Bakuhansei kokka ni okeru 'tōjin' 'karasen' mondai no suii." *Higashi Ajia to Nihon: kōryū to henyō*. Fukuoka: Kyushu University 21st Century COE Program, 2004, 17–32.
———. *Edo bakufu no taigai seisaku to engan keibi*. Azekura shobō, 2010.
———. "Iemitsu seikenki no engankeibi taisei ni tsuite." *Hakusan shigaku* 35 (Apr. 1999): 83–104.
———. "Shōhō nen no Porutogaru shisetsusen raikō wo meguru taisaku." *Nihon rekishi* 643 (Dec. 2001): 59–75.
———. "Shōtoku–Kyōhō ki karasen mondai e no daimyō ke no taiō." In *Higashi Ajia kaiiki ni okeru kōryū no shoso*. Fukuoka: Kyūshū daigaku, 2005, 77–89.
Matsutake Hideo. "Feyton go jiken to 19 seiki shotō no kaiun jisei." *Tōnan Ajia kenkyū nenpō* 33–34 (1992): 1–52.
McClain, James. *Japan: A Modern History*. New York: W. W. Norton, 2002.
"Minutes of a Communication between the Governor of Nagasaki and Rear Admiral Sir James Stirling, October 18, 1854." *British and Foreign State Papers, 1855–56*, vol. XLVI. London: William Ridgway, 1865, 716–17.
Mitani Hiroshi. *Escape from Impasse: The Decision to Open Japan*. Translated by David Noble. International House of Japan, 2006.

———. *Perii raikō*. Yoshikawa kōbunkan, 2003.

———. "Tempō-Kaei ki no taigai mondai." *Nihon rekishi taikei* 3 (Aug. 1988): 1127–51.

Miyake Hidetoshi, ed. *Tōsen hyōryūki*. Kita Kyūshū daigaku komonjo kenkyū kai, 1979.

Miyake Satoshi."Kōkaki ni okeru Edo kinaki keiei to Uraga guchi kōzō." *Nihon rekishi* 734 (July 2009): 40–56.

Monroe, Henry. "Mineral Wealth of Japan." *Engineering and Mining Journal*, Dec. 9, 1876.

Morinaga Taneo, ed. *Hankachō*. Vol. 1. Nagasaki: Nagasaki kenritsu toshokan, 1958.

Morley, B. M. *Henry VIII and the Development of Coastal Defense*. London: Stationery Office Books, 1977.

Morris-Suzuki, Tessa. *The Technological Transformation of Japan: From the Seventeenth to the Twenty-first Century*. New York: Cambridge University Press, 1994.

Nagano Susumu. *Sagahan to hansharo*. Shinnihon shuppansha, 2000.

———. "Zairai gijutsu to inyū gijutsu no setten: Saga han no tessei taihō chūzō o megutte." In Sugimoto Akira, ed, *Kindai seiyō bunmei to no deai*. Shibunkaku shuppan, 1989, 46–75.

Nagao Masanori. "Ansei ki kaibōgakari no seidoshiteki kōsatsu." *Hōsei shigaku* 33 (Mar. 1981): 42–60.

Nagasaki kenshi, taigai kōshō hen. Edited by Nagasaki kenshi hensan iinkai. Yoshikawa kōbunkan, 1986.

Nagasakishi yakusho, ed. *Bakufu jidai no Nagasaki, jō kan*. Vol. 1. Kyoto: Rinkawa shoten, 1973.

Nakada Masayuki. *Nirayama daikan Egawa shi no kenkyū*. Yoshikawa kōbunkan, 1998.

Nakai, Kate Wildman. *Shogunal Politics: Arai Hakuseki and the Premises of Tokugawa Rule*. Cambridge, MA: Harvard University Press, 1988.

Nakamura Tadashi. *Kinsei Nagasaki boekishi no kenkyū*. Yoshikawa kōbunkan, 1988.

———. "Sakoku no keisei to Fukuoka han." *Seinan chiikishi kenkyū* 9 (Aug. 1994): 1–38.

———. "Sakokusei no kakuritsu to Fukuoka han." *Seinan chiikishi kenkyū* 10 (1995): 1–22.

———. "Shimabara no ran to Saga han." *Kyūshū bunkashi kenkyūjo kiyō* 24 (Mar. 1979): 57–105.

———. "Shimabara no ran to sakoku." *Iwanami kōza Nihon rekishi 9, kinsei* 1. Iwanami shoten, 1963, 227–62.

Nakamura Tadashi and Takano Nobuharu. "Nagasaki keibi to zaisei kiki no shinkō." In *Zoku Saga han no sōgō kenkyū*, ed. Fujino, 499–559. Yoshikawa kōbunkan, 1987.

Nakano Reishirō, ed. *Nabeshima Naomasa kōden*. 7 vol. Kōshaku Nabeshima ke hensanjo, 1920–21.

Nichols, Frederick. *Honest Thieves: The Violent Heyday of English Smuggling*. London: Heinemann, 1973.

Nihonshi jiten. Edited by Asao Naohiro, Uchino Shun'ichi, and Tanaka Migaku. Kadokawa shinpan, 1996.

Nirayama juku nikki: Takashima ryū hōjustu shiryō. Edited by Ishii Iwao. Nirayama: Nirayama chō yakusho, 1970.

Nishimura Keiko. "Edo bakufu no nukeni torishimari rei o meguru hōishiki no henkan." *Nihon joshidaigaku kiyō*, 23 (1973): 11–36.

———. *Kinsei Nagasaki bōeki to kaiun seido no tenkai*. Bunken shuppan, 1998.

Notehelfer, Fred. "Notes on Kyōhō Smuggling." *Princeton Papers in East Asian Studies, I: Japan*, 1–32. Princeton, NJ: Princeton University Program in East Asian Studies, 1972.

Ōhashi Shūji. "Kindai tetsu kōgyō no akebono." In *Saikō to yakin*, edited by Nagahara Keiji, 211–44. Nihon hyōronsha, 1983.

Oliphant, Laurence. *Narrative of the Earl of Elgin's Mission to China and Japan, in the Years 1857, 1858 and 1859*, vol. 2. New York: Harper and Brothers, 1860.

Osborn, Sherard. *A Cruise in Japanese Waters*. London: William Blackwood and Sons, 1859.

Pacheco, Diego. "The Founding of the Port of Nagasaki and Its Cession to the Society of Jesus." *Monumenta Nipponica* 25, nos. 3–4 (1970): 303–23.

Pérotin-Dumon, Anne. "The Pirate and the Emperor: Power and the Law on the Seas, 1450–1850." In *The Political Economy of Merchant Empires*, edited by James D. Tracey, 196–227. New York: Cambridge University Press, 1997.

Plutschow, Herbert. *Historical Hakodate: Foreigners' Views of the City in the Second Half of the Nineteenth Century*. Hakodate: Hokkaidō International Foundation, 1991.

Ravina, Mark. *Land and Lordship in Early Modern Japan*. Stanford, CA: Stanford University Press, 1999.

———. *The Last Samurai: The Life and Battles of Saigo Takamori*. Hoboken, NJ: Wiley, 2003.

Roberts, Luke. *Performing the Great Public Peace: Political Space and Open Secrets in Tokugawa Japan*. Honolulu: University of Hawai`i Press, 2012.

Rodger, N. A. M. *The Command of the Ocean: A Naval History of Britain, 1649–1815*. New York: W. W. Norton, 2004.

———. *The Safeguard of the Sea: A Naval History of Britain, 660–1649*. New York: W. W. Norton, 1997.

Ruddle, Kenneth, and Tomoyama Akimichi. "Sea Tenure in Japan and the Southwestern Ryukyus." In *A Small Sea of Boats*, edited by John Cordell, 337–70. Cambridge, MA: Cultural Survival, 1989.

Saga ken kinsei shiryō. 25 vols. Saga: Saga kenritsu toshokan, 1993–2013.

Saga kenshi hensan iinkai, *Saga kenshi,* vol. 2, Saga: Saga ken, 1967–68.

Sakai, Robert. "Shimazu Nariakira and the Emergence of National Leadership in Satsuma." Albert Craig and Donald Shively, eds. *Personality in Japanese History*. Berkeley: University of California Press, 1970, 209–23.

Sakoku jidai: Taigai ōsetsu kankei shiryō. Edited by Katagiri Kazuo. Kondō shuppan, 1972.

Satō Masao. *Shinagawa daiba shikō*. Rikogakusha, 1997.

Serizawa Masao. *Yōshiki seitetsu no hōga: ransho to hansharo*. Agune gijutsu sentaa, 1991.
Shapinsky, Peter. "With the Sea as Their Domain: Pirates and Maritime Lordship in Medieval Japan." In *Seascapes, Littoral Cultures and Trans-Oceanic Exchanges*, edited by Jerry Bentley, Kären Wigen, and Renate Bridenthal, 221–38. Honolulu: University of Hawai`i Press, 2007.
Shibata Kazuo. "Fukuoka han no Tempō kaikaku." In *Kyūshū bunkashi kenkyūjo kiyō* 27 (Feb. 1982): 235–79.
Shimazu Nariakira. *Shimazu Nariakira monjo*. 3 vols. Yoshikawa kōbunkan, 1959–.
Smith, Henry. D., III, and Amy G. Poster, eds. *Hiroshige: One Hundred Famous Views of Edo*. New York: George Braziller, 1986.
Sugitani Akira. *Nabeshima kansō*. Chūō kōronsha, 1992.
Suzuki Kahoru. *Tokugawa Ieyasu no Supein gaikō: Mukai Shōkan to Miura Anjin*. Shinjinbutsu ōraisha, 2010.
Suzuki Yasuko. *Nagasaki bugyō no kenkyū*. Shibunkaku, 2007.

Takayanagi Shinzō and Ishii Ryōsuke, eds. *Ofuregaki Kampō shūsei*. Iwanami shoten, 1934.
Takeda Mariko. *Sakoku to kokkyō no naritate*. Dōseisha, 2005.
Takemoto Tomoyuki. "Chōshū han no Sōshū keibi ni miru azukaridokoro keiei to minseishiso." *Kaikokushi kenkyū* 5 (May 2005): 96–110.
Takeno Yōko. *Hakata no gōshō*. Fukuoka: Ashi shobō, 1980.
———. *Han bōekishi no kenkyū*. Kyoto: Minerva shobō, 1979.
Tanji Kenzō. "Kōkaki ni okeru Edo wan bōbi mondai to ikokusen toriatsukai rei." In *Taigai kankei to seiji bunka, dai san*. Yoshikawa kōbunkan, 1974, 211–55.
Tempō go nen shintatsu shichi gatsu itsuka hassoku Oranda honkoku sen tōrai no ki. Akitsuki Kuroda ke monjo. Kyūshū bunka shi kenkyūjo, Kyūshū daigaku.
Tempō roku nen kugatsu Oranda sen hogake mikakushi no ki. Akitsuki Kuroda ke monjo. Kyūshū bunka shi kenkyūjo, Kyūshū daigaku.
Toby, Ronald. *State and Diplomacy in Early Modern Japan: Asia in the Development of the Tokugawa Bakufu*. Stanford, CA: Stanford University Press, 1991.
Totman, Conrad. *The Collapse of the Tokugawa Bakufu, 1862–1868*. Honolulu: University of Hawai`i Press, 1980.
———. *Politics in the Tokugawa Bakufu, 1600–1843*. Berkeley: University of California Press, 1967.
Toyama Mikio. *Nagasaki bugyō: Edo bakufu no mimi to me*. Chūō kōronsha, 1988.
Tronson, J. M. *Personal Narrative of a Voyage to Japan, Kamtschatka, Siberia, Tartary, and Various Parts of Coast of China*. London: Smith, Elder, 1859.
Tsukahira, George. *Feudal Control in Tokugawa Japan: The Sankin Kōtai System*. Cambridge, MA: East Asian Research Center, Harvard University, 1966.
Turnbull, Stephen. *Strongholds of the Samurai: Japanese Castles, 250–1877*. Oxford: Osprey Publishing, 2009.

Van der Velde, Paul. "The Interpreter Interpreted: Kaempfer's Japanese Collaborator Imamura Genemon Eisei." In *The Furthest Goal: Engelbert Kaempfer's Encounter with Tokugawa Japan*, edited by B. M. Bodart-Bailey and Derek Massarella, 44–58. Sandgate: Japan Library, 1995.

Van der Velde, Paul, and Rudolf Bachofner, trans. and eds. *The Deshima Diaries, Marginalia, 1700–1740*. Japan-Netherlands Institute, 1992.

Vann, James Allen. *The Making of a State: Württemberg: 1593–1793*. Ithaca, NY: Cornell University Press, 1984.

Vaporis, Constantine. *Tour of Duty: Samurai, Military Service in Edo, and the Culture of Early Modern Japan*. Honolulu: University of Hawai`i Press, 2008.

Wakabayashi, Bob Tadashi. *Anti-Foreignism and Western Learning in Early-Modern Japan: The New Theses of 1825*. Cambridge, MA: Harvard University Press, 1986.

Walker, Brett. *The Conquest of Ainu Lands: Ecology and Culture in Japanese Expansion, 1590–1800*. Berkeley: University of California Press, 2006.

Walthall, Anne. *Social Protest and Popular Culture in Eighteenth Century Japan*. Tucson: University of Arizona Press, 1986.

Westney, D. Eleanor. "The Military." In *Japan in Transition from Tokugawa to Meiji*, edited by Marius B. Jansen and Gilbert Rozman, 168–94. Princeton: Princeton University Press, 1986.

White, James. *Ikki: Social Conflict and Political Protest in Early Modern Japan*. Ithaca, NY: Cornell University Press, 1995.

———. "State Growth and Popular Protest in Tokugawa Japan." *Journal of Japanese Studies* 14, no. 1 (1988): 1–25.

Wigen, Kären. *A Malleable Map: Geographies of Restoration in Central Japan: 1600–1912*. Berkeley: University of California Press, 2010.

Wilson, Noell. "Tokugawa Defense Redux: Organizational Failure in the *Phaeton* Incident of 1808." *Journal of Japanese Studies* 36, no. 1 (2010): 1–32.

Yamamoto Hideki. "Karasen uchiharai taisei no naritate to tenkai." In *Chiiki shakai no tenkai to bakuhansei shihai*, edited by Mori Yasuhiko, 461–86. Meichō shuppan, 2005.

Yamamoto Hirofumi. *Nagasaki kikiyaku nikki: Bakumatsu jōhō sensō*. Chikuma shinsho, 1999.

———. *Sakoku to kaikin no jidai*. Azekura shobō, 2003.

———. *Sankin kōtai*. Kodansha gendai shinsho no. 1394, 1998.

Yamawaki Teijirō. *Nagasaki no Tōjin bōeki*. Yoshikawa kōbunkan, 1964.

———. *Nukeni: Sakoku jidai mitsu bōeki*. Nihon keizai shinbunsha, 1965.

Yamori Kazuhiko. *Toshizu no rekishi, Nihon-hen*. Kōdansha, 1975.

Yao Keisuke. "Sakokuka no Fukuoka han to kantōshina kaiiki shakai." *Fukuoka kenshi, Fukuoka han tsūshihen*. vol. 2, Fukuoka: Nishi Nihon bunka kyōkai, 2000, 253–303.

Yanai Kenji, ed. *Tsūkō ichiran zokushū*. 5 vols. Osaka: Seibundo, 1968–73.

Yasutaka Hiroaki. *Kinsei Nagasaki shihō seido no kenkyū*. Kyoto: Shibunkaku, 2010.

Yokohama shishi. Vol. 2. Yokohama: Yūrindō, 1979.

Yonemoto, Marcia. "Maps and Metaphors of Japan's 'Small Eastern Sea' in Tokugawa Japan (1603–1868)." *Geographical Review* 89, no. 2 (Apr. 1999): 169–87.

Yoshida Masahiko. *Bakumatsu ni okeru Ō to hasha*. Perikan sha, 1997.

Zhao Gang. *The Qing Opening to the Ocean*. Honolulu: University of Hawai`i Press, 2013.

Index

Italic page numbers refer to figures and maps.

Harvard East Asian Monographs
(titles now in print)

7. Chao Kuo-chün, *Economic Planning and Organization in Mainland China: A Documentary Study, 1949–1957*
13. S. M. Meng, *The Tsungli Yamen: Its Organization and Functions*
31. Madeleine Chi, *China Diplomacy, 1914–1918*
36. Peter Frost, *The Bakumatsu Currency Crisis*
38. Robert R. Campbell, *James Duncan Campbell: A Memoir by His Son*
39. Jerome Alan Cohen, ed., *The Dynamics of China's Foreign Relations*
40. V. V. Vishnyakova-Akimova, *Two Years in Revolutionary China, 1925–1927,* trans. Steven L. Levine
41. Meron Medzini, *French Policy in Japan during the Closing Years of the Tokugawa Regime*
46. W. P. J. Hall, *A Bibliographical Guide to Japanese Research on the Chinese Economy, 1958–1970*
47. Jack J. Gerson, *Horatio Nelson Lay and Sino-British Relations, 1854–1864*
48. Paul Richard Bohr, *Famine and the Missionary: Timothy Richard as Relief Administrator and Advocate of National Reform*
50. Britten Dean, *China and Great Britain: The Diplomacy of Commercial Relations, 1860–1864*
51. Ellsworth C. Carlson, *The Foochow Missionaries, 1847–1880*
53. Richard M. Pfeffer, *Understanding Business Contracts in China, 1949–1963*
55. Ranbir Vohra, *Lao She and the Chinese Revolution*
60. Noriko Kamachi, John K. Fairbank, and Chūzō Ichiko, *Japanese Studies of Modern China Since 1953: A Bibliographical Guide to Historical and Social-Science Research on the Nineteenth and Twentieth Centuries, Supplementary Volume for 1953–1969*
61. Donald A. Gibbs and Yun-chen Li, *A Bibliography of Studies and Translations of Modern Chinese Literature, 1918–1942*
62. Robert H. Silin, *Leadership and Values: The Organization of Large-Scale Taiwanese Enterprises*
63. David Pong, *A Critical Guide to the Kwangtung Provincial Archives Deposited at the Public Record Office of London*

69. Eric Widmer, *The Russian Ecclesiastical Mission in Peking during the Eighteenth Century*
73. Jon Sigurdson, *Rural Industrialism in China*
74. Kang Chao, *The Development of Cotton Textile Production in China*
75. Valentin Rabe, *The Home Base of American China Missions, 1880–1920*
78. Meishi Tsai, *Contemporary Chinese Novels and Short Stories, 1949–1974: An Annotated Bibliography*
80. Endymion Wilkinson, *Landlord and Labor in Late Imperial China: Case Studies from Shandong by Jing Su and Luo Lun*
84. J. W. Dower, *Empire and Aftermath: Yoshida Shigeru and the Japanese Experience, 1878–1954*
85. Martin Collcutt, *Five Mountains: The Rinzai Zen Monastic Institution in Medieval Japan*
86. Kwang Suk Kim and Michael Roemer, *Growth and Structural Transformation*
89. Sung Hwan Ban, Pal Yong Moon, and Dwight H. Perkins, *Rural Development*
92. Edward S. Mason, Dwight H. Perkins, Kwang Suk Kim, David C. Cole, Mahn Je Kim et al., *The Economic and Social Modernization of the Republic of Korea*
93. Robert Repetto, Tai Hwan Kwon, Son-Ung Kim, Dae Young Kim, John E. Sloboda, and Peter J. Donaldson, *Economic Development, Population Policy, and Demographic Transition in the Republic of Korea*
94. Parks M. Coble, Jr., *The Shanghai Capitalists and the Nationalist Government, 1927–1937*
96. Richard Wich, *Sino-Soviet Crisis Politics: A Study of Political Change and Communication*
97. Lillian M. Li, *China's Silk Trade: Traditional Industry in the Modern World, 1842–1937*
98. R. David Arkush, *Fei Xiaotong and Sociology in Revolutionary China*
100. James Reeve Pusey, *China and Charles Darwin*
101. Hoyt Cleveland Tillman, *Utilitarian Confucianism: Chen Liang's Challenge to Chu Hsi*
102. Thomas A. Stanley, *Ōsugi Sakae, Anarchist in Taishō Japan: The Creativity of the Ego*
103. Jonathan K. Ocko, *Bureaucratic Reform in Provincial China: Ting Jih-ch'ang in Restoration Kiangsu, 1867–1870*
104. James Reed, *The Missionary Mind and American East Asia Policy, 1911–1915*
105. Neil L. Waters, *Japan's Local Pragmatists: The Transition from Bakumatsu to Meiji in the Kawasaki Region*
106. David C. Cole and Yung Chul Park, *Financial Development in Korea, 1945–1978*
107. Roy Bahl, Chuk Kyo Kim, and Chong Kee Park, *Public Finances during the Korean Modernization Process*
108. William D. Wray, *Mitsubishi and the N.Y.K., 1870–1914: Business Strategy in the Japanese Shipping Industry*
109. Ralph William Huenemann, *The Dragon and the Iron Horse: The Economics of Railroads in China, 1876–1937*
111. Jane Kate Leonard, *Wei Yüan and China's Rediscovery of the Maritime World*

117. Andrew Gordon, *The Evolution of Labor Relations in Japan: Heavy Industry, 1853–1955*
119. Christine Guth Kanda, *Shinzō: Hachiman Imagery and Its Development*
121. Chang-tai Hung, *Going to the People: Chinese Intellectual and Folk Literature, 1918–1937*
123. Richard von Glahn, *The Country of Streams and Grottoes: Expansion, Settlement, and the Civilizing of the Sichuan Frontier in Song Times*
124. Steven D. Carter, *The Road to Komatsubara: A Classical Reading of the Renga Hyakuin*
126. Bob Tadashi Wakabayashi, *Anti-Foreignism and Western Learning in Early-Modern Japan: The "New Theses" of 1825*
127. Atsuko Hirai, *Individualism and Socialism: The Life and Thought of Kawai Eijirō (1891–1944)*
129. R. Kent Guy, *The Emperor's Four Treasuries: Scholars and the State in the Late Chien-lung Era*
130. Peter C. Perdue, *Exhausting the Earth: State and Peasant in Hunan, 1500–1850*
131. Susan Chan Egan, *A Latterday Confucian: Reminiscences of William Hung (1893–1980)*
132. James T. C. Liu, *China Turning Inward: Intellectual-Political Changes in the Early Twelfth Century*
134. Kate Wildman Nakai, *Shogunal Politics: Arai Hakuseki and the Premises of Tokugawa Rule*
137. Susan Downing Videen, *Tales of Heichū*
138. Heinz Morioka and Miyoko Sasaki, *Rakugo: The Popular Narrative Art of Japan*
139. Joshua A. Fogel, *Nakae Ushikichi in China: The Mourning of Spirit*
140. Alexander Barton Woodside, *Vietnam and the Chinese Model: A Comparative Study of Vietnamese and Chinese Government in the First Half of the Nineteenth Century*
141. George Elison, *Deus Destroyed: The Image of Christianity in Early Modern Japan*
144. Marie Anchordoguy, *Computers, Inc.: Japan's Challenge to IBM*
146. Mary Elizabeth Berry, *Hideyoshi*
147. Laura E. Hein, *Fueling Growth: The Energy Revolution and Economic Policy in Postwar Japan*
148. Wen-hsin Yeh, *The Alienated Academy: Culture and Politics in Republican China, 1919–1937*
149. Dru C. Gladney, *Muslim Chinese: Ethnic Nationalism in the People's Republic*
150. Merle Goldman and Paul A. Cohen, eds., *Ideas Across Cultures: Essays on Chinese Thought in Honor of Benjamin L Schwartz*
151. James M. Polachek, *The Inner Opium War*
152. Gail Lee Bernstein, *Japanese Marxist: A Portrait of Kawakami Hajime, 1879–1946*
154. Mark Mason, *American Multinationals and Japan: The Political Economy of Japanese Capital Controls, 1899–1980*
155. Richard J. Smith, John K. Fairbank, and Katherine F. Bruner, *Robert Hart and China's Early Modernization: His Journals, 1863–1866*
157. William Wayne Farris, *Heavenly Warriors: The Evolution of Japan's Military, 500–1300*

159. James B. Palais, *Politics and Policy in Traditional Korea*
161. Roger R. Thompson, *China's Local Councils in the Age of Constitutional Reform, 1898–1911*
162. William Johnston, *The Modern Epidemic: History of Tuberculosis in Japan*
163. Constantine Nomikos Vaporis, *Breaking Barriers: Travel and the State in Early Modern Japan*
164. Irmela Hijiya-Kirschnereit, *Rituals of Self-Revelation: Shishōsetsu as Literary Genre and Socio-Cultural Phenomenon*
165. James C. Baxter, *The Meiji Unification through the Lens of Ishikawa Prefecture*
166. Thomas R. H. Havens, *Architects of Affluence: The Tsutsumi Family and the Seibu-Saison Enterprises in Twentieth-Century Japan*
167. Anthony Hood Chambers, *The Secret Window: Ideal Worlds in Tanizaki's Fiction*
168. Steven J. Ericson, *The Sound of the Whistle: Railroads and the State in Meiji Japan*
169. Andrew Edmund Goble, *Kenmu: Go-Daigo's Revolution*
170. Denise Potrzeba Lett, *In Pursuit of Status: The Making of South Korea's "New" Urban Middle Class*
171. Mimi Hall Yiengpruksawan, *Hiraizumi: Buddhist Art and Regional Politics in Twelfth-Century Japan*
173. Aviad E. Raz, *Riding the Black Ship: Japan and Tokyo Disneyland*
174. Deborah J. Milly, *Poverty, Equality, and Growth: The Politics of Economic Need in Postwar Japan*
175. See Heng Teow, *Japan's Cultural Policy toward China, 1918–1931: A Comparative Perspective*
176. Michael A. Fuller, *An Introduction to Literary Chinese*
177. Frederick R. Dickinson, *War and National Reinvention: Japan in the Great War, 1914–1919*
178. John Solt, *Shredding the Tapestry of Meaning: The Poetry and Poetics of Kitasono Katue (1902–1978)*
179. Edward Pratt, *Japan's Protoindustrial Elite: The Economic Foundations of the Gōnō*
180. Atsuko Sakaki, *Recontextualizing Texts: Narrative Performance in Modern Japanese Fiction*
181. Soon-Won Park, *Colonial Industrialization and Labor in Korea: The Onoda Cement Factory*
182. JaHyun Kim Haboush and Martina Deuchler, *Culture and the State in Late Chosŏn Korea*
183. John W. Chaffee, *Branches of Heaven: A History of the Imperial Clan of Sung China*
184. Gi-Wook Shin and Michael Robinson, eds., *Colonial Modernity in Korea*
185. Nam-lin Hur, *Prayer and Play in Late Tokugawa Japan: Asakusa Sensōji and Edo Society*
186. Kristin Stapleton, *Civilizing Chengdu: Chinese Urban Reform, 1895–1937*
187. Hyung Il Pai, *Constructing "Korean" Origins: A Critical Review of Archaeology, Historiography, and Racial Myth in Korean State-Formation Theories*
188. Brian D. Ruppert, *Jewel in the Ashes: Buddha Relics and Power in Early Medieval Japan*
189. Susan Daruvala, *Zhou Zuoren and an Alternative Chinese Response to Modernity*

191. Kerry Smith, *A Time of Crisis: Japan, the Great Depression, and Rural Revitalization*
192. Michael Lewis, *Becoming Apart: National Power and Local Politics in Toyama, 1868–1945*
193. William C. Kirby, Man-houng Lin, James Chin Shih, and David A. Pietz, eds., *State and Economy in Republican China: A Handbook for Scholars*
194. Timothy S. George, *Minamata: Pollution and the Struggle for Democracy in Postwar Japan*
195. Billy K. L. So, *Prosperity, Region, and Institutions in Maritime China: The South Fukien Pattern, 946–1368*
196. Yoshihisa Tak Matsusaka, *The Making of Japanese Manchuria, 1904–1932*
197. Maram Epstein, *Competing Discourses: Orthodoxy, Authenticity, and Engendered Meanings in Late Imperial Chinese Fiction*
199. Haruo Iguchi, *Unfinished Business: Ayukawa Yoshisuke and U.S.-Japan Relations, 1937–1952*
200. Scott Pearce, Audrey Spiro, and Patricia Ebrey, *Culture and Power in the Reconstitution of the Chinese Realm, 200–600*
201. Terry Kawashima, *Writing Margins: The Textual Construction of Gender in Heian and Kamakura Japan*
202. Martin W. Huang, *Desire and Fictional Narrative in Late Imperial China*
203. Robert S. Ross and Jiang Changbin, eds., *Re-examining the Cold War: U.S.-China Diplomacy, 1954–1973*
204. Guanhua Wang, *In Search of Justice: The 1905–1906 Chinese Anti-American Boycott*
205. David Schaberg, *A Patterned Past: Form and Thought in Early Chinese Historiography*
206. Christine Yano, *Tears of Longing: Nostalgia and the Nation in Japanese Popular Song*
207. Milena Doleželová-Velingerová and Oldřich Král, with Graham Sanders, eds., *The Appropriation of Cultural Capital: China's May Fourth Project*
208. Robert N. Huey, *The Making of 'Shinkokinshū'*
209. Lee Butler, *Emperor and Aristocracy in Japan, 1467–1680: Resilience and Renewal*
210. Suzanne Ogden, *Inklings of Democracy in China*
211. Kenneth J. Ruoff, *The People's Emperor: Democracy and the Japanese Monarchy, 1945–1995*
212. Haun Saussy, *Great Walls of Discourse and Other Adventures in Cultural China*
213. Aviad E. Raz, *Emotions at Work: Normative Control, Organizations, and Culture in Japan and America*
214. Rebecca E. Karl and Peter Zarrow, eds., *Rethinking the 1898 Reform Period: Political and Cultural Change in Late Qing China*
215. Kevin O'Rourke, *The Book of Korean Shijo*
216. Ezra F. Vogel, ed., *The Golden Age of the U.S.-China-Japan Triangle, 1972–1989*
217. Thomas A. Wilson, ed., *On Sacred Grounds: Culture, Society, Politics, and the Formation of the Cult of Confucius*
218. Donald S. Sutton, *Steps of Perfection: Exorcistic Performers and Chinese Religion in Twentieth-Century Taiwan*

219. Daqing Yang, *Technology of Empire: Telecommunications and Japanese Expansionism in Asia, 1883–1945*
220. Qianshen Bai, *Fu Shan's World: The Transformation of Chinese Calligraphy in the Seventeenth Century*
221. Paul Jakov Smith and Richard von Glahn, eds., *The Song-Yuan-Ming Transition in Chinese History*
222. Rania Huntington, *Alien Kind: Foxes and Late Imperial Chinese Narrative*
223. Jordan Sand, *House and Home in Modern Japan: Architecture, Domestic Space, and Bourgeois Culture, 1880–1930*
224. Karl Gerth, *China Made: Consumer Culture and the Creation of the Nation*
225. Xiaoshan Yang, *Metamorphosis of the Private Sphere: Gardens and Objects in Tang-Song Poetry*
226. Barbara Mittler, *A Newspaper for China? Power, Identity, and Change in Shanghai's News Media, 1872–1912*
227. Joyce A. Madancy, *The Troublesome Legacy of Commissioner Lin: The Opium Trade and Opium Suppression in Fujian Province, 1820s to 1920s*
228. John Makeham, *Transmitters and Creators: Chinese Commentators and Commentaries on the Analects*
229. Elisabeth Köll, *From Cotton Mill to Business Empire: The Emergence of Regional Enterprises in Modern China*
230. Emma Teng, *Taiwan's Imagined Geography: Chinese Colonial Travel Writing and Pictures, 1683–1895*
231. Wilt Idema and Beata Grant, *The Red Brush: Writing Women of Imperial China*
232. Eric C. Rath, *The Ethos of Noh: Actors and Their Art*
233. Elizabeth Remick, *Building Local States: China during the Republican and Post-Mao Eras*
234. Lynn Struve, ed., *The Qing Formation in World-Historical Time*
235. D. Max Moerman, *Localizing Paradise: Kumano Pilgrimage and the Religious Landscape of Premodern Japan*
236. Antonia Finnane, *Speaking of Yangzhou: A Chinese City, 1550–1850*
237. Brian Platt, *Burning and Building: Schooling and State Formation in Japan, 1750–1890*
238. Gail Bernstein, Andrew Gordon, and Kate Wildman Nakai, eds., *Public Spheres, Private Lives in Modern Japan, 1600–1950: Essays in Honor of Albert Craig*
239. Wu Hung and Katherine R. Tsiang, *Body and Face in Chinese Visual Culture*
240. Stephen Dodd, *Writing Home: Representations of the Native Place in Modern Japanese Literature*
241. David Anthony Bello, *Opium and the Limits of Empire: Drug Prohibition in the Chinese Interior, 1729–1850*
242. Hosea Hirata, *Discourses of Seduction: History, Evil, Desire, and Modern Japanese Literature*
243. Kyung Moon Hwang, *Beyond Birth: Social Status in the Emergence of Modern Korea*
244. Brian R. Dott, *Identity Reflections: Pilgrimages to Mount Tai in Late Imperial China*
245. Mark McNally, *Proving the Way: Conflict and Practice in the History of Japanese Nativism*

246. Yongping Wu, *A Political Explanation of Economic Growth: State Survival, Bureaucratic Politics, and Private Enterprises in the Making of Taiwan's Economy, 1950–1985*
247. Kyu Hyun Kim, *The Age of Visions and Arguments: Parliamentarianism and the National Public Sphere in Early Meiji Japan*
248. Zvi Ben-Dor Benite, *The Dao of Muhammad: A Cultural History of Muslims in Late Imperial China*
249. David Der-wei Wang and Shang Wei, eds., *Dynastic Crisis and Cultural Innovation: From the Late Ming to the Late Qing and Beyond*
250. Wilt L. Idema, Wai-yee Li, and Ellen Widmer, eds., *Trauma and Transcendence in Early Qing Literature*
251. Barbara Molony and Kathleen Uno, eds., *Gendering Modern Japanese History*
252. Hiroshi Aoyagi, *Islands of Eight Million Smiles: Idol Performance and Symbolic Production in Contemporary Japan*
253. Wai-yee Li, *The Readability of the Past in Early Chinese Historiography*
254. William C. Kirby, Robert S. Ross, and Gong Li, eds., *Normalization of U.S.-China Relations: An International History*
255. Ellen Gardner Nakamura, *Practical Pursuits: Takano Chōei, Takahashi Keisaku, and Western Medicine in Nineteenth-Century Japan*
256. Jonathan W. Best, *A History of the Early Korean Kingdom of Paekche, together with an annotated translation of* The Paekche Annals *of the* Samguk sagi
257. Liang Pan, *The United Nations in Japan's Foreign and Security Policymaking, 1945–1992: National Security, Party Politics, and International Status*
258. Richard Belsky, *Localities at the Center: Native Place, Space, and Power in Late Imperial Beijing*
259. Zwia Lipkin, *"Useless to the State": "Social Problems" and Social Engineering in Nationalist Nanjing, 1927–1937*
260. William O. Gardner, *Advertising Tower: Japanese Modernism and Modernity in the 1920s*
261. Stephen Owen, *The Making of Early Chinese Classical Poetry*
262. Martin J. Powers, *Pattern and Person: Ornament, Society, and Self in Classical China*
263. Anna M. Shields, *Crafting a Collection: The Cultural Contexts and Poetic Practice of the* Huajian ji 花間集 *(Collection from among the Flowers)*
264. Stephen Owen, *The Late Tang: Chinese Poetry of the Mid-Ninth Century (827–860)*
265. Sara L. Friedman, *Intimate Politics: Marriage, the Market, and State Power in Southeastern China*
266. Patricia Buckley Ebrey and Maggie Bickford, *Emperor Huizong and Late Northern Song China: The Politics of Culture and the Culture of Politics*
267. Sophie Volpp, *Worldly Stage: Theatricality in Seventeenth-Century China*
268. Ellen Widmer, *The Beauty and the Book: Women and Fiction in Nineteenth-Century China*
269. Steven B. Miles, *The Sea of Learning: Mobility and Identity in Nineteenth-Century Guangzhou*
270. Man-houng Lin, *China Upside Down: Currency, Society, and Ideologies, 1808–1856*

271. Ronald Egan, *The Problem of Beauty: Aesthetic Thought and Pursuits in Northern Song Dynasty China*
272. Mark Halperin, *Out of the Cloister: Literati Perspectives on Buddhism in Sung China, 960–1279*
273. Helen Dunstan, *State or Merchant? Political Economy and Political Process in 1740s China*
274. Sabina Knight, *The Heart of Time: Moral Agency in Twentieth-Century Chinese Fiction*
275. Timothy J. Van Compernolle, *The Uses of Memory: The Critique of Modernity in the Fiction of Higuchi Ichiyō*
276. Paul Rouzer, *A New Practical Primer of Literary Chinese*
277. Jonathan Zwicker, *Practices of the Sentimental Imagination: Melodrama, the Novel, and the Social Imaginary in Nineteenth-Century Japan*
278. Franziska Seraphim, *War Memory and Social Politics in Japan, 1945–2005*
280. Cynthia J. Brokaw, *Commerce in Culture: The Sibao Book Trade in the Qing and Republican Periods*
281. Eugene Y. Park, *Between Dreams and Reality: The Military Examination in Late Chosŏn Korea, 1600–1894*
282. Nam-lin Hur, *Death and Social Order in Tokugawa Japan: Buddhism, Anti-Christianity, and the* Danka *System*
283. Patricia M. Thornton, *Disciplining the State: Virtue, Violence, and State-Making in Modern China*
284. Vincent Goossaert, *The Taoists of Peking, 1800–1949: A Social History of Urban Clerics*
286. Charo B. D'Etcheverry, *Love after* The Tale of Genji*: Rewriting the World of the Shining Prince*
287. Michael G. Chang, *A Court on Horseback: Imperial Touring & the Construction of Qing Rule, 1680–1785*
288. Carol Richmond Tsang, *War and Faith:* Ikkō Ikki *in Late Muromachi Japan*
289. Hilde De Weerdt, *Competition over Content: Negotiating Standards for the Civil Service Examinations in Imperial China (1127–1279)*
290. Eve Zimmerman, *Out of the Alleyway: Nakagami Kenji and the Poetics of Outcaste Fiction*
291. Robert Culp, *Articulating Citizenship: Civic Education and Student Politics in Southeastern China, 1912–1940*
292. Richard J. Smethurst, *From Foot Soldier to Finance Minister: Takahashi Korekiyo, Japan's Keynes*
293. John E. Herman, *Amid the Clouds and Mist: China's Colonization of Guizhou, 1200–1700*
294. Tomoko Shiroyama, *China during the Great Depression: Market, State, and the World Economy, 1929–1937*
295. Kirk W. Larsen, *Tradition, Treaties and Trade: Qing Imperialism and Chosŏn Korea, 1850–1910*
296. Gregory Golley, *When Our Eyes No Longer See: Realism, Science, and Ecology in Japanese Literary Modernism*

297. Barbara Ambros, *Emplacing a Pilgrimage: The Ōyama Cult and Regional Religion in Early Modern Japan*
298. Rebecca Suter, *The Japanization of Modernity: Murakami Haruki between Japan and the United States*
299. Yuma Totani, *The Tokyo War Crimes Trial: The Pursuit of Justice in the Wake of World War II*
301. David M. Robinson, ed., *Culture, Courtiers, and Competition: The Ming Court (1368–1644)*
302. Calvin Chen, *Some Assembly Required: Work, Community, and Politics in China's Rural Enterprises*
303. Sem Vermeersch, *The Power of the Buddhas: The Politics of Buddhism During the Koryŏ Dynasty* (918–1392)
304. Tina Lu, *Accidental Incest, Filial Cannibalism, and Other Peculiar Encounters in Late Imperial Chinese Literature*
305. Chang Woei Ong, *Men of Letters Within the Passes: Guanzhong Literati in Chinese History, 907–1911*
306. Wendy Swartz, *Reading Tao Yuanming: Shifting Paradigms of Historical Reception (427–1900)*
307. Peter K. Bol, *Neo-Confucianism in History*
308. Carlos Rojas, *The Naked Gaze: Reflections on Chinese Modernity*
309. Kelly H. Chong, *Deliverance and Submission: Evangelical Women and the Negotiation of Patriarchy in South Korea*
310. Rachel DiNitto, *Uchida Hyakken: A Critique of Modernity and Militarism in Prewar Japan*
311. Jeffrey Snyder-Reinke, *Dry Spells: State Rainmaking and Local Governance in Late Imperial China*
312. Jay Dautcher, *Down a Narrow Road: Identity and Masculinity in a Uyghur Community in Xinjiang China*
313. Xun Liu, *Daoist Modern: Innovation, Lay Practice, and the Community of Inner Alchemy in Republican Shanghai*
314. Jacob Eyferth, *Eating Rice from Bamboo Roots: The Social History of a Community of Handicraft Papermakers in Rural Sichuan, 1920–2000*
315. David Johnson, *Spectacle and Sacrifice: The Ritual Foundations of Village Life in North China*
316. James Robson, *Power of Place: The Religious Landscape of the Southern Sacred Peak (Nanyue* 南嶽*) in Medieval China*
317. Lori Watt, *When Empire Comes Home: Repatriation and Reintegration in Postwar Japan*
318. James Dorsey, *Critical Aesthetics: Kobayashi Hideo, Modernity, and Wartime Japan*
319. Christopher Bolton, *Sublime Voices: The Fictional Science and Scientific Fiction of Abe Kōbō*
320. Si-yen Fei, *Negotiating Urban Space: Urbanization and Late Ming Nanjing*
321. Christopher Gerteis, *Gender Struggles: Wage-Earning Women and Male-Dominated Unions in Postwar Japan*
322. Rebecca Nedostup, *Superstitious Regimes: Religion and the Politics of Chinese Modernity*

323. Lucien Bianco, *Wretched Rebels: Rural Disturbances on the Eve of the Chinese Revolution*
324. Cathryn H. Clayton, *Sovereignty at the Edge: Macau and the Question of Chineseness*
325. Micah S. Muscolino, *Fishing Wars and Environmental Change in Late Imperial and Modern China*
326. Robert I. Hellyer, *Defining Engagement: Japan and Global Contexts, 1750–1868*
327. Robert Ashmore, *The Transport of Reading: Text and Understanding in the World of Tao Qian (365–427)*
328. Mark A. Jones, *Children as Treasures: Childhood and the Middle Class in Early Twentieth Century Japan*
329. Miryam Sas, *Experimental Arts in Postwar Japan: Moments of Encounter, Engagement, and Imagined Return*
330. H. Mack Horton, *Traversing the Frontier: The* Man'yōshū *Account of a Japanese Mission to Silla in 736–737*
331. Dennis J. Frost, *Seeing Stars: Sports Celebrity, Identity, and Body Culture in Modern Japan*
332. Marnie S. Anderson, *A Place in Public: Women's Rights in Meiji Japan*
333. Peter Mauch, *Sailor Diplomat: Nomura Kichisaburō and the Japanese-American War*
334. Ethan Isaac Segal, *Coins, Trade, and the State: Economic Growth in Early Medieval Japan*
335. David B. Lurie, *Realms of Literacy: Early Japan and the History of Writing*
336. Lillian Lan-ying Tseng, *Picturing Heaven in Early China*
337. Jun Uchida, *Brokers of Empire: Japanese Settler Colonialism in Korea, 1876–1945*
338. Patricia L. Maclachlan, *The People's Post Office: The History and Politics of the Japanese Postal System, 1871–2010*
339. Michael Schiltz, *The Money Doctors from Japan: Finance, Imperialism, and the Building of the Yen Bloc, 1895–1937*
340. Daqing Yang, Jie Liu, Hiroshi Mitani, and Andrew Gordon, eds., *Toward a History beyond Borders: Contentious Issues in Sino-Japanese Relations*
341. Sonia Ryang, *Reading North Korea: An Ethnological Inquiry*
342. Susan Huang, *Picturing the True Form: Daoist Visual Culture in Traditional China*
343. Barbara Mittler, *A Continuous Revolution: Making Sense of Cultural Revolution Culture*
344. Hwansoo Ilmee Kim, *Empire of the Dharma: Korean and Japanese Buddhism, 1877–1912*
345. Satoru Saito, *Detective Fiction and the Rise of the Japanese Novel, 1880–1930*
346. Jung-Sun N. Han, *An Imperial Path to Modernity: Yoshino Sakuzō and a New Liberal Order in East Asia, 1905–1937*
347. Atsuko Hirai, *Government by Mourning: Death and Political Integration in Japan, 1603–1912*
348. Darryl E. Flaherty, *Public Law, Private Practice: Politics, Profit, and the Legal Profession in Nineteenth-Century Japan*
349. Jeffrey Paul Bayliss, *On the Margins of Empire: Buraku and Korean Identity in Prewar and Wartime Japan*
350. Barry Eichengreen, Dwight H. Perkins, and Kwanho Shin, *From Miracle to Maturity: The Growth of the Korean Economy*

351. Michel Mohr, *Buddhism, Unitarianism, and the Meiji Competition for Universality*
352. J. Keith Vincent, *Two-Timing Modernity: Homosocial Narrative in Modern Japanese Fiction*
354. Chong-Bum An and Barry Bosworth, *Income Inequality in Korea: An Analysis of Trends, Causes, and Answers*
355. Jamie L. Newhard, *Knowing the Amorous Man: A History of Scholarship on* Tales of Ise
356. Sho Konishi, *Anarchist Modernity: Cooperatism and Japanese-Russian Intellectual Relations in Modern Japan*
357. Christopher P. Hanscom, *The Real Modern: Literary Modernism and the Crisis of Representation in Colonial Korea*
358. Michael Wert, *Meiji Restoration Losers: Memory and Tokugawa Supporters in Modern Japan*
359. Garret P. S. Olberding, ed., *Facing the Monarch: Modes of Advice in the Early Chinese Court*
360. Xiaojue Wang, *Modernity with a Cold War Face: Reimagining the Nation in Chinese Literature Across the 1949 Divide*
361. David Spafford, *A Sense of Place: The Political Landscape in Late Medieval Japan*
362. Jongryn Mo and Barry Weingast, *Korean Political and Economic Development: Crisis, Security, and Economic Rebalancing*
363. Melek Ortabasi, *The Undiscovered Country: Text, Translation, and Modernity in the Work of Yanagita Kunio*
364. Hiraku Shimoda, *Lost and Found: Recovering Regional Identity in Imperial Japan*
365. Trent E. Maxey, *The "Greatest Problem": Religion and State Formation in Meiji Japan*
366. Gina Cogan, *The Princess Nun: Bunchi, Buddhist Reform, and Gender in Early Edo Japan*
367. Eric C. Han, *Rise of a Japanese Chinatown: Yokohama, 1894–1972*
368. Natasha Heller, *Illusory Abiding: The Cultural Construction of the Chan Monk Zhongfeng Mingben* 中峰明本 *(1263–1323)*
369. Paize Keulemans, *Sound Rising from the Paper: Nineteenth-Century Martial Arts Fiction and the Chinese Acoustic Imagination*
370. Simon James Bytheway, *Investing Japan: Foreign Capital, Monetary Standards, and Economic Development, 1859–2011*
371. Sukhee Lee, *Negotiated Power: The State, Elites, and Local Governance in Twelfth-Fourteenth China*
372. Ping Foong, *The Efficacious Landscape: On the Authorities of Painting at the Northern Song Court*
373. Catherine L. Phipps, *Empires on the Waterfront: Japan's Ports and Power, 1858–1899*
374. Sunyoung Park, *The Proletarian Wave: Literature and Leftist Culture in Colonial Korea, 1910–1945*
375. Barry Eichengreen, Wonhyuk Lim, Yung Chul Park, and Dwight H. Perkins, *The Korean Economy: From a Miraculous Past to a Sustainable Future*
376. Heather Blair, *Real and Imagined: The Peak of Gold in Heian Japan*

377. Emer O'Dwyer, *Significant Soil: Settler Colonialism and Japan's Urban Empire in Manchuria*
378. Martina Deuchler, *Under the Ancestors' Eyes: Kinship, Status, and Locality in Premodern Korea*
379. Joseph R. Dennis, *Writing, Publishing, and Reading Local Gazetteers in Imperial China, 1100–1700*
380. Cathy Yeh, *The Chinese Political Novel: Migration of a World Genre*
381. Noell Wilson, *Defensive Positions: The Politics of Maritime Security in Tokugawa Japan*
382. Miri Nakamura, *Monstrous Bodies: The Rise of the Uncanny in Modern Japan*
383. Nara Dillon, *Radical Inequalities: China's Revolutionary Welfare State in Comparative Perspective*